Schooling Diaspora

SCHOOLING DIASPORA

*Women, Education, and the Overseas
Chinese in British Malaya and Singapore,
1850s–1960s*

Karen M. Teoh

OXFORD
UNIVERSITY PRESS

OXFORD
UNIVERSITY PRESS

Oxford University Press is a department of the University of Oxford. It furthers
the University's objective of excellence in research, scholarship, and education
by publishing worldwide. Oxford is a registered trade mark of Oxford University
Press in the UK and certain other countries.

Published in the United States of America by Oxford University Press
198 Madison Avenue, New York, NY 10016, United States of America.

© Oxford University Press 2018

First issued as an Oxford University Press paperback, 2020

Library of Congress Cataloging-in-Publication Data
Names: Teoh, Karen M., author.
Title: Schooling diaspora : women, education, and the overseas Chinese
in British Malaya and Singapore, 1850s–1960s / Karen M. Teoh.
Description: New York, NY : Oxford University Press, 2018. |
Includes bibliographical references and index.
Identifiers: LCCN 2017026624 (print) | LCCN 2017041595 (ebook) |
ISBN 9780190495626 (Updf) | ISBN 9780190495633 (Epub) |
ISBN 9780190495619 (hardback) | ISBN 9780197533345 (paperback)
Subjects: LCSH: Chinese—Education—Malaysia—History. |
Chinese—Education—Singapore—History. |
Girls' schools—Education—Malaysia—History. |
Girls' schools—Education—Singapore—History. | BISAC: HISTORY / Asia / General. |
EDUCATION / History. | POLITICAL SCIENCE / Colonialism & Post-Colonialism.
Classification: LCC LC3089.M3 (ebook) | LCC LC3089.M3 T43 2018 (print) |
DDC 370.8209595—dc23
LC record available at https://lccn.loc.gov/2017026624

Portions of this book in an earlier form were previously published as the following book
chapter and journal articles, and are reprinted here with permission: "Breaking Down Barriers
in Chinese Female Education," in *Chinese Women: Their Malaysian Journey*, ed. by Neil Khor
(Malaysia: MPH Publishing, 2010); "Exotic Flowers, Modern Girls, Good Citizens: Female
Education and Overseas Chinese Identity in British Malaya and Singapore, 1900s–1950s,"
Twentieth-Century China 35, no. 2 (April 2010): 25–51; "The Burden of Proof: Gender, Cultural
Authenticity and Overseas Chinese Women's Education in Diaspora," *Intersections: Gender and
Sexuality in Asia and the Pacific* 36 (December 2014), http://intersections.anu.edu.au/issue36/
teoh.htm; and "Domesticating Hybridity: Straits Chinese Cultural Heritage Projects in
Malaysia and Singapore," *Cross-Currents: East Asian History and Culture Review* 5, no. 1
(May 2016): 115–46.

For my teachers, and for teachers everywhere.

CONTENTS

ACKNOWLEDGMENTS

In a book about schools, it seems only fitting to start by acknowledging my profound debt to the teachers and mentors I have had the good fortune to work with over the years. Beatrice Bartlett, Henrietta Harrison, Philip Kuhn, Kristin Mulready-Stone, Mary Steedly, Michael Szonyi, Hue-Tam Ho Tai, Robert Travers, and Robin Winks shaped my intellectual trajectory and expanded my horizons. A Chinese proverb says that it takes ten years to nurture a tree but a hundred years to train people of ability—I hope my teachers are consoled by the fact that this book, while a long time coming, did not take quite that long to be published.

The following individuals read parts of this book at various stages and offered invaluable suggestions, or nudged me to sharpen my thinking through scholarly discussion: Fan Ruolan, Henrietta Harrison, Miriam Kingsberg, Matt Klingle, Belinda Kong, Patrick Rael, Lien Ling-ling, Lin Man-houng, Pär Cassel, Chie Ikeya, Caroline Reeves, Sylvia Rodrigue, Bettina Scholz, Amy Houston, Penny Sinanoglou, and Elizabeth Sinn. My editor, Susan Ferber, patiently and efficiently shepherded this manuscript to publication, while my project manager, Maya Bringe, helped it through its crucial last stages of production. Two anonymous readers for the Press improved this work with their insightful comments. To the many people who gave thoughtful feedback at the conferences and workshops where I presented my research, I extend my thanks. Needless to say, any and all errors of fact or interpretation that remain in this work are my own.

The research for this book stretched across several countries and relied on help from a small army of people. In Malaysia, I am grateful to Loh Wei Leng, Shanthi Thambiah, and the History Department and Gender Studies Program at Universiti Malaya. Without assistance from Chui Kah Peng, Sr. Brede Forde, Lye Ming Pao, Neil Khor, Ong Kian Ming, and Tan Liok Ee, my research would not have progressed beyond its initial stages. In Singapore, the Asia Research Institute hosted me as a research affiliate and the National University of Singapore offered ready access to its libraries and resources. Paul Kratoska, Lee Ching Seng, and Ng Chin Keong shared their considerable knowledge and expertise. In China, Xiamen University in Fujian, Zhongshan University in Guangdong, and the Fuzhou Qiaolianhui (Fuzhou Association of Returned Overseas Chinese) facilitated my research. Liao Shaolian, Li Minghuan, and Zhuang Guotu guided me with equal parts warmth and astuteness, while Lin Zhuodong was a tireless interview coordinator. Lien Ling-ling, Lin Man-houng, the Institute of Modern History at Academia Sinica, and the Center for Chinese Studies in Taipei extended hospitality and mentorship that helped me complete this project. My gratitude also goes to several girls' schools and alumni associations that gave me access to their archives and networks: Kuen Cheng Girls' School Alumni Association, the Holy Infant Jesus Provincialate of Malaysia, Penang Chinese Girls' High School, Nanyang Girls' High School, Raffles Girls' Secondary School, and St. Margaret's Secondary School. One of my greatest debts is to the women whom I interviewed, many of whose names and identifying details in this book have been changed for reasons of confidentiality. Sitting with them and listening to their stories was the most eye-opening and rewarding part of my research. Without their generosity, openness, and good humor in sharing their experiences, the book would have been impossible. I hope I have done them justice.

This book is informed by my personal encounters with education and the overseas Chinese world in postcolonial Southeast Asia. I grew up and attended school in Malaysia and Singapore. Having graduated from two of the institutions discussed in this book—Kuen Cheng Primary School and Raffles Girls' School—I was able to use alumni connections to locate sources and interviewees. My ethnic Chinese heritage has also shaped my consciousness about the complexities of being both the observer and the observed in diasporic space, and of claiming insight from the vantage point of the Western academy where I am now situated.

A room of one's own is a good place to start, but writers also need time, money, and material. I received institutional and financial support at several crucial junctures throughout this project: a series of grants for research travel and writing from Harvard University and the Harvard Asia Center; a Post-doctoral Fellowship at Bowdoin College from the Consortium for Faculty Diversity at Liberal Arts Colleges; a Taiwan Fellowship from the Ministry of Foreign Affairs and Center for Chinese Studies in Taiwan; a Research Publication Grant from the American Association of University Women; and Professional Development Grants from Stonehill College. I am grateful to the History Department and Asian Studies Program of Bowdoin College for holding a workshop to discuss my research with members of their faculty. The History Department of Stonehill College has been a collegial professional home in my continuing journey as a teacher and scholar, and the College has generously supported me with vital research leave and grants. I owe many thanks to librarians at several institutions, especially at Harvard-Yenching Library at Harvard University and MacPhaidin Library at Stonehill College, who were ever ready to help me with my research needs. If there are any other individuals or groups whom I have inadvertently omitted, please accept my apologies and appreciation.

Throughout the writing of this book, friends and family smoothed my path and sustained my spirits. For literally and figuratively giving me shelter, I thank Petrina Kow and Sung Lingun, Maria Stalford, Merlina Manocaran, Shika Pappoe, Claudine Riley and Meredith Faggen, and Suzanne Lye. For non-intellectual but essential companionship, I acknowledge my dog Dante. Taymin and Paul Chang Bin Liu encouraged and aided my work in Taiwan. Cate Liu, Chloe Tan, and Lucas Tan helped me keep in mind the promise and energy of youth. Tan Tang Yew provided crucial technical aid. To my sisters Celine Teoh and Adele Teoh, my lifelong companions and friends: I don't know what I'd do without you. Loving gratitude goes to my earliest teachers: my mother, Chin Cheng Mei, for her belief in me and for telling me when I was young that I should travel as much and as widely as possible, and my father, Teoh Eng Chooi, whose enthusiasm for Chinese history and culture started me on this path in the first place. My maternal and paternal grandparents' diasporic journeys gave rise to mine. In particular, I would like to remember my grandmothers Fu Mei Yoke and Ong Ching Geok, whose talents for survival and compassion in times of hardship are an inspiration.

Last but never least, heartfelt thanks to my husband Joe for his unstinting love, support, and sense of humor—what an education we have had together. And to my son Benjamin, who brings me great joy and from whom I am learning so much: someday, when you are a teenager, hopefully this book will prove that your mother does know a thing or two.

A NOTE ON SPELLING AND TERMINOLOGY

Most Chinese words in this book have been transliterated with *hanyu pinyin* romanization, with simplified Chinese characters also given for key terms. Where transliteration of names or terms has been established by contemporaneous sources and was in common usage, I follow the conventions of the period in question, for example, Liew Yuen Sien, Kuen Cheng, *towkay*. Chinese surnames precede given names, except in cases where individuals have adopted Western-style names. The word "medium" with reference to schools, as in "Chinese-medium," indicates the main language of instruction and is used interchangeably with the descriptors "Chinese-language" or "Chinese."

Schooling Diaspora

Introduction

Women, Education, and Overseas Chinese Identity

On an October morning in 1951, the principal of Nanyang Girls' School in Singapore was walking to work when a group of youths threw a toxic solution of nitric acid on her.[1] Liew Yuen Sien survived and served at Nanyang's helm for another fifteen years, but she suffered painful chemical burns to her face, eyes, and shoulders and could only resume work after three years of recovery. Liew's attackers were never caught. One of the few descriptions of them on the official record is that they were simply "Chinese ruffians." Contemporary opinion was that the assault was an act of retribution by local Chinese Communist sympathizers for Liew's cooperation with British colonial authorities against them.[2] Perpetrators and victim alike were ethnic Chinese.

The attack on Liew Yuen Sien emerged from the collision of political issues within the overseas Chinese community of Southeast Asia: China's quest for national modernization; female education as a key component of this quest; and overseas Chinese efforts to live within an unstable matrix of national, diasporic, and colonial demands. Liew's professional credentials illustrate this complexity. An active proponent of Chinese schools and girls' education in Singapore, Liew was principal of Nanyang Girls' School for forty years. She won a Chinese Nationalist (Kuomintang) government award in 1940, an Order of the British Empire in 1958, and a Singaporean presidential medal in 1967. She was hailed by much of the Chinese community as an active contributor to their welfare but also strongly criticized by some of her co-ethnics for her acquiescence to British anti-Communist pressure.

This episode of intra-ethnic violence is an extreme example, but it reveals the potentially explosive nature of the politics of education in colonial Malaya and Singapore. It also points to an intractable problem in identity formation: the question of authenticity, and who gets to determine what it means to be loyal to one's ethnicity and country. There were sharp, sometimes deadly, divisions within the overseas Chinese community and between various ethnic groups in these colonies throughout the early to mid-twentieth century. These divisions were exacerbated by a linguistically plural system of schooling established under British colonial auspices. The British East India Company had taken over the strategically important trading ports of Penang (1786), Singapore (1819), and Melaka (1824), merging them as the Straits Settlements in 1826. Home to Malays, Chinese, South Asians, Eurasians, and several other ethnic or national groups, these settlements came under direct English Crown control in 1867. They were further amalgamated with other territories on the Malay Peninsula to form British Malaya, which lasted until national independence in 1957. Throughout the first half of the twentieth century, the British colonial government viewed schools, especially local Chinese schools, as breeding grounds for political activism and sought to control them through strict regulation.

The attack on Liew Yuen Sien occurred during the Malayan Emergency of 1948–60, when local Communist insurgents, most of whom were ethnic Chinese, turned their attention from resisting the Japanese Occupation during World War II to fighting British imperialism using guerilla tactics. Like many other Chinese schools in Malaya and Singapore at the time, Nanyang Girls' School had been home to youth Communist activity and was under colonial scrutiny. In late 1951, Nanyang was forced to close until Liew agreed to disband student organizations and shut down the school's dormitories, both of which were hotbeds of political activism.[3] Government suspicion of local Chinese schools persisted beyond the Malayan Emergency, well into the postcolonial era, and remains a flashpoint in the cultural politics of modern Malaysia and Singapore.

There is an additional, gendered component to Liew's attack: not only was she a woman whose status derived from her stewardship of a girls' school, but the assault on her involved acid intended to disfigure her person. Increasingly available as a result of industrialization, sulfuric acid became a popular weapon in the United States and Western Europe, especially in labor clashes during the eighteenth century and domestic assaults during the nineteenth century.[4] By the late nineteenth and twentieth centuries, chemical attacks in civilian society were largely associated with sexual jealousy or revenge. The majority of victims were women whose prospects for marriage, work, and social acceptance would presumably be ruined by facial disfigurement.[5] In the mid- to late twentieth century, the incidence of acid attacks in Asia and the Middle East began to rise.[6] The persistence of such attacks today represents gender-specific hostility, typically relating to a woman's assertion of independence in defiance of someone else's claim to her personhood.

In the case of Liew Yuen Sien, the body of a successful and influential female community leader became the literal point of convergence for public politics, personal animus, and a gender-specific mode of violence. That this incident took place almost exactly a hundred years after the founding of the first girls' schools in Malaya and Singapore is a grim reminder that female education has had a long and uneven road to acceptance.

This book is a history of educated overseas Chinese women in British Malaya and Singapore from the 1850s to the 1960s, during more than a century of British imperialism, Chinese and Southeast Asian nationalism, and patriarchy. It examines the motivations and strategies of missionaries, colonial authorities, and Chinese reformists and revolutionaries for educating girls, and the impact that this education had on identity formation among overseas Chinese women and larger society. Combining institutional and personal viewpoints, it explores the girls' schools in which these women studied and worked, both those where the primary language of instruction was English and those where it was Chinese. These schools were sometimes also called English-language or English-medium and Chinese-language or Chinese-medium schools, respectively. Some of these institutions spread missionary and imperial influence; others nurtured powerful Asian ethnonational sentiments. The chapters that follow relate the previously untold stories of the students and teachers in these pioneering schools and trace how ethnic Chinese women came to dominate these institutions—in terms of numbers, as agents of change, and as targets of consternation by British and Chinese authorities.

Overseas Chinese female education in these colonies was a force for transformation and a battleground of ideologies during an era of national reinvention. Girls' schools could reproduce social and cultural norms, but they could also be disruptive, giving overseas Chinese women options to be colonial subjects, transnational actors, patriotic national citizens, or some combination of these roles. These institutions exposed diasporic women to a different set of pressures and limitations than were experienced by women within the Chinese nation. Educated overseas Chinese women confronted tensions emanating from intersecting or outright conflicting forces: empire, country of ethnic origin, country of settlement, and a transnational community's effort to find the stable ground of an authentic ethno-national identity amid geo-political upheaval.

Educated overseas Chinese women enjoyed freedoms their mothers and grandmothers could not have imagined. Yet they also found that the promises of gender equality and national belonging were still heavily qualified by the social conventions and political needs of not just one, but several, different nation-states and cultural frameworks. The opportunities for transcending gender stereotypes were unevenly distributed across groups with different socioeconomic and politico-cultural affiliations. Chinese women in diaspora found that failing to conform to any number of state priorities could lead to social disapproval, marginalization, and even deportation. The cost of being transnational was that one could end up stateless after all. Overseas Chinese communities were mindful of these perils, and one of the key considerations in their efforts to advance female education was how it could support their self-consciously cultivated image as a stable, modern, and desirable population in their new countries of settlement.[7]

Historically, the logic behind girls' schools was straightforward and paradoxical. Many patriarchal societies had long regarded the formal education of girls and women as a luxury at best and a breach of morality at worst. But in the nineteenth century, female education became part of civilizational improvement, particularly in Western Europe and North America but also in parts of East and Southeast Asia.[8] Girls' schools were safe enclosures where young females could be shielded from the unseemly gaze of men. In colonial Southeast Asia, such schools ranged from charitable missions operated by nuns who rescued orphans and prostitutes to elite institutions for the daughters of the wealthy and powerful. These schools could tailor their curricula according to certain ideals of femininity, emphasizing domestic skills such as sewing and cooking, or, later, training for so-called women's work in teaching, nursing, or secretarial jobs. Founding bodies behind such educational efforts, such as churches, governments, and local community organizations, could shape these institutions according to their ideologies. Girls' schools would help produce what society needed, in the form of better wives and mothers, or workers and citizens of developing nation-states, while ensuring compliance with desired ideals.

At the same time, the concept of female education never completely shed the aura of deviation, even danger, which surrounded its beginnings. In colonial Malaya and Singapore, schools had to reassure parents that their daughters would be protected by bamboo fences around their campuses, and that covered rickshaws chaperoned by matrons would shield girls from the public gaze as they were escorted to and from school.[9] Although the greatest threat to the survival of these schools was lack of funds, politicians and community leaders placed further obstacles in the way by constantly questioning the content, standards, and necessity of female education. Both male and female critics focused on how schools exposed girls and women to the moral and socioeconomic perils of modernity.

Girls' schools offered a controlled environment that could create and modulate change through careful socialization. They also opened up the possibility of contamination and subversion. This is not to diminish the bold and visionary female educators who helped to launch these efforts, nor the students and teachers who animated these institutions and used their education to great personal and public benefit. In fact, educated women showed great determination and creativity even as they had to bear the triple burden of ethno-national, diasporic, and colonial expectations. Yet there were also unintended consequences to the growth of girls' schools. The support of male-dominated institutions, such as the above-mentioned churches and state governments, was essential to their long-term success. At the very least, administrators, teachers, students, and alumna of these schools had to balance their pioneering work with the agendas of patriarchal sponsors and social environments.

This type of tension is not unique to girls' schools. Boys' schools and co-educational schools have also proven capable of reproducing a status quo as well as generating independent thought and radical change. A classic example is British Indian education, which was intended to cultivate a population of English-speaking natives as low-level civil servants. However, this system also introduced notions of personal liberty and national freedom to indigenous elites, giving rise to a class of local anti-imperialist intellectuals.[10] What is unique in this case—the experience of female education and the overseas Chinese in British Malaya and Singapore—is how this history illuminates and alters understandings of overseas Chinese women, a group that has so far been depicted in limited ways.

The circulation of Chinese people, goods, capital, and ideas in Southeast Asia has been documented from at least the tenth century onward, and written histories of these migrations abound.[11] Although it is not the aim of this book to delve into the details of these histories, it is important to foreground a few significant terms and concepts in overseas Chinese and Southeast Asian studies. When referring to Chinese migrants, I use the terms "ethnic Chinese" and "overseas Chinese" interchangeably, while acknowledging that some scholars consider the latter term problematic because it wrongly suggests an innate political or nationalistic affiliation with the Chinese state. However, both have become accepted if imperfect terms of reference for ethnic Chinese peoples outside China. Similarly, using "diaspora" to describe this community can be controversial, as the term has a complex history and can wrongly evoke notions of shared political sympathies or a desired return to a homeland.[12] As for geographic matters, "British Malaya" and "Singapore" describe the present-day national entities of Peninsular or Western Malaysia and Singapore. These states were grouped as a single administrative unit under British colonial rule from 1867. Malaya gained national independence in 1957 and was renamed Malaysia in 1963; Singapore separated from Malaysia in 1965. In Chinese, *Nanyang* means the "Southern Seas," that is, Southeast Asia.

Malaya and Singapore's sizes and demographic compositions were markedly different, but because they were considered parts of a larger unit of governance during the British colonial administration, this book looks at both venues collectively. For example, in the 1930s, Malaya was a peninsula of approximately 50,000 square miles with a population that was more than half indigenous Malay but with a significant one-third Chinese minority, whereas Singapore was a 247-square-mile island with a population that was more than three-quarters Chinese.[13] Yet the emergence of English and Chinese schools and the developing tensions between nationalist Chinese and British colonials followed similar patterns in both locales. More important, familial, economic, and political ties connected many overseas Chinese in this region and contributed to a sense of common identity.

In-migration of ethnic Chinese to British Malaya and Singapore surged in the eighteenth century, largely due to internal unrest and the easing of restrictions on outmigration in China, combined with the rise of European imperialism and growing labor needs of the British in Southeast Asia.[14] In these multi-ethnic colonies, the British administration also struggled to maintain control over a majority population of indigenous Malays as well as a minority of migrant Chinese and Indian workers.[15] (In Malayan and Singaporean colonial history, the term "Indian" refers to the primarily southern Indian peoples who migrated to these territories from the late nineteenth to the early twentieth centuries, with the encouragement of the British colonials in both sending and receiving societies. The population was overwhelmingly Tamil, with a smaller percentage of Telegu and Malayalee, and also included some north Indians from Punjab, Bengal, and Gujarat.) Norms of Chinese economic migration, whereby men would leave home to sojourn or settle abroad for work opportunities, and the mostly physical nature of available jobs meant that the migrant population was largely male. Insofar as they were part of the Chinese migratory current flowing around Southeast Asia and the rest of the world, women were noted on the historical record mostly as victims of trafficking for prostitution.

Female education began to take root in Malaya and Singapore in the nineteenth century. As in other colonial settings, these girls' schools both reflected and complicated notions of gender and ethnicity that were unique to each locale. British authorities were initially skeptical about local female education and took little action to support it. The earliest appearances of any kind of formal instruction for girls during the first half of the nineteenth century were tentative and uneven. Small, ad hoc classes on basic literacy and needlework for a handful of students at a time were organized by wives of missionaries in port settlements, where trade had attracted mixed populations of colonialists and immigrants from other parts of Asia.[16] Most were adjuncts to larger boys' schools, and many shut down after a few years of operation due to lack of funds or students, or the departure of the missionaries in charge.

By the mid-nineteenth century, the female education movement acquired a new momentum. A critical mass of European missionaries, with some support from the British authorities, founded English girls' schools in these colonies. These institutions were intended for the daughters of European colonials and Eurasians resident in the tropics, but also for daughters of the indigenous Malays and the large Chinese and Indian migrant populations. School founders at this early stage included nuns from French Catholic, British Protestant, and American Methodist orders, and the British administration. Schools started out teaching basic literacy and domestic skills such as sewing and cooking, and later added subjects such as mathematics, literature, and geography; eventually they offered vocational classes such as teacher training and accountancy programs. At the turn of the twentieth century, the sizable ethnic Chinese community in Malaya and Singapore also began to establish Chinese girls' schools, whose enrollments over the next few decades came to exceed the English girls' schools. The Chinese girls' schools drew from American and Western European models of education but remained Chinese in cultural and political orientation. They offered not just alternative learning but an alternative paradigm that competed with the colonially sanctioned English schools. They were also self-consciously modern, emphasizing a curriculum that was similar to that in boys' schools, sometimes eschewing the domestic arts altogether. Newly arrived immigrants signed up as founders, donors, students, and teachers in both these Chinese institutions and English girls' schools.

Throughout the nineteenth and early twentieth centuries, women were a minuscule fraction of the overseas Chinese population. In the 1920s, changes in Chinese and European colonial policies permitted greater female migration, but their numbers were still small. However, by the early twentieth century, ethnic Chinese girls and women dominated the ranks of students and teachers in English- and Chinese-language girls' schools alike. For example, in 1836, there were only 361 women to 2,956 men among the Chinese in Malaya, and 7,229 women to 22,755 men among the Chinese in Singapore.[17] In 1850, there were still only 2,239 women to 25,749 men among the Chinese in Malaya—an increase in absolute numbers of women but an even more uneven sex ratio of 1 to 12.[18] Between 1881 to 1890 and 1891 to 1900, Chinese female immigrants were only 3.4 percent and 5.2 percent, respectively, of the overall number of immigrants in Malaya.[19] The female-to-male ratio among the Chinese population in Singapore was approximately 1:5 in 1911, 1:2 in 1931, and just under 1:1 in 1957.[20] Yet, by the late 1930s, there were more than fifty Chinese girls' schools across Malaya. In the major urban centers of Penang, Kuala Lumpur, and Melaka alone, more than 10,000 Chinese female students were enrolled. English girls' schools in the same areas had an estimated 6,800 Chinese female students.[21] In short, the presence and influence of ethnic Chinese females in girls' schools was much greater than their general population numbers would suggest.

Educated Chinese women were equipped to engage in the public sphere as never before. They had the option of paid and socially respectable work outside the home. Through organized extra-curricular activities such as sports, performing arts, student government, and alumni associations, female graduates were exposed to new avenues for intellectual and personal expression. As tensions of European empire and Asian nationalisms seeped into classrooms, these students gained awareness of and opportunities for participation in transnational political movements—movements that were built on connections and networks that made reference to but also transcended national boundaries, such as overseas Chinese nationalism. The chapters to follow detail these new developments, showcasing the rich internal and external world that educated overseas Chinese women could envision.

Although the vista of possibilities was wider than before, the roads that educated women could actually travel were not as numerous or as extensive as they appeared. Women could study and work, but their primary roles were still located squarely within the home and family. They enjoyed greater freedom of movement and a broader range of intellectual, socioeconomic, and political activities than in previous generations, but they remained under intense scrutiny with regard to their moral purity and femininity. They were inspired to political activism by the rhetoric of equality, modernization, and anti-colonialism that emanated from an ancestral homeland undergoing radical transformation, yet their responses were constrained by their circumstances as an ethnic minority living under British rule. As overseas Chinese women emerged from the domestic sphere into the public realm, the type of school they attended defined their cultural and political affiliations, regardless of the ambivalence or complexity that each individual might have felt. They were perceived as being Chinese nationalist if they attended Chinese schools, and pro-Western if they attended English schools. Girls' education became a politically charged issue that divided the overseas Chinese community by creating an artificially dichotomous choice between ethnic loyalty and Westernization.

To authorities, managing the female population through formal training suited the agenda of modernization, according to the needs of empire or nation. At the same time, girls' schools continued to stress the importance of traditional feminine virtues, such as modesty and domesticity. In the postcolonial era, state ideologies continued to shape the female education experience through gendered curricula, privileging women's domestic roles, sometimes more strongly than during colonial times, even as social attitudes shifted and the economic value of female labor outside the home increased.

Against this backdrop, the value of a closer look at girls' schools and overseas Chinese women becomes clear. Whereas the paradoxes of female education are well studied in terms of national histories, they are less well understood in terms of immigrant populations, particularly one that was at once influential and discriminated against in its places of settlement.[22] While much has been written about overseas Chinese political identities and overseas Chinese women, respectively, the relationship between the two is infrequently examined.[23] Transnational and diasporic Chinese studies have flourished over the past two decades, but the literature on overseas Chinese women and gender remains uneven and overshadowed by a male-centered, politically, and economically focused historiography. To the extent that scholars have examined this population, the focus has tended to be on marriage and family, or on women at extreme ends of the social scale: privileged wives and daughters in elite families or prostitutes and *mui tsai* (Cantonese for "little sister," a euphemism for enslaved bondmaids) on the lowest rung of society's ladder. Other books tend to be anecdotal explorations of individual lives or subgroups, still mostly concentrating on women as exceptional individuals or oppressed subalterns.[24]

But as Liew Yuen Sien's story demonstrates, the lens of female education offers a different, more comprehensive view of overseas Chinese women's history. Myriad forces acted on Chinese women in diaspora, from sources as global in scale as nation and empire, and as intimate as family and personal relationships. Formal education in girls' schools ensured that significant numbers of overseas Chinese girls and women came into direct contact with these forces, suggesting that the classroom is the place to seek more information about women's lives. The process of identity construction among overseas Chinese women does not fit into models that earlier scholars applied to the Chinese diaspora, which typically relied on occupation and migrant generation as determinants of identity patterns and degree of affiliation with China.[25] For most women, who either did not work in the typically male-dominated occupations used in these models or whose politico-cultural orientations have not been studied systematically, how did they think about being Chinese? And what was their legacy to future generations of overseas Chinese? For those in or influenced by girls' schools, the conventional challenges of female education combined with the specific anxieties of overseas Chinese existence. As such, the tug-of-war between modernization and conservatism in female education was overlaid with concerns about how to craft a sense of cultural authenticity and socioeconomic stability that would strengthen overseas Chinese status without threatening authorities in diaspora or in China. All these factors merged to produce an even more densely woven web of demands, options, and obligations for overseas Chinese girls and women.

So how did a community in which men condemned their own women as languishing in a state of "ignorance and degradation" come to be a leader in female education?[26] What happened when these educated overseas Chinese women intellectually and physically moved across the boundaries of empire and nation-state, sometimes repeatedly? Or when diasporic women became vital players in national modernizations? Historians of China and of colonial Southeast Asia have explored female education as a battleground for apparent opposites: progressives versus conservatives, imperialists versus the indigenous.[27] But what about migrant or transnational populations who did not clearly belong to one side or another?

Answers to these questions lie in the lives of educated overseas Chinese women. These women built for themselves a wide range of sociocultural identities that reflected their diverse and transnational environment. However, the politics of the education that empowered their choices also constrained their ability to fully live out those identities. The stories in this book include those of Southeast Asia–born teenagers who ran away to China in the 1940s and 1950s to join the Communist movement; convent schoolgirls who immersed themselves in British culture and went into careers teaching English literature and European geography; and sisters from the same household divided by the language of their education. They reveal the surprising reach of transnational female affiliations and networks in an age and a community that has mostly appeared to be male dominated. Overseas Chinese women joined, maintained, and managed networks in school, workplaces, associations, and politics. They expanded notions of labor and social relations in Chinese and European colonial societies. They were at the center of political debates over language and culture in education and were vital actors in the struggles over twentieth-century national belonging. Often considered a marginal population in overseas migration, Chinese women in fact took bold, creative, and complex actions to participate in global networks.

There are, of course, limitations to using girls' schools as a window into the lives of overseas Chinese women, or any community of women. Formal education was by no means the only way in which gender norms and social expectations were reinforced. Before and after girls' schools were established, informal learning took place within one's family and community, where a wide range of knowledge, practices and traditions would be transmitted from one generation to another. Socioeconomic class, too, limits the use of schools as a means for analyzing an entire community. Up to World War II, attending school was largely the province of wealthier classes, although there were special provisions in English and Chinese schools alike for the poor and indigent. Formal education cannot be assumed to be the only cultural process molding children and youth, and even for those who did attend school, other forms of knowledge acquisition or living circumstances might have buffered the impact of any state-sanctioned ideological influence.[28]

All the same, the society-wide symbolism of modern female education and its importance to institutions of authority justify attention to this seemingly small and privileged subset of women. Educated overseas Chinese women contended with an elite male discourse that linked ethnicity and authenticity with gender and nation. This motif recurred in the Chinese nation, and also among the overseas Chinese community, in the British colonial milieu, and in the early nationalist movements of Malaya and Singapore. The female education project, by and among the overseas Chinese of British Malaya and Singapore, was crucial in envisioning ethnic Chinese status and belonging in multiple sites: country of ethnic origin, colony and nation of settlement, and the spaces in between. Girls' schools, and the girls and women who studied and worked in them, were important actors in engendering the Chinese diaspora.[29]

As in the nation, overseas Chinese girls' schools were emblems of modernity and ideological battlegrounds for women's changing social and political roles. Female education in the age of the nation-state confronted a paradox of having to champion both modernity and tradition. In the diaspora, there was an additional struggle over how educated and modernized women, at once of and outside the nation, could help propagate an authentic ethno-national identity that would represent the overseas Chinese community in their adopted homelands, while maintaining a lifeline to cultural tradition during a period of turbulent geo-political change. Ambivalence about the pro-Western associations of the former and sensitivities about the implication of backwardness associated with the latter only exacerbated the internal conflict. This struggle was not part of a straightforward opposition between East versus West, or nation versus empire. Rather, it was part of a global and multicultural conversation that cut across different transnational diasporas.[30]

Any analysis that uses the concept of "modernization" as an organizing principle necessarily has artificial boundaries. Scholarship and lived experience alike have shown that definitions of modernity are as multifarious and subjective as the human beings who invoke its existence.[31] As problematic as the concept of modernity may be, it is important to foreground it in this book due to its centrality in the female education project and the changing societies in which it unfolded. For men and women alike, modernization was a goal to which they aspired and a benchmark for the girls' schools in which they were involved. They applied the term and their multiple understandings of it in establishing these institutions, in designing and implementing curricula, in their discourses of teaching and learning, and, for the female graduates of these schools, in constructing their identities. At times, the archetype of the Modern Girl or Modern Woman became a foil that the educated Chinese woman could use to prove her own intellectual and sociopolitical importance, or a caricature that opponents of "excessive" female liberation could use to censure girls' schools.[32] The contradictions of modernity became the contradictions of these women's academic, professional, and personal lives.

Among the overseas Chinese of colonial Malaya and Singapore, modernity had additional meanings. It could be a way of aligning oneself with a newly nationalistic and changing China; of acquiring greater economic or social advantage in colonial, national, or transnational contexts; of asserting a particular brand of Western, Chinese, Southeast Asian, or other cultural identity; or some combination thereof. For all these variations and permutations, however, one common feature of modernity as conceived of in these visions was constant reference to something other than oneself. The implication of this feature is that one's current state is unsatisfactory and that one has to move toward a different state, already embodied by someone or something else.[33] In such a framework, the seeker of modernity may well be setting herself up to fall short or to feel that she is betraying some element of herself. Modernization is hence asymptotic—one is always approaching it but the target is constantly out of reach.

Closer scrutiny of overseas Chinese female education also complicates certain pieces of received wisdom about other East-West dichotomies. Insofar as historians have looked at female education in British Malaya and Singapore, usually in the context of education in general, there has been a sense that English-language or Western education was more influential than Chinese-language education for modernizing Asian societies and peoples. Yet a deeper look at overseas Chinese girls' schools suggests an alternative interpretation. Commentators during the colonial period and beyond, Western as well as Chinese, argued that English education was more "modern" because its approach appeared to be more oriented toward introducing scientific learning. This modern learning included the most up-to-date knowledge in areas from geography to mathematics to the fine arts, in notions of physical fitness and democracy, and at least a foreshadowing, if not always a resounding endorsement, of gender equality.[34] English girls' schools aimed to correct the flaws of traditional Asian attitudes toward women. Throughout the twentieth century, the image of the more progressive and sophisticated English school alumna pulling ahead of her more conservative Chinese-educated peers has persisted.

However, a comparison of the two types of girls' schools during the first half of the twentieth century shows that Chinese institutions were in fact more clearly focused on imparting notions of scientific learning, secularism, non-domestic careers, and political awareness. In large part, this was due to the struggle for modernization and the rise of nationalism in China at this time. Unlike English girls' schools, Chinese girls' schools did not regularly offer domestic science, de-emphasizing the importance of cooking, sewing, and housekeeping as necessary skills for an educated woman. The more express political awareness and activism on the part of Chinese female students and teachers was also striking. Although English education unquestionably introduced new ideas and practices for Chinese girls and women, it is by no means clear that Western education was more modern, progressive, or emancipating for overseas Chinese. If anything, Chinese female education, and the women that it produced, often challenged Anglo-American patriarchal norms and appeared to some contemporaries to be more politically and socially progressive, even radical, than its Western counterpart.

Given the volume and frequency of migration in the nineteenth and early twentieth centuries, it is logical to take note of non-nation-based groups spread across the globe, and not just to polities or identity concepts defined by the geographic and ideological boundaries of nations.[35] Scholars have already established the links between female education and national modernization in late nineteenth and early twentieth-century China, but there is as yet little discussion of how the women in one of the largest migrant groups in history featured in the capacious and disputed gaps between nations and empires.[36] Girls' schools attended by ethnic Chinese in colonial Southeast Asia were shaped by three major forces: early twentieth-century China, Western imperialism, and the missionary-colonial complex in Asia. Each force was driven by a specific concern: national rejuvenation in the first and "the civilizing mission" in the second and third. Each power grappled with its own internal inconsistencies and competing interests, such that the overseas Chinese denizens of girls' schools had to contend with a bewildering array of paradoxical expectations. In diaspora as in the nation, women had to embody tradition and the "essential truth" of a nation or civilization, while also representing progress through their education and participation in modern society. For migrant Chinese, especially from the second generation onward, the colonial context created the additional opportunity and burden of integrating new cultural influences with existing practices. As a study of ethnic Chinese in Japan-ruled Manchukuo once asked: "Can a Chineseness be denied to those who seek their identity in their own cosmopolitan traditions?"[37] The case of diasporic female education shows that the answer, at times, is unfortunately yes—although this does not prevent overseas Chinese from seeking their own brand of Chineseness anyway.

This confusion of pressures for educated overseas Chinese women is a microcosm of the overseas Chinese experience in Southeast Asia and beyond, perhaps even of major diasporas throughout the world.[38] As a particular group finds a new way to climb above its existing and often disadvantaged position in the sociocultural hierarchy, its erstwhile superiors may cautiously respect its newly apparent skills, but also suspect it of subverting a natural and desirable order. Whether their sojourns abroad were voluntary or coerced, ethnic Chinese outside of China have often been associated with an almost uncanny ability to adapt and assimilate to local conditions. They would intermarry with indigenous peoples; dominate specific economic niches, especially that of merchant, middleman, or some version of capitalist enterprise; and blend local languages, customs, religions, and even sociopolitical practices with their own. At the same time, overseas Chinese have also often been cast as the perpetual "other": ethnically exclusive in their business endeavors, clannish and insular in their adherence to cultural norms from their ancestral homelands, and outsiders whether resident in a particular locale for one generation or five.[39] The latter perception has been especially invidious when linked to suspicions of economic or political disloyalty to their adopted country and has resulted in anti-Chinese prejudice over hundreds of years in Southeast Asia. In the twentieth century alone, practically every modern nation-state in the region has witnessed anti-Chinese violence. Billed in scholarly and popular literature alike as some of the most adaptable and flexible migrants in the world, the overseas Chinese are also subject to persistent racial stereotyping and hostility.

Educated overseas Chinese women and the overseas Chinese community as a whole have a shared theme of simultaneous disarticulation from their origins and inability to disengage completely from others' perceptions of their essential character. Distanced from traditional Chinese definitions of womanhood, were Chinese female students able to achieve greater emancipation? Unmoored from their ethno-national origins in China, were individuals able to break free from reified categories of race and nation? More often than not, the answer to both questions was no. This is not to deny agency to the girls and women who used education to expand their opportunities and those of others, or to refute the fact that migrant Chinese were able to construct new and innovative cultural-political identities. Nor is the purpose of this book to argue that authentic personhood and cultural identity are entirely subject to validation by entities external to the self. However, it is important to acknowledge historical reality: the grip of racial, national, and gendered categories remained strong, whether from the perspective of the ancestral homeland or the adopted country. For those who had left traditional confines, such as emigrant Chinese, or girls and women who ventured outside the home for modern schooling, their options were in fact more numerous than before. Yet they would be plagued by stubborn prejudices about the untrustworthiness of the immigrant, the China-oriented nationalism of the ethnic Chinese, and the importance of cultivating the "right" kind of woman as a symbol of her cultural or political community. The purported flexibility of the Chinese migrant and the liberation of the educated overseas Chinese woman were not entirely fictional, but, because of unrelenting external pressures, they would never completely be true.

The wide-ranging nature of transnational Chinese women's educational networks made research for *Schooling Diaspora* a similarly transnational quest. Recreating connections between colonial Southeast Asia, the imperial metropole, and a globally dispersed community required pursuit of historical information in four countries: present-day Malaysia, Singapore, England, and China. Print sources from government archives, schools, private homes, alumni associations, and convents were in multiple languages: English, Mandarin Chinese, Malay, and French. This book's richest and most distinctive historical sources are oral histories of educated overseas Chinese women that I conducted in person and collected from archives. I interviewed nearly fifty women in Malaysia, Singapore, and southeastern China about their academic, professional, and personal lives. In addition, I drew from recorded interviews with nearly a hundred local Chinese women at the Oral History Center of the National Archives of Singapore. Although oral histories can be fragmentary, uneven, and deeply subjective, they are nonetheless crucial for excavating a sense of lived experience and otherwise undocumented details about the past. These interviews capture the voices of educated overseas Chinese women and their self-narratives or representations.

Context for overseas Chinese female migration and education was provided by late Qing and early Republican official reports on overseas Chinese education outreach, British Colonial Office records, and the annual reports of the colonial Ministry of Education for the Straits Settlements and the Federated Malay States from the turn of the twentieth century. These reports included details of school curricula, enrollment numbers, school inspectors' evaluations, and photographs of activities such as sports and theater. The administrative records and archives of some of the oldest and most influential English-language and Chinese-language girls' schools gave close insight into the workings of these institutions. So did information from periodicals, such as collections of school magazines and major Chinese-language newspapers, particularly those published by and for overseas Chinese in Malaya and Singapore.

The chapters that follow are organized thematically and chronologically, with some overlap given the simultaneous nature of developments in English-language and Chinese-language education. Chapter 1 examines the British Malayan and Singaporean colonial politics of education in general, girls' schools in particular, and their relationship to imperial attitudes concerning the overseas Chinese. Chapter 2 traces the origins of the earliest English girls' schools in the settlements, paying particular attention to the role of their French Catholic and British Protestant missionary founders, and to the intra-ethnic tensions that grew out of the linguistically plural education system that evolved under colonial rule. Chapter 3 examines how the culturally hybrid Peranakan or Straits Chinese—so-called because they had lived and intermarried for generations in the Straits Settlements of British Malaya and Singapore—reacted to the rise of female education and its implications for the sociocultural status of their community, and their efforts to establish the first Singapore Chinese girls' school for local residents. In Chapter 4, the political dynamics and personal impact of overseas

Chinese female education appear through the writings of students and teachers in school magazines and local newspapers, which highlight tensions between the modernizing mission and ethno-cultural conservatism in Chinese girls' schools of the era. Chapter 5 delves into personal perspectives, focusing on the self-narratives of women from Chinese girls' schools in Malaya and Singapore who re-migrated to China during the 1940s and 1950s to participate in revolution and nation-building. The concluding chapter looks beyond the colonial era to the age of independent statehood in Malaysia and Singapore, and to the continuing evolution of female education. This coda underscores the longevity of gender role assignations in state educational policy, and the delicate relationship between ethnic and gender politics in multicultural, postcolonial nations.

Although the nation-state dominates recent history, the continuous movement of people and ideas across the globe has been more the norm than the exception in the longer chronology of human civilization. Unlike authorities and elites in the nation-state, less powerful groups participating in migration are often neglected or misrepresented in official historical accounts. Tending to the margins of history, as in the case of overseas Chinese women of Southeast Asia, shows us where and how it is possible to correct this imbalance. Diaspora, rather than a satellite of communities orbiting around an ancestral homeland, is for most people their true home and originator of their identities. This perspective suggests that complicated transnational affiliations are not something to eliminate or justify but rather something to understand, and sometimes, embrace.

CHAPTER 1

A Little Education, a Little Emancipation

The Colonial Politics of Female Education, 1850s–1950s

In 1950, a year after China's Communist revolution, British authorities in Malaya decided to sponsor a dozen ethnic Chinese female teachers from local Chinese-language schools to attend a training course in England. The goal was to push back against leftist influences among the overseas Chinese. The training would help create "a wholesome atmosphere in the Chinese Schools" and "to make the Chinese more Commonwealth-minded . . . [or] . . . whatever gains we may achieve against Communism will prove wholly illusory."[1] This plan ran into some difficulties, as the indigenous Malay Conference of Rulers protested that this scheme showed favoritism toward the Chinese, causing the British official in charge to suggest that the Malays did not fully grasp the political import of the training:

> The point that the Chinese sorely needed indoctrination while the Malays did not left [the Malay Rulers] unmoved, and they argued that if Malays were included both they and the Chinese would benefit from the mutual contact. I cannot say whether this was the real reason or whether it was a wish that Malay women might be present to see what was afoot, or possibly no more than a desire that they should share in what is doubtless regarded, in some quarters, as an attractive joyride.[2]

This observation had been written in a draft of a telegram to the secretary of the Federated Malay States, but was removed from the final version in what may have been an attempt at tact, given the tense state of

Chinese-Malay relations at the time. Eventually, half the places in the program were given to Malay female teachers, and the training course proceeded. Unlike other teacher-training schemes designed for educated Malay women at the time, this program had an explicit political agenda that targeted the uncertain subject status of the ethnic Chinese in the colonies and saw educated Chinese women as agents of political and social change who "sorely needed indoctrination." This was an especially pressing need in view of the armed insurrection being staged by local Chinese Communist guerillas against the British government, in what came to be known as the Malayan Emergency of 1948–60.

What led to the differential policy concerning educated Malay and Chinese women in British Malaya and Singapore? And what was the British role in creating, or exacerbating, these discrepancies? To address these questions, this chapter traces why and how the British colonial regime intervened in the education of local girls in Malaya and Singapore from the mid-nineteenth to mid-twentieth centuries, and what this reveals about imperial associations between race, gender, and nationalism, particularly with regard to the overseas Chinese. The chapter first examines the evolution of British educational policies in these colonies, then considers the impact of these policies on the development of Chinese-language girls' schools. A fuller picture of female education in this corner of empire requires more in-depth exploration of the English and Chinese girls' schools in question than can be dealt with in this chapter, but the remaining chapters of the book will concentrate on those schools and their denizens. Here the focus is on how an early period of relative inattention by the British in this area created spaces for missionary societies and the local Chinese community to establish linguistically plural and sometimes private educational enterprises in the mid-nineteenth and early twentieth centuries, respectively. In both cases, the colonial administration increased its involvement several decades after the schools had been founded, but for different reasons: in English schools, to bring the curriculum in line with racialized notions of femininity, and in Chinese schools, to combat the threat of rising Chinese nationalism.

British policies toward Chinese female students were driven more by political than social considerations. Governmental concerns over managing the ethnic Chinese population outweighed the gender-specific assumptions that characterized educational policies for Malay female students. Of all the measures taken to increase British influence over private Chinese-language schools from the 1920s onward, virtually none can be found that target the education of Chinese females, as distinct from Chinese males. The 1950 training program was meant for female teachers in all Chinese schools, not just girls' schools, which contrasts with the attention paid to gender-specific curricula in English-language and Malay-language girls' schools during this period.

Colonial education from the late nineteenth century onward was aimed at training local girls and women in cooking, handicrafts, and hygiene. In the annals of local English missionary girls' schools, for example, there are records of frequent visits to the school by the British Inspector, whose reports include careful notes on students' progress in embroidery and handicrafts.[3] Yet little such mention is made in official records with regard to Chinese girls' schools. In a 1931 annual government report on education, three pages of detailed information on lace-making, weaving, and physical education in Malay girls' schools is followed by a half-page of data and no curricular description of Chinese vernacular schools for girls.[4] Debates in the 1940s and 1950s over the curriculum of Chinese schools, male and female, argued over their orientation toward China instead of Malaya, Singapore, and the British Empire. Efforts to redress this imbalance focused on recruiting and training teachers and principals of local origins, and on replacing China-published textbooks with textbooks and curricula with a more Malayan political and social orientation.[5] Up to the point of decolonization in the late 1950s and early 1960s, comparatively scant attention was paid to revising the largely non-gender-specific curriculum of Chinese girls' schools, which devoted significantly less classroom time to domestic science and whose school publications included writings by female students and teachers on progressive topics such as equality of the sexes, modern womanhood, marriage and divorce, and women's right to a career.

Given that colonial anxieties over gender, sexuality, and race were common across European empires, and female education would presumably be a key arena for these concerns, why is there so little evidence of this when it came to Chinese girls and women in Malaya and Singapore?[6] One explanation lies in the unique position of the ethnic Chinese in the British colonial order. As economic brokers and foreign nationals whose subject positions were not clearly established, they contributed to the operation but also the potential undermining of the imperial project in ways that eclipsed gender-specific issues. While schools designed for indigenous Malay and immigrant Indian girls were targets for racialized notions of gender, Chinese girls' schools were, at least in their early years, regarded as one more form of self-government among a non-indigenous, apparently sojourning population.[7] The shift from relative neglect to close monitoring of these schools was part of a larger preoccupation by the British with the containment of overseas Chinese nationalism. This rising sentiment was an alternative locus of power within the colonial state and summoned the specter of Chinese anti-imperialism and radicalism. This explanation does not imply that colonial administrators lacked awareness of or anxiety over such issues as sexual propriety, marriage customs, and hygiene practices in the Chinese community. Institutions such as orphanages attached to European missionary-run girls' schools and welfare homes for indigent females played a major role in monitoring the sexual health and morality of Chinese women.[8] Rather, a combination of circumstance and choice led the British to focus on the political rather than the domestic in Chinese girls' schools.

COLONIAL POLICIES ON EDUCATION: FROM LAISSEZ-FAIRE TO INCREASING INVOLVEMENT

As in other parts of the colonial world, imperial control in British Malaya and Singapore developed gradually and unevenly. The evolving nature of colonial rule led to a contingent approach to educational policy. British authority in Malaya and Singapore underwent several transformations after it was formally established in 1826. That year, Penang, Singapore, and Melaka (acquired by the East India Company in 1786, 1819, and 1824, respectively) were combined to create the Straits Settlements. These settlements were managed variously by the East India Company Presidency in India, followed by the Presidency of Bengal, and eventually, in 1851, the governor-general of India. The East India Company and the India Office benefited financially from the flourishing trade of the Straits Settlements but did not invest a great deal of energy or care in the administration of these territories, causing frustrated merchants in the settlements to petition successfully for the transfer of control to the London-based Colonial Office in 1867.[9] Up to this point, policy decisions, including those on education, which might have been taken by local leaders such as the British Resident of Singapore, were often overruled by the government in India. Thereafter, even though the British monarch and Colonial Office were empowered to overturn any ordinances passed by local legislatures in the settlements, this right was seldom exercised.[10] Colonial administrators were hence better able to effect policy changes at the local level, although officials in the colonies and metropole continued to wrangle over such matters occasionally.

Similar conditions applied elsewhere in Malaya. To protect their trading interests, the British government took over the states of Selangor, Perak, Pahang, and Negri Sembilan (the Federated Malay States) in 1896, and Perlis, Kedah, Terengganu, Kelantan, and Johor (the Unfederated Malay States) in 1914, each headed by a British Resident or Advisor. These arrangements remained in place until the Japanese invasion and occupation of these territories during World War II. After 1945, decolonization and national independence movements brought about a series of transitional administrations, with increasing local representation but a sustained British influence, up to Malayan independence in 1957 and Singaporean independence in 1963.

During the early to mid-nineteenth century, the colonial stance on education in these territories was one of detached interest. Efforts to establish schools for local residents in Singapore and Malaya in earlier decades had met with polite indifference at best and active discouragement at worst by senior colonial officials. Even the influential Stamford Raffles, who acquired Singapore for the East India Company in 1819, did not garner a great deal of official support when he sought to create an educational institution for what he called the "sons of the higher order of natives."[11] Instead, it was missionaries from France, Britain, and the United States, along with a number of charitable organizations and individuals, who were most active in establishing schools in the Straits Settlements and Malay States from the early nineteenth century onward. These schools could be divided into several categories. There were the English-language Free Schools that were typically set up by private individuals but that enjoyed the patronage of the government before being fully taken over by them in later years. They were called "free" not because they did not require school fees, but because they were open to students of all races and religions. Then there were English missionary schools that received colonial grants-in-aid but that were mostly supported by groups such as the London Missionary Society, the Roman Catholic mission, the American Methodist mission, and the Anglican Church. Eventually, the government also established and operated its own English and Malay schools. Finally, there were private vernacular schools, especially Chinese-language ones, which appeared from the mid- to late nineteenth century onward and did not receive government aid.[12]

In the early to mid-nineteenth century, these schools' intended students were European, Eurasian, or local Malay, Chinese, and Indian boys. Some institutions made efforts to create sub-branches that would cater to female students, but enrollment was typically very low and the all-girl classes or schools were unsustainable for more than a few years at a time. An early girls' school, established in 1817 in conjunction with the Penang Free School (which is regarded as the first English-language boys' school in the Straits Settlements), closed in 1821 due to lack of funds, and another girls' school attached to the Melaka Free School also closed in 1855.[13] A missionary-operated Chinese Girls' School in Penang opened in 1827, teaching needlework and basic literacy, but it, too, was short-lived.[14] By the mid-nineteenth century, there was only one known Malay girls' school, which had been established by a clergyman and his wife and sister.[15] Like male education, female education proceeded through the efforts of many different groups, some numbering no more than three or four individuals, each with its own agenda. Aside from the difficulty for these groups of being a scattered minority, one of their greatest challenges in the early years was simply attracting enough students and financial support to stay open.

Most of these early English-language girls' schools were founded by missionaries who were concerned with the spiritual and moral welfare of local children. Institutions such as the Convent of the Holy Infant Jesus, St. Margaret's School, and Raffles Girls' School were originally intended as shelters for poor, orphaned, or otherwise indigent girls. Their goals were to protect these girls from moral corruption and to provide a basic education in literacy and home-making skills. The first of these institutions to enjoy success and longevity arose in the mid-nineteenth century. At this point the British colonial government was willing to provide financial support and encouragement but was not deeply involved or invested in the operations of these schools. In this loosely managed setting, private entities had significant latitude in their educational endeavors. Schools using various languages of instruction, such as English, Malay, Tamil, and Chinese, were allowed to take root and flourish. The British found this ad hoc system of linguistically plural schools adequate for the short term but became concerned upon realizing that private vernacular education could serve as a channel for ideologies that were inimical to imperial control.

During the latter half of the nineteenth century, British interest in local education increased, but with ambivalence over how much and what type of schooling should be offered to indigenous children. In 1854 and 1857, the Court of Directors of the East India Company issued dispatches to the governor of the Straits Settlements, specifying the parameters of British educational policy in India and Southeast Asia. While education was viewed as a "sacred duty" on the part of the British government, it was also supposed to refrain from disrupting indigenous traditions and, as such, was meant to focus on schooling in local vernacular languages and to provide for those in rural districts.[16] Where English education could be implemented, the language should be taught not as an end in itself but as a means for producing a supply of "intelligent, diligent and honest servants to work for the [East India] Company."[17] During this stage of the imperial project, formal education was often a means of simultaneously creating and forestalling change.

Indigenous peoples were regarded as backward and in need of civilizational improvement, but they were also required to remain in certain socioeconomic and cultural positions that would be most beneficial to the colonial order. Cautious administrators in Malaya argued in 1890 that if education was to be provided to locals, it should produce a very specific outcome:

> [English] could not be well-taught except in a very few schools, and I do not think it is at all advisable to attempt to give to the children of an agricultural population an indifferent knowledge of a language that to all but the very few would only unfit them for the duties of life and make them discontented with anything like manual labour . . . . [Vernacular education], the Koran, and something about figures and geography, this knowledge and the habits of industry, punctuality, and obedience that they will gain by regular attendance at school will be of material advantage to them.[18]

This opinion was echoed by the State Inspector of Schools for Perak in 1895:

> It is *not* advisable to teach English indiscriminately . . . . It is the mere smattering of English and English ideas that is harmful, and which in India causes the country to "swarm with half-starved, discontented men, who consider manual labour beneath them because they know a little English." . . . A simple, vernacular education will, however, tend to make them better citizens and more useful members of the community.[19]

This view was a commonplace among British officials, whose extension of schooling to the local population had a deliberately stunted reach. Among Malay boys, for example, their goal was to "make the son of the fisherman or peasant a more intelligent fisherman or peasant than his father had been, and a man whose education will enable him to understand . . . his own lot in life."[20] The reluctance to offer English-language education to the indigenous population included girls' schools. Raffles Girls' School in Singapore, which had been established by a private board of trustees in 1844, was described by the governor of the Straits Settlements in 1855 as an institution for the daughters of "poor Protestant parents," in which vernacular languages were not taught because the school was not meant for "natives and heathen females."[21] This characterization indicated that English education was not appropriate for local female children because it would unsuit them, as it would boys, to their supposed station in colonial society.

Despite these misgivings, the British were content to allow private entities to take the lead in establishing schools, especially when they would reduce the financial and administrative burden on the government by doing so. To support these efforts, the government provided supplementary financial assistance called grants-in-aid, which from 1870 onward required that the aided school be open to all races and creeds and that religious instruction be optional.[22] Official enthusiasm for this arrangement was expressed in publications such as the *Straits Settlements Annual Report on Education for 1894*, which observed that the cost per student to the government was half the amount at an "aided" or missionary school than at a government school, and recommended that "missionaries and other bodies" should be allowed to undertake the work of the government English schools wherever possible.[23]

After the handover of the Straits Settlements from the East India Company to the Colonial Office in 1867, the colonial administration paid closer attention to education. By 1872, committees that had been set up to study the schooling system in the colonies recommended that greater efforts should be made to expand educational opportunities for indigenous boys and girls, and that a dedicated inspector of schools should be appointed to monitor the condition and operations of local institutions. These were the beginnings of a department of education overseeing Malaya and Singapore.[24]

This imperial vision of educational needs in the colonies did not include all groups. Widely perceived as a non-indigenous and sojourning population, the ethnic Chinese did not appear to have the same claim to government-provided schooling as did the Malays. Colonial legislation for managing the Chinese population was primarily centered on issues of law and order, and this was true of women as well as men. It was this approach that laid the foundation for British policies toward Chinese female education.

COLONIAL CONTROL, THE ETHNIC CHINESE, AND WOMEN

The earliest colonial policies concerning Chinese girls and women centered on maintaining social harmony. When indigenous systems for maintaining social welfare or conflict resolution were in jeopardy and threatened economic stability, the British decided to step in with new laws governing marriage and divorce practices, and to rein in social ills such as prostitution and the keeping of bondmaids. These policies were part of a greater effort to regulate an increasingly large and influential Chinese migrant population in the colonies. Government intervention in girls' schools can thus be seen as an extension of an overall strategy for imperial control and management of race relations.

Throughout most of the eighteenth century and part of the nineteenth, British authorities in Malaya and Singapore had limited control over the activities of the Chinese immigrants in their territories. With scant knowledge of Chinese dialects and social organization, and little interest in the daily lives of the Chinese as long as they performed their economic functions, colonial administrators practiced indirect rule by appointing specific Chinese leaders as "Kapitan Cina" or "captains" of their community. These leaders were in charge of maintaining order among their people, which gave a certain degree of autonomy to the ethnic Chinese. However, the authority of the Kapitan Cina was largely confined to his own dialect group and was also dependent on the support of armed Chinese secret societies.[25] These secret societies in turn grew from strength to strength, both in terms of membership and their control over a range of profitable enterprises, from revenue farms to "vice trades" such as gambling, opium, and prostitution. At the same time, Chinese immigrants were also organizing themselves into more benign groups that were based on affiliations such as ancestral kinship, home district, and professional trade. These associations, also known as *bang* or *huiguan* depending on their type of organizing principle, offered practical aid ranging from employment opportunities to repatriation of an immigrant's body to China for burial, and created a sense of mutual aid and community.

When the Kapitan system appeared to be failing in the mid-nineteenth century, with dialect group and secret society rivalries erupting in violent riots and disruption to social and economic stability, the British decided to intervene. Even before this crisis, some segments of the British community were beginning to put pressure on the colonial authorities to "fulfill its moral obligations as a Christian government."[26] This referred to clamping down on illicit activities, such as gambling and opium smoking, and eradicating the influence of Chinese secret societies. However, British attempts to exercise greater control in Chinese affairs were resented and resisted by the Chinese for several decades.

In the 1870s came the establishment of the Chinese Protectorate. British men who were trained in Chinese dialects were brought to the colonies to help the administration understand and manage the Chinese population. These Protectors of the Chinese, as they were officially titled, were to communicate with and mediate conflicts with the Chinese directly, which presumably would help to win favor with the community. One of the justifications for the existence of Chinese secret societies was their role in protecting newly arrived immigrants and in resolving disputes on their behalf, even if only with rough justice and self-interest to guide them. By passing legislation empowering the Protector of the Chinese to defend the interests of the most vulnerable among Chinese immigrants—newly arrived migrant laborers, and girls and women who were forced into prostitution and bondmaid servitude—the British sought to supplant the secret societies and give some Chinese an alternative recourse for legal protection.[27]

The government enacted further legislation that aimed at reducing illegal or abusive treatment of immigrants, with special attention devoted to Chinese women involved in the vice trades. Such legislation also served the purpose of increasing colonial surveillance and management over local society. An 1877 Immigrant and Anti-Crimping Ordinance, forbidding the coercive recruitment of Chinese labor, opened the way to the registration of newly arrived Chinese workers. In 1881, the Protector of Chinese was charged with enforcing the Contagious Disease Ordinance, a piece of legislation that had existed since 1870 and that enabled the government to inspect brothels and prostitutes to prevent the spread of venereal diseases. In 1885, a Society for the Protection of Chinese Women and Children in the Straits Settlement was organized to suppress the kidnapping and trading of girls and women and to rescue victims of these crimes. These intentions were given some legislative heft by the passage of the Protection of Women and Girls Ordinance in 1887. Taken together, these actions show a colonial preoccupation with managing physical and moral hygiene, at the time considered to be essential components of an orderly and civilized society, through the regulation of women's bodies.[28]

From the management of social health and order through legislation, it was only a short distance to addressing the problem at its source by molding people's minds and behavior. Formal education appeared to be a promising means of influencing the public, especially as private groups such as missionaries had since the mid-nineteenth century been using schools as shelters for indigent youth and centers for proselytization in Malaya and Singapore. However, government educational policy as it developed over the next several decades was not total or monolithic. Imperial interests, driven by metropolitan powers and local officials seeking to preserve their control over their territories and resources, were tempered by a range of restrictions and countervailing forces. Long-standing attitudes toward particular ethnic groups shaped trends in colonial policy. Ethnic Chinese communities were often treated as less entitled to governmental concern or services than indigenous peoples, at least until their activities posed a threat to social order. Financial limitations, missionary influence, changing notions of the extent and purpose of state involvement in social services, and the relative strength of various groups that desired some measure of control over their children's schooling experience—all had a profound impact on the development of the education system in Malaya and Singapore, a system that was characterized by decentralization and linguistic pluralism.[29]

COLONIAL POLICIES ON EDUCATION: A NEW FOCUS ON GIRLS' SCHOOLS

British colonial attention to female education entered a new phase in the 1890s, nearly two decades after the 1872 educational report that inspired the creation of a Department of Education and other measures for monitoring local schools. This sea change was likely spurred by a series of reforms in Victorian England, where education in general and female education in particular were on the rise. Between the 1840s and the 1880s, women in the metropole gained access to universities and vocational training, while government decrees extended the right to free primary education across society.[30] In the colonies, the official interest in girls' schooling was driven by a combination of pragmatism and a sense of moral duty. By equipping girls and women with basic work skills, education would give them the means for economic survival and keep them from becoming social problems in the form of prostitutes, indentured servants, or indigents. To some, female education was also an instrument for improving the homemaking and mothering skills of local women, part of the civilizing mission for which the government felt it should bear some responsibility, especially with regard to the indigenous Malay population. Officials made concerted efforts to persuade Malay parents to send their daughters to government-operated girls' schools. They proffered attractions such as placing schools close to residential areas, so that girls would not have to be exposed to the outside world for any longer than necessary to get to class, and introducing classes in needlework, lace-making, and silk sarong weaving, with the hope that these measures would bring Malay girls into contact with Western ideas of education long enough to be changed by them.[31]

No doubt the flurry of activity by missionaries in this area, while relieving the government of some of the financial and practical onus involved, also caused some anxiety over the administration's lack of influence over their female subjects. It may have been with a mixture of awe and concern that officials in 1894 noted: "While Missionary bodies have done so much for boys' schools, they have done almost everything for female education. A few years ago there was no demand for the education of girls; that the attitude of parents has changed is due . . . to the work of the Convents and other Missionary Schools."[32] In 1895, the British Inspector of Schools in

Kuala Lumpur, Frank W. Harris, noted that one obstacle to the establishment of a government girls' school was that there were already a number of privately organized girls' schools in existence. Even with enrollments of less than twenty students each, they were competition for the colonial authorities. At the same time, Harris expressed confidence that parents would prefer a government girls' school because it would be able to provide "certified female teachers," and that he would endeavor to find out "how many Chinese may be expected to appreciate the advantages" of this provision.[33] Such a school was indeed established in August 1896, with an enrollment of eighteen students whose average age was eight.[34] While the eventual success of this school is unclear from the historical record, it is intriguing to note the importance accorded to the attendance of Chinese students. Their presence would have mattered because the numbers of Chinese were larger in this area, and they were therefore more likely to bring with them the financial revenue that the Department of Education needed.

Some administrators were skeptical about the necessity of female education. Frank Swettenham, British Resident of the Federated Malay States and eventually governor of the Straits Settlements, remarked in 1899: "It might be that a little education, a little emancipation, is what the Malay woman chiefly needs. I doubt it."[35] But others were more adamant about the necessity of local girls' schools, primarily because of the vital role that women played as mothers and as the earliest teachers that their children would encounter. The director of education for the Straits Settlement in 1906 argued:

> The greatest obstacle to all educational efforts [is] the indifference on the part of the Asiatic population to the education of girls, and the consequent ignorance and faulty home influence of the women. In spite of anything that can be done for the boys, even they can never be satisfactorily educated in the true sense of the word unless the intellectual level of their mothers and sisters is raised.[36]

This belief in the importance of raising the "intellectual level" of women so that they could better serve empire or nation was common among male elites throughout the world at the turn of the twentieth century and is more extensively discussed in Chapter 3.

Domestic practices were a matter of sufficient concern that they were added to the official curriculum advocated by the Department of Education in 1893, under the subject name of "Domestic Economy."[37] According to yet another director of education, improvement of women's skills in this area would help raise the standard of living in the colonies, in terms of literal and metaphorical health:

> The ignorance of women is a formidable obstacle to progress especially in such matters as sanitary education and hygiene. Many of them live in a heavy, murky atmosphere of ignorance and superstition. Education will provide light and ventilation essential for development and vigorous life.[38]

The value that education could add to a woman's potential role as a wife was a point of leverage for advocates of girls' schools. In Singapore, St. Margaret's School, which was originally founded as a shelter for poor or orphaned Chinese girls, was noted in the 1920s for its "service" of providing Christian Chinese wives to local Chinese male converts.[39] For the Malay community, British education officials in 1931 found satisfaction in knowing that "thoughtful Malays [now] recognize the need of supporting an attempt to educate girls to be the intellectual peers of their husbands."[40] Interestingly, the criteria for being an "intellectual peer" in the 1930s were still confined to domestic skills, albeit those that were more leisure-related than practical, such as "cookery, clay modeling, paper-cutting [and] drawn thread work."[41] An educated local female populace was seen by colonial authorities as an important asset in the quest for civilization and modernization, a view that was shared by many local elites and nationalist movements around the world. At the same time, colonial authorities assumed the right to determine and delimit the type of education that would be most appropriate for native peoples, as illustrated in the case of Malay girls and women. Anything more than a little learning, then, was a dangerous thing, and education for local girls was often confined by the parameters of traditional gender roles within a patriarchal structure.

Over the course of several decades, the British colonial government felt that it had been reasonably successful in promoting female education in Malaya at large and among the Malay community in particular. The first Lady Supervisor of Malay Girls' Schools was appointed in 1928, a position that was continued until 1932 when financial restrictions caused the temporary suspension of this post.[42] By the 1930s and 1940s, official reports on education took pride in noting an increase in enthusiasm for female education "among all the races," an "anxiety" for the same among the Malays, and "notable victory" in the operation of Malay girls' schools.[43] This was considerable progress from the early days, when "prejudice and conservatism" among local peoples kept girls from attending school:

> For years the girls of all races remained as it were, caged, hidden in the background, rarely seen and deprived of all the contacts that make life rich and full.

In course of time all this was changed and much of the credit must go to the teachers of these first girls' schools, mainly Eurasians, who refused to lose heart. The girl of Malaya is very different from her sister of yesterday: she possesses charm, force, energy, personality and conversational vivacity.[44]

There was, however, one significant wrinkle in this narrative of success. The Chinese vernacular schools, privately established and operated with little to no colonial involvement, were a source of interest and frustration to colonial officials. In its annual reports, the Department of Education provided comprehensive details on English and Malay schools, but comparatively sparse information about the Chinese-language and Tamil-language schools. The government had decided early on to concentrate its resources and efforts on providing education for the indigenous population and had opted to leave the Chinese and Indian communities to their own devices. The Indian population was small and its schools few; educational opportunities for Indian girls were rare, save for exceptions such as the Anglo-Tamil Schools (later included among the Methodist Girls' Schools), which were operated by the American Methodist mission. The Chinese population, on the other hand, was both numerous and increasingly active in the educational sphere. At the turn of the twentieth century, local Chinese girls were already beginning to dominate both missionary and government English-language schools. Their attendance was sufficiently desired by British officials that as early as 1897 there were suggestions to offer Chinese-language classes in government girls' schools or even to establish government-sponsored Chinese vernacular girls' schools to attract them.[45] From the 1900s on, social and political events in China sparked a new movement in Chinese-language female education, which, by the late 1930s, would eventually outstrip English girls' schools in their enrollments. Officials noted these developments but found them difficult to track and regulate as most of these privately operated schools remained beyond the purview of the colonial state. In the 1920s, the British colonial administration began to turn from relative disinterest in Chinese female education to a stronger interventionist approach.

EXAGGERATED NATIONALISM AND UNPATRIOTIC COSMOPOLITANISM: OVERSEAS CHINESE FEMALE EDUCATION

The Fifth Educational Conference of Malaya took place in 1939 and was attended by delegates from the Department of Education, Department of Health, and various educational institutions from across Malaya and

Singapore, including government, missionary, and private Tamil and Chinese vernacular schools. The main committee took a firm stance on using education to inculcate a strong but measured sense of pro-British patriotism. "One of the main objects of education," it was stated in the opening speech, was to prepare youth "to steer successfully between the Scylla of an exaggerated nationalism and the Charybdis of an unpatriotic cosmopolitanism."[46] Although the reference was not explicit, it clearly pointed to parts of the ethnic Chinese population, which was suspected of either being too closely bound to the cause of Chinese nationalism, or too loosely affiliated with the British imperial world to be anything but dangerously cosmopolitan. This statement reflects the increasing politicization of Chinese vernacular education over the previous decades, which aroused consternation on the part of the British educational authorities.

The same speech from 1939 noted that there had been a "marked advance" in the education of Malay girls, whose schooling was vital to the project of the colonial state: "By training the girl we bring education into the home, and the girl, so trained, as a wife and mother helps the cause of education in the State."[47] The government promised to continue its efforts on this front, with "further facilities for the education of Malay girls in the way of the training of teachers, the supervision of schools and the provision of more schools . . . engaging the earnest attention of the Department of Education."[48] While Malay female education was singled out for praise and attention, and English-language girls' schools were discussed at some length at other points in the conference, Chinese and Indian female education were not. This pattern was reflected in the annual reports of the Departments of Education in the Straits Settlements and Federated Malay States, in which lengthy reports on the conditions and operations of Malay and English girls' schools outweighed the cursory reports on Chinese and Indian female education. Although lack of information on these privately run, non-English institutions could be part of the explanation, there remains the question of why the students of these other schools did not appear to be considered in the same category as Malay girls and what, if any, official educational policies were directed toward them.

This is not to suggest that the colonial administration had paid no attention to female education in the local Chinese community in earlier decades. In 1898, an official discussion over the possible establishment of a government Chinese girls' school in Kuala Lumpur dwelled on the reluctance of parents to send their daughters to a school, as they were thought to have "a great dread" of their children being kidnapped, and proposed a number of measures, such as having a tall bamboo hedge surrounding the school building, to assuage parents' fears.[49] Education officials noted the increasing numbers of Chinese girls in missionary, government, and Chinese vernacular schools in the late nineteenth and early twentieth centuries. They wrote, in 1911, that Chinese girls would "beg to continue their schooling" even after their parents considered them too old and in 1929 that several of them would stay in school long enough to matriculate and go on to train as professionals, mostly in teaching.[50] The recruitment of Chinese girls for government schools was desirable, as in the case of the 1895 Kuala Lumpur school. The colonial administration consistently supported the ethno-culturally hybrid Peranakan or Straits Chinese community, who founded the Singapore Chinese Girls' School in 1899. Immediately after World War II, the Department of Education recorded that more than half the students in English-language girls' schools were ethnically Chinese, a far greater proportion than population numbers would suggest.[51] At a minimum, the demand for girls' schooling among the ethnic Chinese was noted by the British as a positive development.

Nonetheless, negative cultural assumptions about vernacular education and the Chinese community as a whole colored British opinion of Chinese girls' schools. The growing strength of Chinese nationalism gave colonial administrators pause, particularly from the 1910s onward. Some accounts put the total number of Chinese primary and secondary schools on the Malay Peninsula in 1938 at 1,032, "developed entirely from the financial resources of the Chinese community."[52] Chinese schools for boys and girls alike created a literal and figurative space for transmitting a distinct cultural and political identity, making them sites for alternative forms of identification that often eluded the control of imperial power. The British government did not have easy access to their inner workings, as most Chinese schools typically refused government grants and therefore stood independent from colonial oversight. Through these schools, influence from China in the form of textbooks, teachers, and political beliefs was able to reach the local community. As fears about "exaggerated nationalism" and "unpatriotic cosmopolitanism" came to shape colonial policy, Chinese female education became subsumed as part of a larger challenge—the management of a politicized and economically influential ethnic population—rather than being treated as a crucible in which state-approved wives and mothers could be forged. This dynamic was reinforced by the fact that the ethnic Chinese who had settled in the British colonies were neither indigenous nor completely foreign, so did not have a reassuringly fixed sociopolitical position relative to the imperial state.

Chinese girls' schools in Malaya and Singapore were modeled along Western lines but with a Chinese cultural orientation. The medium of instruction was Mandarin Chinese; history, geography, and literature focused mainly on China; and most textbooks were obtained from Chinese publishers.[53] Unlike Malay and English girls' schools, Chinese girls' schools emphasized non-gender-specific curricula, with much less time spent on domestic science than in missionary girls' schools. These schools prospered throughout the 1920s and 1930s, such that by 1937, the number of students in Chinese girls' schools in Penang, Kuala Lumpur, and Melaka stood at 10,620, exceeding the 6,844 enrolled in English girls' schools.[54] Given that the former type of institution would have had an almost entirely Chinese student body, whereas the latter would have included a mix of Chinese, Indian, Malay, and Eurasian students, it is reasonable to speculate that Chinese girls occupied the largest percentage of all school-going or educated females in British Malaya and Singapore during this period.

As the colonial administration grew uneasy over the ethnic, cultural, and political assertion of the Chinese community through its schools, officials sought to exert more control in the educational sphere. These efforts took the form of government ordinances and programs that were supposedly designed to maintain consistent educational standards but were in fact also aimed at monitoring political activities, particularly those of Chinese schools that were suspected of being hotbeds for ethnic nationalism or radicalism. Such fears were magnified by the events surrounding the May Fourth movement in 1919, when anti-Japanese protests in China spread to Malaya, with violent demonstrations by Chinese schoolteachers and students in Singapore, Penang, and Kuala Lumpur leading to the British declaration of martial law in the first two territories.[55]

With a rising tide of ethno-national fervor sweeping outward from China and lapping at the shores of overseas Chinese communities, most Chinese schools in Malaya and Singapore elected not to accept government grants-in-aid and hence remained opaque to imperial view. When British authorities passed an ordinance in 1920 requiring the registration of all private schools, teachers, and managers; another in 1923 establishing a system of financial grants for Chinese schools; and yet another in 1924 creating an Inspector of Chinese Schools, the objects of these legislative measures were reluctant to comply. The 1920 school registration ordinance theoretically applied to all schools but was targeted at Chinese ones and sought to expand colonial control by giving the government the power to close schools that failed to meet official standards concerning management, sanitation, and the curriculum.[56] Later amendments to these ordinances adopted a less punitive approach, offering expanded financial assistance to Chinese schools that were willing to open themselves to inspection in 1923, and providing incentive grants for Chinese schools that had Junior

Cambridge-certified instructors teaching more than a certain number of hours of English language each day.[57]

Despite these enticements and the real need for financial assistance in many Chinese schools, there was a continued reluctance to meet the requirements that would qualify them for aid.[58] In some cases, the response was outright protest, as principals of Chinese institutions, including prominent leaders of girls' schools, risked government censure and even deportation by resisting these attempts at surveillance and control. British educational authorities described these measures as part of an overall plan to standardize and improve local schools. Chinese schools found these efforts intrusive and imperialistic. Matters were not improved by the fact that full understanding by the British administration of the ethnic Chinese population was often colored by cultural assumptions and misperceptions, as illustrated by the example of official committees that were concerned with the promotion of "social hygiene" in the colonies. One such committee argued in 1925 that one of the best ways to address the problems of prostitution and general moral malaise was through education. Its rationale was that teaching "sex hygiene" to Chinese children should be easier than with Western children because the former "is said to have full knowledge of sex matters at a comparatively early age."[59]

These tensions became increasingly problematic as significant portions of the overseas Chinese community grew more politicized throughout the 1930s and 1940s. Chinese schools appeared to be staging grounds for the assertion of overseas Chinese ethnic identity and resistance to foreign encroachment. Chinese girls' schools were not exempt from this influence, and in fact had grown out of the political and cultural ferment that characterized the early twentieth-century experience for Chinese overseas. Two of the most prominent and long-running Chinese girls' schools in Malaya and Singapore were Kuen Cheng Girls' School, founded in 1908 in Kuala Lumpur, and Nanyang Girls' School, founded in 1916 in Singapore. In both schools' histories, there are connections with reformers and revolutionaries of early twentieth-century China. Kuen Cheng numbers among its earliest proponents the reformist Kang Youwei, and one of Nanyang's original founders is said to have been the revolutionary Sun Yat-sen.[60] Apart from their non-gender-specific curriculum, these institutions also promoted notions of gender equality, careers outside the home, and Chinese culture and nationalism. In times of political crisis, Chinese-educated girls and women became even more noticeable public actors, joining protests against the Japanese in World War II, guerilla campaigns against Western imperialism in the postwar period, and pro-China nationalist movements from the 1950s.

Throughout this period, official reports on Chinese girls' schools during the first half of the twentieth century critiqued both the lack of domestically oriented training in the curriculum and the supposedly sub-standard quality of teachers in these institutions. Yet, when it came to educational policy, British attention focused only on the latter problem. While issues with the curriculum could be at least partially explained by so-called cultural differences and did not offer ready opportunities for official intervention, the quality of teachers was an area in which colonial authorities were able to justify their involvement and hold these institutions to external standards, thus wresting some control over a dangerously autonomous site within the Chinese community. Despite colonial solicitousness over gender-specific curricular issues in English and Malay girls' schools, little such concern was directed at Chinese girls' schools, which were viewed more as part of a larger political problem than as important training grounds for female colonial subjects.

For the Departments and Inspectors of Education, regulating the standard of teaching in all schools was one of their raisons d'être. In the late nineteenth and early twentieth centuries, much ink was spilled in the pages of annual education reports and missives between colony and metropole on the challenge of obtaining adequately trained instructors for local girls' schools.[61] Authorities took special interest in teacher training programs, hoping to generate a pool of local talent to supplement the well qualified but undoubtedly expensive specialists who were brought in from England to teach classes, assist in inspecting schools, and design curricula. The Kuala Lumpur government girls' school established in 1896 was confident that one of its main attractions for local Chinese parents would be its staff of certified teachers.[62] Of course, administrators wanted all teachers to conform to specific, standardized, and Western philosophies of education. From the 1920s to the 1950s, annual reports on education devoted entire sections to detailing local teacher training programs and the inadequacies of Chinese schools on this front, especially in equipping teachers with English-language skills and "modern" pedagogical methods. Authorities favored European approaches such as those of Friedrich Froebel, the early nineteenth-century founder of the kindergarten and pre-primary child education methods, whose reformist educational measures were later criticized as racial, classist, and exclusionary.[63] British colonials gave credit to the "Froebel-minded women officers" they had employed to develop a sound primary education program in these settlements.[64] Evidently, it was a priority to cultivate a class of educators who were trained according to colonial norms of schooling, and who would also be willing to uphold them. In the government's view, this was a vital means for extending their influence into the Chinese community.

On the curricular front, official criticisms of Chinese girls' schools ranged from the superficial, such as the "noise" that would emanate from the "chorus methods of teaching reading," which were "a nuisance to neighbouring classes," to the more substantial, such as the list of things that Chinese girls' schools lacked:

> There is no specific feminine tradition of education, and girls follow the same curriculum as boys . . . . [T]here is no Domestic Science, there is no physical training especially designed for girls. There is no particular hygiene taught relating to the part girls will play as mothers in charge of homes . . . . There is little real craft developed in any school. The schools are severely handicapped by bad premises (one is in an old temple), by lack of furniture, and by lack of equipment and apparatus.[65]

In the 1940s, a number of official reports on education in Singapore observed disapprovingly that teaching of domestic science in Chinese girls' schools had "made little headway" and was regarded with "only moderate enthusiasm."[66] In the Federation of Malaya, the Director of Education recorded that with only one exception, Chinese middle schools for girls offered no instruction in domestic science, even though, in his opinion, "there can be no reasonable doubt that Chinese parents would appreciate the inclusion in the curriculum of a subject bearing directly on the career of marriage."[67] Regardless of British opinion, up to the point of decolonization in the 1950s, the curriculum of privately operated Chinese girls' schools remained largely the prerogative of the institution itself. The government was only able to intervene in terms of demanding that they use more "Malayanized" classroom materials, that is, no China-oriented or China-published textbooks.

Chinese-language girls' schools stood out as separate and separatist entities, seemingly neither dependent on nor interested in the colonial approach to formal education. British authorities were willing to tolerate this situation as long as they believed that private community efforts at schooling would save the imperial government money, time, and effort. But as the Department of Education became increasingly interventionist, and burgeoning Chinese nationalism became more of a threat, the British administration undertook more concerted efforts to track the goings-on in these schools and to bring them under state influence. During the post–World War II period, when the Malayan Emergency of 1948–60 saw local Chinese Communist guerillas in armed conflict with British and Malayan authorities, suspected Communist activists were monitored, arrested, and sometimes deported. These individuals included students and teachers from Chinese girls' schools. A graduate of one of these schools who became a teacher in the 1950s remembers that she and her female colleagues eagerly took part in the locally organized "Torch Movement," in which they went door-to-door in ethnic Chinese neighborhoods urging parents to enroll their children in Chinese-language schools.[68] Given the racial tensions and anti-Communist fears of the time, this was a highly political act that exposed these women to potential persecution. With the "feminization" of the teaching profession from the 1930s and 1940s onward, the influence of Chinese-educated women on the youth of the nation was no small thing.[69] Hence, when female Chinese teachers were targeted in special training schemes, the priority was political indoctrination, not the promotion of traditional gender roles that Chinese girls' schools seemed to be challenging.

As Malaya and Singapore approached independence from British colonial rule in the late 1950s, political stability in a multi-ethnic, multicultural society became ever more an issue of concern. Education continued to be a vital means for cultivating a sense of national identity and belonging, but now along the lines of citizenship and not colonial subjecthood. Still haunted by the twin specters of "exaggerated nationalism" and "unpatriotic cosmopolitanism," advocates of Chinese-language education found themselves struggling to keep their mandate alive amid a new landscape of racial politics, and state interest in female education persisted, albeit with different considerations and scope for action, in the postcolonial era.

Up to and beyond the point of national independence for British Malaya and Singapore, the status of the overseas Chinese community as an intermediate, non-native ethnic population had a profound impact on government policies. To colonial authorities, Chinese girls and women were seen primarily through the lens of nationality and culture, resulting in a clear distinction between measures taken to control them as a group, and measures directed at indigenous Malay women and Malay- or English-language girls' schools. Chinese-language girls' schools were treated as Chinese schools first and as girls' schools second, reflecting the anxiety of British colonial authorities over the political activism and anti-imperialism of the overseas Chinese community. Efforts to control these institutions were driven more by political fears than gender-based concerns, showing that the British viewed the ethnic Chinese, who were neither fully their subjects nor their equals, as a community whose cultural awareness and national pride were more destabilizing to the colonial order than any challenge that their women posed to colonial patriarchy.

Of course, these schools could not and did not serve all segments of society. Nor, as policies concerning the sexual hygiene of the colonies indicate, did they reflect the entirety of British official attitudes toward local girls and women. Formal education was mostly a privilege for the wealthier classes, at least up to World War II. Colonial policies for dealing with Chinese women involved in prostitution and slavery may reflect other, more commonly known imperial perspectives on women, sexuality, and race. Nonetheless, the contrast between British priorities in educational services for the Malays as opposed to the Chinese delineates the different colonial attitudes toward varied groups under imperial control and explains the lacunae within which non-colonial entities such as European missions, Chinese community groups, and the Chinese nation were able to operate with relative freedom.

Despite the existence of a complex bureaucracy, legal codes, and specialized divisions such as the Department of Education, colonial influence was not applied uniformly across different parts of society. It was hamstrung by a variety of factors, such as lack of resources or insufficient knowledge about local conditions, and was often reactive to the most pressing political exigencies of the moment. These characteristics marked the early years of educational policy in colonial Malaya and Singapore. Such a dynamic suggests an intriguing interplay between the two transnational phenomena of colonialism and diaspora. While the former involved formal systems of rule and the latter an informal movement of peoples, it turns out in this case that colonialism was the more ad hoc and improvisational of the two, while the migrant Chinese response to its diasporic situation was to establish standardized structures of cultural preservation.

CHAPTER 2

Barrier against Evil, Encouragement for Good

English Girls' Schools, 1850s–1960s

In 1852, after four arduous months of travel over land and sea, two French nuns from the Order of the Charitable Mistresses of the Holy Infant Jesus (IJ) in Paris arrived on the island of Penang.[1] They had lost two other members of their mission along the way: one sister had become ill and died, and another had run away with the ship's captain when they were docked in Singapore. The task of their mission was to establish a school for girls—an institution that would include a crèche, a nursery, an orphanage, and catechism classes. In providing these services for the indigenous peoples of Malaya, the sisters hoped to win converts for their faith. This was not a new strategy: it had been practiced by their order since its founding in France in the late seventeenth century. However, this was the first time that sisters had traveled so far from home to fulfill their mission, with a special focus on girls and women. According to school histories, such was the dedication of the nuns that while still at home they had practiced sleeping while wrapped up in thick wool blankets even in the heat of summer in order to prepare for the sweltering equatorial climate.

The early years in Penang were full of struggle and anxiety. The sisters were tested by financial shortages, tropical diseases, and local languages, primarily Malay, that they had to learn.[2] Student enrollment was modest and erratic. Ongoing obstacles included resistance by locals to the idea of female education and the hostility of rival missionary orders.[3] But persistence and effort, together with some limited support from the British colonial administration, paid off. The sisters of the IJ Order not only established a flourishing school for girls in Penang—the Convent of the Holy Infant Jesus (CHIJ) on Light Street, otherwise known as Convent Light Street or the IJ Convent of Penang—but also founded a number of convent schools throughout British Malaya. By 1924, there were seven such institutions.[4] By 1941, there were forty-seven convent schools across the peninsula, with yet more throughout Asia in Singapore, Thailand, and Japan.[5] The motto for many of these institutions was "Simple Dans Ma Vertu, Forte Dans Ma Devoir" (Simple in Virtue, Steadfast in Duty). Throughout its period of growth, the IJ schools found that ethnic Chinese girls dominated the student population. According to the chronicles of the IJ Convent in Kuala Lumpur, between 1900 and 1941, the majority of students were Chinese.[6]

For the overseas Chinese in British Malaya and Singapore, English-language (or English) girls' schools offered opportunities for improving their social status, both within their own ethnic communities and vis-à-vis other ethnic groups in the colonies. By enrolling their children in these schools, Chinese families hoped to secure better marriages for their daughters, gain access to the linguistic and cultural capital of their colonial rulers, and associate themselves with Western modernity and affluence. Still, even as English girls' schools opened doors to upward social mobility for some, these institutions embodied and perpetuated imperial hierarchies of gender, class, and race. While this characteristic of colonial education was not unique to Malaya and Singapore, the adaptive responses of the ethnic Chinese shows that the Western civilizing project shaped the identities of migrant and diasporic peoples at least as powerfully as overseas nationalism did. Educated overseas Chinese women were important participants in the building of communal overseas Chinese identity. The class-aspirational quality of English schooling for ethnic Chinese girls in British Malaya and Singapore linked British culture and hopes of socioeconomic status improvement. Because male elites in various societies portrayed women as emblems of progressiveness or civilization for their communities, the linguistic milieu in which girls were educated came to be invested with political and cultural meaning. The language of their education could determine the socioeconomic class to which women and their community would eventually belong and would furthermore be part of a cultural orientation, which they, as mothers and teachers, were uniquely positioned to impart to their families and children. The less benign outcome of this dynamic, however, was the enduring intra-communal suspicion, even hostility, that emerged between English-educated and Chinese-educated overseas Chinese in the postcolonial era.

This chapter looks at the development of English girls' schools in Malaya and Singapore from the late nineteenth to the mid-twentieth centuries. It traces their origins as providers of social welfare services and their role in the quest for status improvement for the local Chinese population. It focuses on one of the most widespread and influential organizations in the area of female education: missionary girls' schools, particularly the Order of the Infant Jesus (IJ). Less than a century after their arrival in colonial Malaya and Singapore, the French Catholic IJ Order had not only founded one of the largest and best regarded girls' schools in the region but had also established nearly fifty other branch schools throughout the peninsula.[7] Other missionary groups belonging to the Church of England and the American Methodist Church also founded a large network of girls' schools, working with the permission, if not always the full assistance, of the British colonial administration. The last section of this chapter turns to ethnic Chinese women who attended these schools around the mid-twentieth century and how the politics of language may have alienated them from their Chinese-educated sisters. Over time, English missionary girls' schools in these colonies became closely affiliated with the perpetuation of Anglo-American sociocultural and political values. These institutions reinforced traditional and patriarchal gender norms even as they introduced new possibilities for women's work. They reified colonial socioeconomic categories even as they offered some chances for social mobility, and heightened awareness of racial differences even as they gave diverse ethnic groups a common linguistic and cultural reference point in the form of English, often Christian, socialization. Generations of students passed through these schools, many of whom became teachers, one of the few professions that educated women found genuinely open to them. As ethnic Chinese girls and women became a demographically significant portion of students and teachers in these schools, they were deeply influenced by this education as they in turn shaped the schools' development.

The value that some overseas Chinese placed on an English-language education in the British colonies became a point of bitter contention from the 1920s onward. While parts of the Chinese community saw English girls' schools as a crucial means of improving the lot of their women, others saw them as foreign institutions that undermined the integrity of Chinese identity. To pro-Chinese education factions, English schools destroyed certain traditions, such as knowledge of Chinese language and history, and were anti-progressive in supporting colonialism and smothering the rise of Chinese nationalism. In so doing, they argued, these schools hampered the modernization of Chinese girls and women, and hence of the Chinese people and nation. Other groups in the Chinese community had no such reservations in sending their daughters to English schools, or, in the case of the Peranakan Chinese, creating their own brand of Sino-English female education. This conflict played out not only in the realm of public politics but also in the personal experiences and attitudes of educated Chinese women.

THE MORAL ORIGINS OF ENGLISH-LANGUAGE GIRLS' SCHOOLS

The motto of Raffles Girls' School, one of the oldest English girls' schools in Singapore, is "Filiae Melioris Aevi," or "Daughters of a Better Age." Introduced in 1953, the slogan communicates a message of progressiveness and female empowerment. Yet the chief objective of this school, when it was founded in 1844, was "to shelter the girls from the many temptations to which they were exposed, the provision of some sort of education being but a secondary consideration."[8] This shift of female education from preventive measure to positive mission reflects the origins of English-language girls' schools in British Malaya and Singapore, which were originally intended as rescue centers for orphans, indigents, or "fallen women" before they became learning institutes for daughters from middle- and upper-class homes. To carry out this work, religious societies and the British administration relied on nuns, wives of missionaries, and certified teachers from Europe and America to accomplish that which had been neglected in the colonies thus far, "for want of what only women can do."[9]

In the mid- to late nineteenth century, major port settlements such as Penang and Singapore were vibrant trading communities, complete with the promise and perils of a socioeconomically diverse and rapidly urbanizing environment. One of the most notable demographic characteristics of the large ethnic Chinese communities in these settlements was the unbalanced gender ratio. Because the colonial administration specifically sought immigrant labor for agricultural, mining, and trade purposes, and also because the countries from which this labor originated (in this case, China and India) did not have a strong tradition of female outmigration, the result was a predominantly male migrant population. In Penang, for example, Chinese men outnumbered Chinese women by a ratio of 50:1 in 1879, 40:1 in 1883, and 20:1 in 1892–1902.[10]

In this setting, the illicit trafficking of girls and women for prostitution became a lucrative trade and a serious social problem. The British administration sought to bring Chinese immigration and social welfare issues, including the protection of girls and women, under control in the 1870s.

However, their efforts were often stymied by groups such as Chinese secret societies that profited from such activities and by the government's own ambivalence. Viewing prostitution as a necessary evil and hoping to control it rather than drive it underground, the British allowed prostitutes to enter Straits Settlements ports up to 1927 and did not outlaw brothels until 1930.[11] An 1870 Contagious Diseases Ordinance decreed that brothels were subject to inspection and required prostitutes to undergo medical examinations. By 1885, medical authorities in Penang warned the government that venereal disease was growing out of control and suggested that prostitution in that settlement was a predominantly Chinese problem, with 10,362 out of 11,335 of registered hospital admissions of prostitutes being Chinese cases.[12] Furthermore, of all the registered prostitutes the authorities regularly examined, including those of Japanese, Indian, and European origin, the Chinese were the most numerous.[13] Matters grew worse after the repeal of the Contagious Diseases Ordinance, which meant that brothels were no longer obliged to report on the health of their workers. During this period of crisis, private groups stepped into the breach, taking over from or supplementing the struggling government's efforts. Such groups ranged from associations of Chinese business community leaders seeking to engage in social uplift causes to European and American missionaries who combined social welfare services for girls and women with the formal structures of female education.

Missionaries sought to rescue these girls from lives of vice and debasement via religiously based schooling. In Singapore, St. Margaret's School was founded in 1842 by Maria Dyer, wife of the Reverend Samuel Dyer from the London Missionary Society; school chronicles state that she was motivated by her horror in observing the sale of young Chinese girls to be used as *mui tsai*, or enslaved bondmaids, in local households.[14] St. Margaret's curriculum included rehabilitation through instruction in basic literacy, domestic arts such as cooking and sewing, and the absorption of Christian values. Eventually, these girls were to be placed in arranged marriages with local Christian Chinese men, some of whom were too poor to be able to obtain a bride otherwise.[15] In 1852, a French Catholic priest in Singapore called for the founding of the Convent of the Holy Infant Jesus (CHIJ) in order to "provide religious and secular education for poor Catholic and non-Catholic girls and also shelter for poor widows, orphans, and girls rescued from brothels."[16] For the Methodist Girls' School (MGS), established in Singapore in 1887, the vision was that an "educated Christian womanhood of Malaya, touching the new civilization at its most vital points—its home, its schools and its religion—will bear no small part in forming the character of its citizenry."[17] The first Chinese girl reported to have enrolled at MGS in Singapore was Siauw Mah Li, whose father entrusted her to the school's founder, Sophia Blackmore, in 1897.[18] After being baptized in the church and educated at the school for several years, Siauw taught at MGS. She married Kung Tian Siong, a Melaka-born Chinese Christian who graduated from MGS's "brother school," the Anglo-Chinese School in Singapore and who was reportedly a seventy-second-generation descendent of Confucius. According to Blackmore, Siauw and Kung's religious conversions—Kung was a lay preacher for the Methodist Church—were topics of gossip and criticism:

> [Siauw's] husband is an earnest Christian and an active worker. His mother is not a Christian, and her friends tell her that her children are lost to her because they are Christians. "I cannot see how that can be," she replies. "First, my children do not gamble. They do not smoke opium. They do not go to places of iniquity and my daughter-in-law does not spend all her time dressing up before a looking-glass, but keeps her eyes open to see how she can help me."[19]

In short, girls' schools arose not simply as educational institutions but also as essential providers of welfare and moral improvement for society as a whole.

During this period, new ideas about education were filtering into Southeast Asia through colonials, missionaries, and migrants. These included the notion of educating girls using rational or scientific techniques to become better wives, mothers, and workers.[20] The cultural production of the modern, educated person encompassed the subset of the modern, gendered person—the feminine ideal who would best support colony or nation. However, female education struggled to balance the demands of modernity with powerful beliefs about gender roles. In nineteenth- and early twentieth-century Europe and the United States, girls' schools continued to focus on conventionally female skills: needlework, cooking, and other domestic tasks. Admittedly, schooling for certain elite groups of women had not always been confined to domestic subjects. The gender-differentiated curriculum was in fact absent in the nineteenth-century US high school and only pervaded the national system after New Liberal ideology argued that intellectual development was extraneous to what ought to be a practical schooling process, especially in an increasingly industrialized age.[21] However, women who enjoyed such an education were typically members of upper socioeconomic classes who did not need practical domestic skills as much as knowledge of how to manage household staff. In imperial China, there were similar patterns. Some women of elite families from the tenth century onward acquired more than a basic literacy through private tutorship and were sufficiently well versed in classical texts, literature, and history to have their talents remarked upon favorably by their male contemporaries.[22] But this was an unusual luxury confined to a small and privileged class. For the vast majority of girls who attended school during the modern era, their curriculum was "a shadow version of the male curriculum from which it was adapted, providing lower-status, attenuated versions of some key subjects."[23] This pattern is significant to female education in Asia, as European and American models of education were carried to China and Southeast Asia during the nineteenth and early twentieth centuries by missionaries and colonials and were circulated between East, South, and Southeast Asian states.[24]

By the late nineteenth century, more ethnic Chinese settlers with families in British Malaya and Singapore began to entertain the thought of sending their daughters to school. Although their constituency was relatively small and their social impact limited to specific portions of society, missionary-run schools for girls in China were beginning to gain social acceptance in the 1880s and 1890s, around the same time that some Chinese elites began to seriously consider emulating Japan and the West in establishing public education for girls.[25] In China during the 1900s, foreign missionaries introduced home economics (*jiazheng* 家政) to create "good homemakers" who would help them reform Chinese families in the Western Christian mode, consistent with the model later adopted by missionary girls' schools in Southeast Asia.[26] Middle- to upper-class urban elites, particularly the ethnic Chinese, were realizing the value that a formal education could now impart to a young woman's prospects of marrying well and of reflecting a certain respectability on her family and community. These diasporic Chinese elites would eventually lead the way in supporting girls' schools by enrolling their daughters as students and through financial contributions. One such beneficiary of these actions was the IJ Order, which founded the oldest and second oldest continuously operating missionary girls' schools in Malaya and Singapore, respectively.

The survival of the IJ Order's schools was not assured in their early decades, and other pioneering English-language girls' schools followed a similarly long and often arduous path toward eventual success in the mid-twentieth century. Although the first documented English girls' school in Malaya appeared as early as 1817 in Penang, very few Chinese students enrolled.[27] The Chinese population in Malaya and Singapore at this time still largely consisted of male laborers, artisans, and merchants, with few women and children. Even for Chinese girls who were present, formal education was atypical. The earliest schools failed to thrive, and female education for the Chinese continued to be more of a novelty than a norm. The opening of the IJ schools and, later on, greater attention to education by British colonials in the later part of the nineteenth century brought some change. The London Missionary Society had already made efforts at setting up girls' schools in the Straits Settlements of Melaka and Singapore; in the latter, St. Margaret's School was established in 1842. The American Methodist Church also became involved in female education. In 1887, it established the Tamil Girls' School in Singapore, later renamed the Methodist Girls' School. In Malaya, it began setting up a number of Methodist Girls' Schools (sometimes called Anglo-Chinese Girls' Schools), starting in 1892 in Penang, and continuing in 1897 in the mining town of Ipoh. Another missionary institution, the Chinese Girls' School, later renamed Bukit Bintang Girls' School, was the first girls' school established in the state of Selangor in 1895.[28]

Up until the 1890s, enrollment in these schools was very low and consisted of more European or Eurasian (children with mixed European and local ethnic heritage) than local Chinese, Malay, or Indian girls. At the three main English girls' schools in Penang—the Convent Light Street, Anglo-Chinese Girls' School, and St. George's Girls' School—ethnic Chinese attendees numbered nine, ten, and twenty-one, respectively. But by 1905, the numbers had increased to twenty-three, forty-one, and twenty-eight, respectively.[29] In 1902, the IJ Convent in Kuala Lumpur had enrolled a total of 114 students, of whom thirty-nine, or more than one-third of the total student population, were Chinese.[30] The other students were primarily Eurasian and Indian, with a small proportion of overseas students from other parts of Southeast Asia and the very occasional Malay student. Most of these institutions were located and operated in such a way as to appeal to as many families and students as possible. They were generally situated in urban areas, where there was a larger, denser population and greater likelihood that parents would be willing and financially able to send their daughters to school. Nevertheless, as observed by Elinor Gage-Brown, founder of the Pudu English Girls' School in Kuala Lumpur, in 1901: "It is difficult to persuade the people that education is good for girls."[31] In the earliest days of their operation, missionaries went door to door, appealing to parents to enroll their daughters in school, personally answering questions, and allaying fears about this new social experiment. Apart from not seeing the point of formal education for girls, parents were anxious about exposing their daughters to dangerous societal influences. Missionaries countered this wariness with the argument that formal education was integral to preserving feminine virtue—that such schools were "a barrier against evil and an encouragement for good."[32] Ultimately, increasing numbers of Chinese families were persuaded by a combination of this argument with a pragmatic sense of social aspiration: the risks of engaging in this modern enterprise might be worth the benefits of better marriage prospects and status improvement for their daughters who were growing up in a European colony.

It was not only the mission schools that were strongly focused on a moral and religious mandate. While institutions such as the IJ schools did indeed see their primary goal as "the protection of prostitutes and orphans," the government-sponsored Raffles Girls' School in Singapore also viewed itself in 1855 as "a female school designed for the education and religious training of the children of poor Protestant parents."[33] This premise for establishing girls' schools markedly contrasts with the goals of Chinese-language girls' schools, which were more sharply oriented toward social and political modernization.

CULTURE AND CLASS IN ENGLISH-LANGUAGE GIRLS' SCHOOLS

Of the many ways in which English-language girls' schools differed from their Chinese- language counterparts, perhaps the most profound were their cultural orientation and the socioeconomic classes from which their students were derived. In these schools, English was typically the primary language of instruction. Up to the 1870s, the focus was on needlework and basic literacy. From the 1870s onward, the curriculum expanded to include history, geography, algebra, geometry, literature, art, music, religious knowledge, languages such as French or Latin, and hygiene—similar to the curriculum in most contemporary boys' schools.[34] Although domestic science was not formally established as a subject prior to the early decades of the twentieth century, its components, including cooking, sewing, household management, and what was sometimes called "mothercraft," were always an essential part of instruction in these schools.[35] The first mention of domestic science as a subject in the IJ schools was in 1931. Until the 1940s, science was usually not offered. This was both because of lack of funds, and therefore facilities such as laboratories, and a perception that scientific knowledge was not of practical use to women. In terms of staff, teachers mostly came from abroad in the early decades, arriving from as far away as France, Ireland, England, and the United States. But by the 1910s and 1920s, more locally trained teachers entered the profession and rose up the ranks of school administration, helping to meet the growing local demand for education.

While nominally united in their use of the English language as the medium of instruction, varying characteristics of the schools such as religious affiliation, degree of government involvement, and founding organization led to different experiences and outlooks for their students. For example, Chinese women who attended Catholic schools recalled that the nuns who were their teachers enforced very strict discipline, including corporal punishment at times. Faith was not forced upon them but had an unmistakable presence. Extra-curricular activities were not highly encouraged in the early years, and nuns repeatedly emphasized the importance of feminine virtue—that is, sexual purity.[36] In the American-operated Methodist Girls' Schools, on the other hand, teachers advocated extra-curricular activities as part of a more well-rounded education.

The Western cultural orientation of the English school curricula distinguished these institutions from Chinese and other vernacular schools. Language, literature, history, geography, and religious instruction were based on British or Western European knowledge, with little time or attention devoted to the histories and cultures of Asia or Southeast Asia. As in Western models, schooling was divided into six years of primary and four to six years of secondary levels, with children in the primary grades ranging from approximately six to twelve years of age. Extra-curricular activities such as folk dance, Girl Guides, and drama society were derived from models in girls' schools in the West. English-language girl's schools also apportioned more classroom time to the domestic arts than did Chinese-language girls' schools. Unlike the Chinese schools, needlework and hygiene were always included in the curriculum of the English-language schools. Perhaps because they were more likely than Chinese schools to fall under the purview of colonial administration, Malay and Tamil girls' schools also focused heavily on Western interpretations of appropriate skills for feminine instruction, as suggested by a colonial report on education in the Federated Malay States in 1931:

Malay girls' schools remained for a long time a very hard problem . . . . Despite insuperable obstacles, the Lady Supervisor [of Malay girls' schools] has effected real reforms and caused thoughtful Malays to recognize the need of supporting an attempt to educate girls to be the intellectual peers of their husbands. The curriculum of the girls' schools is no longer dead and uninspiring. Cookery, clay-modelling, paper cutting, drawn-thread work, hygiene taught by Lady Medical Officers are romantic subjects for the little Malay girl compared with what her elder sisters learnt a few years ago. Domestic science is the most popular subject.[37]

The subjects referred to as being studied by Malay girls "a few years ago" were most likely basic literacy—sufficient for reading the Koran by rote, but not for the sake of developing extensive linguistic abilities—and traditional craft work such as sewing and weaving. These skills were likely to have more practical application in the domestic and cottage industry spheres and were the chief attraction of the earliest Malay girls' schools. Few Malay girls attended mission schools, in large part because the Christian environment was regarded by their parents as incompatible with their Muslim faith. English-language girls' schools were mostly attended by European, Eurasian, Chinese, and Indian students, while Chinese-language schools were, for linguistic and cultural reasons, almost entirely dominated by ethnic Chinese.

The emphasis that English girls' schools placed on domestic science carried certain class overtones, as their approach suggested what a woman in a middle- to upper-class household would need to know in order to manage it, likely with the help of servants, and to fill her leisure time. In this view, academic skills were less vital. From the records of the IJ Convent in Kuala Lumpur, entries from 1902 and 1903 note the visits and comments of government school inspectors, whose reports typically begin with praise for the needlework: "most efficient" and "always excellent in the Convent schools."[38] The inspectors also note that reading and arithmetic is "good though less remarkable" and "accurate but slow . . . this slowness is common to most girls' schools." Also in 1902, the records show correspondence from a government Federal Education Officer approving certain changes in the curriculum for hygiene, a precursor to the broader category of domestic science, in which books such as *Lessons on Living* and *A Domestic Economy Reader* impart information on nutrition, materials suitable for making clothing, and "Causes and Simple Treatments for Common Complaints."[39] In addition to needlework and hygiene, students were also trained in music. The school records document a 1902 "Programme for Examination of Music" for piano performance—surely an occupation for girls from more well-to-do family backgrounds, as music lessons were an expensive luxury at the time.[40] The seeming impracticality of these lessons might be explained by the fact that sending daughters to school in the early days of female education was a privilege of the wealthier classes, and there was no need for these girls to learn the more menial aspects of household work. Those who were less well-off were probably already performing domestic chores from a young age and needed no additional training in that area. Over the decades, inculcating a sense of upper-class feminine refinement became an integral part of these schools' mandate. At the centenary celebration for the IJ mission in 1952, the British colonial inspector of schools once again praised its schools for its production of students with "good manners and social graces."[41]

Domestic science as a subject was a challenge in many schools, as there was often insufficient money to buy equipment such as sewing machines and cooking stoves. However, teachers constantly reminded students that they should prepare for their future in the domestic sphere.[42] As a former student of the Convent Light Street in Penang during the 1930s recalls, "All the nuns talked about was becoming a wife and mother."[43] At Assunta Girls' School, another missionary-founded institution near Kuala Lumpur, the headmistress overrode the demands of parents in the 1950s for their daughters to learn commercial science, which would have included the basics of economics and book-keeping. Instead, she made domestic science compulsory in the first three years of secondary education. "The girls were future home-makers," the headmistress noted cheerfully, "and their husbands are now thanking me [for insisting on domestic science]!"[44]

Educational approaches were not the only way in which social class, as a reflection of students' existing or aspirational status, was manifested. The composition of the student body tended to reflect and reinforce pre-existing hierarchies of race and wealth, even though it might encompass different ends of the social spectrum. Mission schools were originally intended as shelters for the poor and unfortunate but evolved over time to become highly regarded institutions to which wealthy members of society, particularly Europeans, could entrust the training of their daughters. When the IJ Convent in Kuala Lumpur was established in 1899, it was a charitable institution, with "only poor girls needing a home or a mother's care" coming through its doors.[45] In 1902, its sister school in Melaka was the type of shelter to which a young Chinese girl "running away from [being forced to work in] a theatre" would flee for refuge.[46] In less than ten years, however, such schools grew to become far more than welfare homes for the destitute. Their provision of academic and religious instruction in a European language and cultural milieu made them a prime destination for elite local families who were amenable to female education. The IJ Convent in Penang in the 1870s and 1880s was already extending its curriculum beyond basic literacy and needlework to include geography, history, French, music, and "Christian virtues."[47] In 1910, the IJ in Kuala Lumpur saw its first student pass the Cambridge Senior Certificate Examination, an internationally recognized qualifying test administered by British authorities.[48] All this while, the Chinese orphans in the convents "left only to get married," equipped with skills in housework and sewing that they had developed under the care of the nuns and as part of their required duties to help earn their keep.[49]

While the charitable aspect remained an important component of these schools, their prestige and fees rendered them fairly exclusive. Formal education was therefore a potential means of social mobility but could also operate as a strong bulwark of colonial privilege. Up to the post–World War II period, "primary and secondary education . . . was not free and English schools generally charged much higher fees than [Chinese] secondary schools."[50] As a result, English-language girls' schools tended to include students from the farthest extremes of the socioeconomic spectrum, including the least and the most wealthy, and those who were already racially and socially marginalized as well as those whose families were located squarely within the upper ranks of the sociocultural hierarchy. Chinese-language schools, on the other hand, were mostly attended by newer generations of migrants or their children and hence encompassed a more limited range of socioeconomic classes and appeared more egalitarian.

In the daily life and operations of English girls' schools, the boundary between elites and non-elites was clearly marked and consolidated by school policies. In the IJ Convent in Penang, there were distinct divisions between "first-class boarders," "second-class boarders," "day students," and orphans. First-class boarders were girls from wealthy, typically European or Eurasian families or Thai royalty who were housed in the best dormitory quarters and given the best food. Second-class boarders were housed in a separate building, while day students were local girls who would go home at the end of each day. The orphans who lived in the school were a separate underclass altogether. As a school history solemnly noted, "during play time [the orphans] were not allowed in any other area of the Convent grounds unless they were on assignments. They were also not allowed to mix with the boarders and day students."[51] Boarders were similarly told that they were "not allowed to mix and speak with the orphans."[52] A former student of the IJ Convent in Penang during the late 1930s and early 1940s remembered that "there was a clear difference" between First- and Second-class Boarders, who lived in different blocks of dormitories.[53] Yet another alumna recalled being discouraged from initiating contact or socializing with the most elite girls in their midst, such as the few Thai or Malay princesses in their classes. "The nuns would ask us 'not to be rude,'" she said, "and this instruction would only come if there was royalty in the class."[54] In St. Margaret's School in Singapore, a former student from the 1930s has distinct memories of the First-class Boarders in her school having the privilege of being seated with the school matron instead of other students at mealtime, enjoying an additional bowl of soup, and being given less homework.[55] The accumulation of these daily reminders served to reflect and perpetuate divisions of race and class.

The combination of moral-religious emphases, a focus on Western culture and domesticity, and clear class divisions in English girls' schools had a particular effect on the Chinese community—not by alienating it, but in fact drawing in significant parts of it. From inception, the IJ convent schools felt the presence and influence of the local Chinese population, in terms of their attendance as students and their involvement as donors. This presence could be humble in nature. Some of the earliest Chinese students at the IJ Convent in Penang were orphans from rescue homes for prostitutes.[56] On the other end of the spectrum, some schools owed their financial well-being, even survival, to charitable donations from prominent local Chinese. IJ archives note the generosity of certain individuals, such as one Hong Kim, "a rich Chinese," who made a sizable contribution to the IJ Convent in Penang during its early years, and another "pagan Chinese" who donated a hearse for a nun's funeral.[57] The establishment of the IJ Convent of Kuala Lumpur in 1899 was heavily dependent on the donation of a house by a wealthy Peranakan Chinese woman for use as the school premises.[58] When the convent seemed on the verge of being overwhelmed by too many orphans and too little money and space, a wealthy Chinese businessman (or *towkay*) came to the rescue:

> The valiant Missionary [leading the school] could no longer restrain her tears; and at this moment, God's messenger appeared in the person of Towkay Goh Ah Ngee. "You are in trouble, Reverend Mother, but what do you think I am here for?" . . . The good Towkay took immediate measures to remove the Sister and children—eighty in all—to his own house . . . providing them with everything necessary, forbidding them to buy anything, while he set about looking for a building which would answer the purpose. Learning that the Victoria Hotel in Brickfields was for sale, Mr. Goh Ah Ngee approached the authorities, requesting them to organize a lottery of which the first prize would be donated to the Sisters to provide them with the funds to purchase the hotel and the surrounding lands. The necessary alterations were paid for by Mr. Goh himself, and he gave $5,000 to buy the house.[59]

At various other junctures in the IJ school annals, notations are made of donations from "generous hearted Chinese Catholics," such as a contribution of $15,000 to a convent school in Johor Bahru in 1927, and visits to the school by "Chinese ladies," church officials "in company with several Chinese towkays," and "rich Chinese gentlemen," presumably to inspect the recipients of their financial contributions.[60] Perhaps this patronage had its price. A handwritten entry in the IJ Kuala Lumpur school diary noting the visit of these Chinese ladies includes an aside in parentheses that the writer, most likely one of the nuns, "was glad when they left."[61] Still, the school annals for this period do not single out any other group, ethnic or otherwise, for their financial support. While Catholic or Protestant Chinese were most likely driven to donate because of their faith or sense of religious community, other Chinese with no such ties to missions may also have been motivated by a cultural tradition of contributing to educational charities, as a morally uplifting and social status-improving act. For overseas Chinese living and doing business in a British colony, building social capital by supporting English educational endeavors would have been strategic as well as praise-worthy.[62]

Chinese students dominated the rolls of most English girls' schools. According to the chronicles of the IJ Convent in Kuala Lumpur, between 1900 and 1941, the majority of students were Chinese. Each year in late January or early February, the annals would note that nearly all the Chinese girls would be absent from classes for a week or more because of the Chinese New Year celebrations; eventually, the school would simply declare a long holiday for the entire school during that festival as the Chinese constituted such a large part of the student body.[63]

Starting from the 1930s , English girls' schools had to compete with an increasing number of local Chinese girls' schools, whose popularity was attributed by missionaries to the fact that "the Chinese wanted a Chinese education."[64] To meet this demand, the IJ Order established a number of schools that conducted classes in Mandarin Chinese, and some of the existing schools introduced Chinese-language classes as part of their curriculum. Ethnic Chinese sisters in the order who had obtained diplomas in teaching were tasked with leading these schools and classes.[65] While these efforts may have made some difference, it was still the distinguishing features of an English education that continued to attract large numbers of Chinese students. Chinese families were keen for their children to acquire Western language skills and the ability to apply them in a European colonial context. Chinese girls continued to constitute the bulk of the student body. In 1933, of 238 students at the IJ Convent in Kuala Lumpur, 122 or more than half had recognizably Chinese names.[66] The next largest group of students had European or Eurasian names, followed by those with Indian or Tamil names, and finally, a very small number of Malay and Japanese names.

An education in English was held in high esteem by many local residents in colonial Malaya and Singapore, not only because it could enable a person to get a well-paying, well-regarded job in the British civil service but also because of its cultural cachet. But the process of acquiring this education was not always easy. Former students of the English mission girls' schools, especially the ethnic Chinese, had negative or difficult experiences that they would often interpret as being based on their race or social status, both in school and in the larger Chinese community.

Reminiscing about their school days, some of these former students had vivid memories of tense moments that illustrated some of the class and cultural conflicts arising from being an English-educated Chinese person living in a British colony. Rose Ong, who was born in 1919 to a family in Penang with origins in Guangdong province, attended the IJ Convent in Penang from primary through secondary school.[67] Interviewed in 2006 about her experiences in formal education, the eighty-six-year-old Ong had vivid recollections of her schoolgirl days and recounted her memories with sharp frankness and occasional mischievousness. One of her older half-sisters attended Chinese-language schools and ended up becoming headmistress of the Penang Chinese Girls' High School, a leading Chinese girls' school in Malaya, but Ong and her other siblings were sent to English-language schools at her father's behest. Ong had little knowledge of English when she first began attending classes at the convent at the age of five. She had fond memories of her Irish kindergarten teacher, Sister Anne, who was responsible for giving her the English name "Rose." But such was her limited understanding of the English language that when she started Primary One the following year, when another nun was taking attendance on the first day of classes, Ong failed to respond when her English name "Rose" was called because she was only accustomed to being addressed by her Chinese name. Impatient with what she took to be insolence, the nun slapped Ong across the face. In later years, her name was to become an issue with yet another Irish nun at the convent. Ong remembers a teacher of English literature "who had been to Oxford and was very snobbish. She used to call us barbarians, and made us memorize [and recite] Robert Burns' poetry with its Scottish accent." This teacher made fun of Ong for what she considered to be the pretentiousness of her name, unaware that it had been conferred by a fellow nun. As Ong recalls: "She would say, 'You think you are very special because you are named Rose? Did you not know that a rose may blossom in the morning but become all shriveled up by afternoon?' . . . I hated Robert Burns, and I hated her!" While traumatic experiences in one's early school years may be a universal possibility, in this case, Ong viewed hers through the lens of race and culture, constructing this aspect of her identity in opposition to what her teacher represented: foreign culture and class elitism. Yet this construction was by no means straightforward, as Ong also sees herself as having absorbed a solid sense of morality and valuable work skills through her convent-based education.

From the late 1950s onward, the former British colonies of Malaya and Singapore were confronted with the excitement and challenges of postcolonial independence. One of the most daunting tasks was creating cohesive national identities for the multi-ethnic, multicultural and multilinguistic population that lived within their borders. The tensions that strained social group relationships, including the politics of language and identity, were felt within families and among children as well as adults, as in the case of the Lu sisters.

Lu Wei and Lu Zhao were somewhat unusual in that their parents migrated to Singapore and then Malaya from northeastern China, unlike most ethnic Chinese in these areas who typically originated from the southwestern provinces of Fujian and Guangdong.[68] Their father was a publisher and writer of Chinese-language books, their mother was a teacher in local Chinese schools, and the sisters began their education in the 1950s immersed in a Mandarin-language environment in local Chinese institutions. After a few years, they moved to an English missionary girls' school, where they participated in a special Mandarin-language program that was aimed at easing students' transition from Chinese to English education. Lu Wei, the older of the two sisters, recalls that the girls in the "Chinese stream" never really mixed with the "English stream" students. Even though they shared teachers and facilities, and despite the fact that most of the students were ethnic Chinese, the two groups would take classes and converse in different languages. Although her experience was one of segregation, Lu Wei did not mind the situation much. She excelled in her studies and went on to a career in Malaysian academia. She felt little connection to the Chinese school system, and throughout her life she "felt quite cut off" from the politics of the overseas Chinese community.

Lu Zhao, on the other hand, had a very different reaction to these years. To this day, she bristles when she speaks of the treatment received by the Chinese-educated girls in the English school; in her view, they were "underdogs" and were "abused" by the teachers, fellow students, and even the principal.[69] Lu Zhao concurs with Lu Wei that there was "no mixing" with the English stream students, but she goes further in charging that the school discriminated against the Chinese stream students by giving them teachers of lesser quality and subjecting them to "nasty comments" on a frequent basis, even as they expected all students to help equally in supporting the school through activities such as fundraising. As a star athlete for the school, she would occasionally go on strike by refusing to participate in key sporting competitions when she wanted to protest what she felt was unfair treatment of the Chinese stream students. When one of her Chinese-language teachers treated her condescendingly, as she was less academically advanced than her English-educated peers, she greatly relished the fact that he was unable to correctly write her given name in Mandarin—an obscure Chinese character chosen by her intellectual father and that was one of the names of Empress Wu Zetian, the only woman to have held the throne in imperial Chinese history. Lu Zhao's father had told her that when she was born, she cried so fiercely that her father decided to name her after a powerful and intimidating female historical personage. In Lu Zhao's opinion, the most enduring lessons she learned from her years in her English school were "how to raise money, and how to stick up for yourself and your comrades." She went on to a career in language translation and teaching.

Personality differences aside—both sisters acknowledge that Lu Zhao is the more rebellious of the two—it is striking to note how the politics of language and education have influenced their sense of being Chinese. Lu Wei adapted readily to the English-language environment and assimilated sufficiently into the postcolonial Malaysian establishment to build a successful career in higher education. She avoided political involvement, especially when it came to the sensitive issue of vernacular Chinese schools. Yet it is she who says she "cannot live without Chinese culture," expressing a passion for Chinese language, literature, and classical Beijing opera that has endured throughout her lifetime.[70] Lu Zhao, on the other hand, moved to Canada for a number of years, where she raised children who did not learn the Chinese language as well as she had hoped. Her emigration was prompted by anger with what she perceived to be the unfairness of the Malaysian political system, in which affirmative action policies favor indigenous Malays over other ethnic groups in economic and educational opportunities. Lu Zhao's deeply felt indignation heightened her sense of being and acting as an ethnic Chinese, but also placed her in a situation where she eventually found herself "able to live without Chinese culture."[71]

The Lu sisters' experiences highlight the multivariable equation that was English education for the overseas Chinese in Malaya and Singapore, and the complexity of Chinese women's responses to it. Over the first several decades of the twentieth century, the decision over whether one's child would attend an English-language or Chinese-language school was tangled up in multiple issues: class, culture, political orientation, ethnic identity, and the role of women in the advancement of the community and nation. Although English girls' schools began as shelters for protecting the physical and moral welfare of women, they soon became pathways for cultural affiliation and social positioning. A significant number of ethnic Chinese subscribed to the belief that an English education would improve their socioeconomic status in a colonial society, especially if such an education could, as asserted by male elites, modernize and improve their women, and hence the community as a whole. Yet the adoption of such an education, and the linguistic and cultural trappings that accompanied it, also became fodder for intra-ethnic conflict within a community struggling to define its cultural identity in a shifting political landscape.

When interviewed about their experiences in English-language girls' schools, a number of ethnic Chinese alumnae typically point to their parents' high regard for things British or practical considerations about the importance of knowing English for getting a job and getting ahead as the main reasons for their enrollment in these institutions. Rose Ong, who attended the IJ Convent in Penang, recalls that her father, who had received only a basic education, was determined that all his children, male and female, should go to school, but not just any kind of school. He believed that the best kind of education in a British colony was an English education. In his opinion, Chinese girls' schools were "for bound-feet women," and graduates from Chinese schools came out to be "letter writers and abacus users."[72] Whereas an English-educated man might find a good job as a chief clerk in a colonial government department, "earning $200 to $300 per month and able to afford a car for his wife and children, making him equivalent to a Chinese official," a Chinese-educated man would "only manage to be a shopkeeper," a low-class occupation as far as Mr. Ong was concerned. Maria Yong, who also attended the IJ Convent in Penang in the 1950s, credits her father and his "very English outlook" for her education in the British system.[73] Yong speculates that her father was seeking to distance himself from a past of which he was not proud. She observes that he came from "a family of carpenters," had an opium-smoker for a father and a gambler for a mother, and carried a "somewhat condescending outlook on Chinese culture." In reaction, he became a Christian and placed tremendous emphasis on the educational achievements of his children, even insisting that Yong study Latin in preparation for training to become a medical doctor. "He really looked up to the British," Yong recalls, and immersed his children in British language and culture as much as possible, "regularly taking us for $3 set lunches so that we could experience English cuisine." In these cases, the association of English language and education with a higher sociocultural status was a determining factor in sending one's daughters to an English school.

In other cases, there were more pragmatic considerations about the realities of living and working in a British colony. Chong Eu Ngoh, whose parents were Chinese educated and whose father was a building contractor, remembers being sent to an English school together with her eight sisters, "in order to be sure to be able to find work."[74] She started attending Treacher Girls' School, a government institution, in the late 1930s. While she had some basic Chinese-language training, she was not encouraged in this area. In fact, she remembers being punished with a fine of one cent ("the equivalent of a day's snack money," she mournfully recalls) for each time that she spoke Chinese in her English school. When Chong eventually went to work for the Ministry of Social Welfare, a position that she would not have been able to acquire had she not graduated from the English system, her educational background sometimes counted against her. In 1953, when she traveled around the country on behalf of the government encouraging local Chinese to accept Malayan citizenship, the Chinese whom she met were hostile, refusing her offer and accusing her of being a "running dog" for the British. "I hardly knew how to respond," said Chong, especially because "I was unable to converse with them in Chinese."

Chong's experience of being rejected by her co-ethnics for her English education speaks to one of the greatest reasons for division among the Chinese in British Malaya and Singapore: one's language medium of education, and therefore one's supposed cultural and political orientation. Parents made decisions about which type of school they would send their children to for a wide variety of reasons: sometimes because of their cultural or political beliefs, but sometimes for pragmatic reasons such as proximity to one's home or how high the school fees were. Yet there were widespread, simplified assumptions among the Chinese about the effects of each type of education. The English-educated would look down on the Chinese-educated for their alleged clannish traditionalism, and the latter or newly arrived Chinese immigrants would despise the former for their supposedly slavish adoration of all things British.

Asked about this divide, the educated Chinese women who were interviewed for this study would often preface their answers by saying they had so little awareness of and interaction with girls from other language streams of education that they had simply no opinion about them at all. This may well have been true in many cases. Female students from opposite sides of the linguistic tracks would have had few opportunities to mingle. Even inter-school extra-curricular activities such as sports meets or debates would have been restricted by language medium. Maria Yong states that as an IJ Convent-attending girl in Penang, she was unaware of the largest Chinese girls' school in her hometown, the Penang Chinese Girls' High School, and gave no thought to its students.[75] As they transitioned into the workforce, graduates would continue to work and socialize among those who were educated in and spoke the same language. Yong describes her years in a teacher training college as marked by the self-segregation of the Chinese-educated women, who were "very close-knit" and did not mingle much with the English-educated women.

In other cases, individuals were much more emphatic or negative in their impressions, and mutual wariness, or even animosity, emerged as a barrier between the two groups. This tension between the English-educated and Chinese-educated Chinese developed to varying degrees of severity, within families as well as among larger segments of the Chinese community, and it has been widespread enough that scholarly articles and literary works have been written about it.[76] In Singaporean society, for example, the Chinese-educated were called *shi bu shi* (a derogatory term that made fun of a Chinese expression for "yes or no?") and were thought to be "conservative, parochial, chauvinistic, politicized and hard-working."[77] The English-educated, on the other hand, were contemptuously dismissed as *er maozi*, a disparaging name for Chinese Christian converts during the Boxer Rebellion era in China, implying that they were fake or second-class foreigners. They also carried the stigma of being "arrogant," "Westernized," and "servile" toward foreign rulers.[78] Some Chinese-educated female interviewees felt that English schoolgirls "looked down on us," "claimed that their hometown was London," and even "emitted Western farts" (*fang yangpi*).[79] Another choice epithet for the English-educated was *ang mo sai*, a Fujianese phrase for "white-people shit," and an insult that was often heard by Tan Liok Ee, an English-educated academic in Malaya who was the only one of her siblings to be sent to an English instead of a Chinese school.[80] She saw a growing divide in her family as being cultural and political as well as linguistic:

> Throughout my childhood, my sense of difference from my siblings was marked less by gender and more by a linguistic and cultural gap . . . . I learnt a different language, which took me into a different body of literature, shaping my mental landscape to think in different ways. The difference in Chinese and English school teaching was most glaring in history—I learnt about the extension of British power and civilization over an empire on which the sun did not set, my brother about how western imperialism had tried to carve up the Chinese melon. Teachers and textbooks in the Chinese schools of the mid-1950s were heavily anti-colonial in spirit . . . . The English schools, even in the late 1950s, essentially imbued us with an Anglophile colonial mentality.[81]

Rose Ong also experienced this tension within her own family. She describes a standing conflict with a younger male relative who was educated in the

Chinese-language school system and who, she says, "is very pleased with himself for this." As Ong wryly observes, "He calls me '*ang mo zao gao*'"— Fujianese for "running dog of the white people"—and "we argue, make up, and then argue again about this."[82]

The impact of this schism was also keenly felt at the broader social level. Chinese school graduates did not have any local Chinese-language college or university options, so they had to go abroad to pursue tertiary education. Both during and after the colonial period, it was also more difficult for a Chinese school graduate, male or female, to gain employment in government service and a number of other economic sectors. This institutionalized handicap for the Chinese-educated led to frustration among their ranks and a dim view of Chinese schools among some of the English-educated. "There was a great deal of hostility towards learning English" among some of the ethnic Chinese, notes Margaret Chang, even though her own family suggested that such antagonism was not universal. Chang's mother was an English-educated teacher of the Chinese language who socialized successfully in both linguistic milieus. Chang's own bilingualism is rooted in a conscious desire to determine her own sense of Chineseness. Still, in general, she notes that her English-educated and Chinese-educated peers "just didn't mix," with accusations flying back and forth of Chinese chauvinism and betrayal of one's cultural roots.[83]

This process of political and cultural polarization through language of education altered the range of identity options available to Chinese women. With the ethnic Chinese community becoming split by broad dividing lines of language, class, cultural orientation, and political ties to China or Britain, women no longer had as much flexibility as they may have had before to interweave the various cultural and ethnic practices that formed the complex fabric of their personal lives. In some instances, growing up in an English school environment may have prompted Chinese women to identify more closely with colonial culture, or with a local Malayan or Singaporean community, rather than a marginalized Chinese position. When asked if they joined any anti-Japanese fundraising efforts during the 1940s, some interviewees said that they "didn't do such things" and seemed to suggest that such activities were inappropriate and socially disruptive. The English-educated Maria Yong remembers that she and her fellow ethnic Chinese teachers in English schools were aware of political controversies surrounding Chinese schools, such as repeated flare-ups during the 1970s and 1980s when the postcolonial Malaysian government sought to minimize or eliminate the role of vernacular schools, to the outrage of non-Malay communities. However, she and her colleagues did not feel the urge to get involved as they were not convinced that any injustices had necessarily been done.[84] "We were more interested in our bread and butter" of teaching, she explains, and "minded our own business." Another English-educated interviewee, who asked to remain anonymous for reasons of political sensitivity, explains that she feels she is very much Chinese, "but not in a nationalistic way. Customs matter, and race matters, but not politics. For example, I have no yearning to go to China."[85] In her opinion, the Chinese-language school system is "not good for the country," and "all problems would be solved if the government abolished vernacular [Chinese- and Tamil-language] schools." Furthermore, while she understands that pro-Chinese school activists in the 1970s and 1980s were driven by cultural pride, she also thinks that they are "too much governed by feeling themselves a part of China."

On the domestic front, some English school graduates found themselves inadvertently passing on to their children their alienation from certain aspects of the overseas Chinese identity that had become too closely tied to Chinese-language education. Asked about how she defined her ethnic identity, Maria Yong expresses some regret that she thinks she neither developed a strong sense of it on her own nor encouraged it in her children by sending them to a Chinese school.[86] Even though she hired a Chinese-language tutor for them for eight years, they never learned the language well. "They suffered the same fate as me," she says, "in terms of hardly being able to speak a word of Chinese." Her career as a teacher in English-language schools only cemented this state of affairs. Upon retirement, she says, "I felt I was in a desert [because] I did not know Chinese culture at all." At that point, she took up a slew of Chinese cultural activities, from calligraphy to playing traditional musical instruments.

Ultimately, the imbrication of the political and the personal has had long-lasting and complex effects in the lives of educated Chinese women. Margaret Chang, who came from a Chinese-speaking background but attended an English girls' school and went on to a career in English-language education, found her and her husband's attempts to teach their children the Chinese language thwarted, mainly because they had re-migrated to Canada and Hong Kong where their children grew up in an English-speaking milieu.[87] This re-migration came about close to the time of Malayan and Singaporean independence from colonial rule—a time when she, and the larger Chinese community in which she lived, had to confront the legacy of the linguistically plural education system that two or three generations of Chinese had experienced. "We began to imagine: what kind of community would we like? What kind of language would we use, or write with? Who would read what we wrote? Such questions obsessed and worried us," she recalls. Although, unlike Yong, Chang feels a clear and strong sense of her ethnic identity, she finds that her political environment had a powerful influence on her family's relationship to Chinese culture. To Chang's mind, "being Chinese is attitudinal." "I have never felt a stranger wherever I have gone," she says, "but I can't help being aware of being Chinese because of others' expectations and assumptions [about me]." This was particularly the case in 1960s Malaya, where ethnic minorities found themselves navigating a political and cultural minefield as they addressed the issue of postcolonial national citizenship in their land of settlement. Although Chang herself feels secure in her Chineseness, she finds that the matter is contested by others who are continuing to grapple over the meaning of overseas Chinese ethnic, cultural, and political identity. This struggle echoes the debates on English- and Chinese-language education that have been taking place since the turn of the twentieth century.

Well into the twentieth century, English-language girls' schools in British Malaya and Singapore were closely identified with the missionary societies and female educators who were responsible for their establishment. These institutions formed in response to needs from a number of constituencies: girls and women who required shelter and livelihoods, socioeconomically elite families who sought basic education for their daughters, and a colonial government that was all too glad to have non-state organizations assist them in helping to manage the local population. As English girls' schools took root, their origins in the provision of social welfare services were matched and largely overtaken by the structures of modern formal education, although their curricula always prioritized the inculcation of Western norms of femininity and domesticity. When the British administration began to intervene, in the name of raising educational quality, they also exercised greater colonial supervision and control. Whether they welcomed or resented this intervention, English girls' schools became part of the imperial architecture in these colonies, helping to uphold and perpetuate certain cultural and racial divisions through their daily operations.

As in many other colonial locales, English-language female education, provided by women for girls and women, contained a number of inherent tensions. While serving the colonial enterprise in some ways, English girls' schools also offered possibilities for social mobility and the formation of new, hybrid cultural identities, for a segment of the population that had previously enjoyed little to no access to education and other activities in the public sphere. What women could and did do in this area was to create openings, however limited and conditional, for transformations in social relationships and hierarchies.

The belief that an English-language education was a ticket to a better life became a contentious issue in the Chinese community. For educated overseas Chinese women in British Malaya and Singapore, school choice was a political gesture that contributed to enduring inter- and intra-ethnic tensions in their domestic and professional lives. These women's experiences are a reminder that plurality does not always lead to pluralism. Whereas Chinese-language schools in Malaya and Singapore have often been faulted for encouraging cultural separatism and Chinese chauvinism, this discussion shows that English-language schools were part of the polarization in the late colonial and early postcolonial periods.[88]

For the overseas Chinese in these colonies, English girls' schools were an opportunity for status improvement and security in their new land of settlement, in a region where their ethnicity and migrant status could be an advantage or handicap depending on which way political winds were blowing. Over the years, enough Chinese took up this opportunity to create a strong presence in this segment of the educational world. However, this was not a simple world in which social mobility could be easily obtained. Apart from the frustrations experienced by Chinese girls within the walls of the convent or other English-language schools, there were also different kinds of class- and culture-related tensions that emerged from the fact of their language of education. As an English education became a marker of social status for male and female students alike, the overseas Chinese in Malaya and Singapore became increasingly divided over the question of whether the adoption of this new marker constituted a betrayal of one's ethnic and cultural identity. This internal conflict, within the individual as well as the Chinese community at large, would be most clearly embodied by the ethno-culturally hybrid Peranakan Chinese.

Figure 1 Baptism of a baby, Convent Light Street, Penang, undated. The Convent Light Street was founded by French Catholic nuns in 1852 and included an orphanage on its premises. Courtesy of Sisters of the Infant Jesus, Malaysia.

Figure 2 Needlework lesson, Convent Light Street, Penang, undated. Some students are dressed in Peranakan attire, reflecting their multicultural heritage. Courtesy of Sisters of the Infant Jesus, Malaysia.

Figure 3 Inspector of Schools, Convent Light Street, Penang, undated. As the British colonial government shifted from inattention to intervention regarding local education in the 1920s, it required regular school inspections in exchange for financial grants. Courtesy of Sisters of the Infant Jesus, Malaysia.

Figure 4 Students from the Junior Cambridge class at drill, Convent Light Street, Penang, 1934. Both colonial and nation-state authorities viewed physical education as a key component of education for the modern female subject or citizen. Courtesy of Sisters of the Infant Jesus, Malaysia.

1939 Staff L-R Philomena Dragon, Maisie Robless, Peggy O'Neill, 7th Muriel Dragon, 8th Gertie Bruins, 9th Ella Vonarnst,
10th Minette Reutens, 14th Annie Eisenberg, 15th Mrs. Nunis, 16th Phyllis Boudeville
Seated L-R Katherine Lowe, Celine Teh, Babs Phillips, Betty Lee, Joan Geddy, Kathleen Robless with white bow.
Far right Zella Healy (Mrs. Bateman); On floor Lucy Koh.

Figure 5 Staff, Convent Light Street, Penang, 1939. As girls' schools expanded to offer Normal or teacher training courses, more local women joined the ranks of professionally trained teachers in girls' schools. Courtesy of Sisters of the Infant Jesus, Malaysia.

Figure 6 Class in session, Convent Light Street, Penang, undated. Courtesy of Sisters of the Infant Jesus, Malaysia.

Figure 7 Maypole, St. Margaret's School, Singapore, 1930s. St. Margaret's Secondary School, School History Exhibit, accessed 2005.

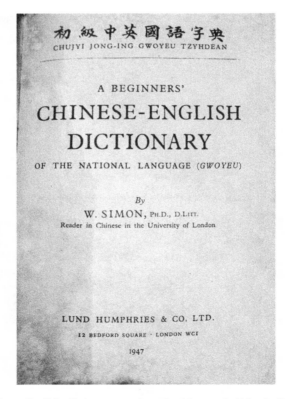

Figure 8 Chinese-English dictionary used at St. Margaret's School, Singapore, 1947. Written and published by British authorities, this book used non-standard Romanized transliteration. St. Margaret's Secondary School, School History Exhibit, accessed 2005.

30th MAY 1939 – 12th Day of 4th MOON

Figure 9 Peranakan or Straits Chinese bride and groom, Singapore, May 30, 1939. Despite the push for modernization by Peranakan male elites from the 1900s on, Straits Chinese women continued to embody the traditional elements of their hybrid cultural heritage, not least in terms of dress. Courtesy of The Intan, Singapore.

Figure 10 Students and teachers of the Singapore Chinese Girls' School, between 1901-23.
Courtesy of the Frank and Frances Carpenter Collection, Library of Congress.

CHAPTER 3

So That They May Be an Honor to You

The Nyonya Problem and the Singapore Chinese Girls'
School, 1890s–1940s

On July 1, 1899, the Singapore Chinese Girls' School (SCGS) opened its doors for the first time, with an Englishwoman, Mary Geary, at its helm as principal. As a self-proclaimed pioneering school, the institution was far from impressive. Its premises were a humble two-story building with a leaking roof, and student enrollment in its first year came to a grand total of seven little girls. It struggled against a widespread reluctance by parents to educate their daughters and had to hire a matron for fifty cents a month to escort students to and from school in a covered sedan, in order to shield the girls from public view. In its first two decades, SCGS nearly closed a number of times due to chronic shortages of funds, erratic student attendance, and high turnover of teachers who were routinely underpaid and under-qualified.[1]

Nonetheless, SCGS survived, increasing its institutional complexity over time. Initially, the school offered the first five years of primary or elementary education—Primaries One and Two, followed by Standards I to III—and included in its curriculum Malay, Mandarin Chinese, arithmetic, geography, music, and sewing classes. In its second year, enrollment jumped to sixty students; by its tenth anniversary in 1909, that number had reached 125.[2] By the late 1900s, the scope of the school had extended to Standard V, a level that qualified a student to sit for the British-administered Junior Cambridge examinations, which would in turn allow her to receive a School

Leaving Certificate and to work as a teacher—although the reality was that students kept dropping out before reaching this level.[3] Every weekday, SCGS maintained a consistent schedule of classes from nine or ten in the morning to two-thirty in the afternoon. Initially, there was no school uniform, and students simply wore their everyday clothing. For many, this consisted of a tunic called the *baju panjang* (Malay for tunic) over a *sarong batik* (a dyed wraparound long skirt), with *kasut manek* (beaded slippers) peeking out beneath the hem, hair pulled back in a tight bun atop the head. For the wealthier girls, a few items of glittering jewelry might adorn their hair, ears, wrists, or dress.[4] This distinctive form of dress marked these students as hailing from the *Peranakan* or Straits Chinese community. Over the decades, SCGS incorporated the external trappings and the internal substance of a formal educational institution. These included uniforms and a school badge, annual prize-giving ceremonies and school fairs, extra-curricular activities such as athletic clubs and the Girl Guides, and, more significantly for the perpetuation of the school, the acceptance of financial aid from and regular inspection visits by the British colonial government.

Although it was not the first or only girls' school in the British colony of Singapore, SCGS was significant in how it captured an era of transition for a multicultural Chinese community. It was the first girls' school founded by the Peranakan or Straits Chinese, a group descended from generations of intermarriage between Chinese male settlers and local Malay women in Southeast Asia from as early as the fifteenth century. The men were called *Baba* and the women *Nyonya*. The name *Peranakan*, derived from a Malay word indicating "child of" or "born of," denoted the local part of their ancestry, while their cultural practices combined Chinese, Malay, and British elements. SCGS reflected this rich tapestry of influences. Its founders were self-described "King's Chinese," referring to King George V of England. Its first several principals were European women, its students were of blended Chinese and Malay heritage, and all were immersed in a linguistic world that aimed for facility in English and Chinese. From this admixture, the modern and enlightened Nyonya was to emerge as an object of pride for and a benefit to her community. To its founders, SCGS was not just a collection of schoolrooms for imparting basic literacy and general knowledge. The institution was a symbol and a cause, a revolutionary first step by a small but highly influential immigrant group in a European colony, signaling its modernity through the education of its women. It was a means for the Straits Chinese to rejuvenate their declining sociocultural status, in a world of hardening colonial and national boundaries that were crowding in on their cosmopolitan existence. Their view is best summarized by a well-known quote from a Peranakan leader and SCGS founder, Lim Boon Keng:

Suffice it to say that no great progress can be made by any people if one half—the greater half it may be—is perpetually kept in a state of ignorance and degradation. Ignorance is infectious, and degradation is contagious. Keep your women in a low, ignorant and servile state, and in time you will become a low, ignorant and servile people—male and female![5]

This chapter examines the role of female education in Straits Chinese efforts to maintain or reclaim their place in colonial Malaya and Singapore, first tracing the history of the community in general and attitudes toward its women in particular, then shifting to a brief profile of the Singapore Chinese Girls' School. Chronologically, this discussion overlaps with time periods discussed in other chapters of this book, but the view is different from the perspective of a group and a school that was neither fully colonial nor Chinese in character. Ideally, the cultural capital and social influence of the Straits Chinese would have allowed them to create a new middle ground that would accommodate their unique hybridity and permit negotiation of a more inclusive Chinese identity. Instead, even as this new identity developed, the politics of European colonialism and Asian nationalisms rendered the occupation of transnational space uncertain and perilous. The discourse of Straits Chinese male elites about educating girls and women echoed voices from imperial and nationalist powers, rather than speaking for the multicultural heritage embodied by their women. To the extent that there was any middle ground, it was narrow and far from neutral.

The Peranakan or Straits Chinese embarked on a quest for cultural reformation at the turn of the twentieth century. This journey was paradoxical in definition and earnest in spirit. It was driven by a genuine desire to recover and re-invent a secure ethno-political identity somewhere between diaspora and empire. The reformation looked to tradition and modernity simultaneously: its goal was to revive certain elements of Chinese culture, such as language, classical literature, and Confucian values, while jettisoning perceived retrogressive tendencies in that same culture, such as superstition and the practice of folk religious rituals—elements that were typically associated with the women of the community.[6] Gender intersected with ethnicity in this view, as the Malay-female aspect of Peranakan heritage was associated with matriarchal practices and ethno-cultural hybridity, both of which had no place in a patriarchal and ethnically purist cultural revival. An educated female populace would help to advance the modernization agenda, as it would not only be a credit to Peranakan sociocultural standing but would also be instrumental in molding future generations. Interestingly, education and feminine subservience were not deemed mutually exclusive:

I have often heard the China-born Chinese say that the Straits-born Chinese cannot control their women folk. By that I suppose is meant that the mistress of the household is not so submissive as the Chinese wife. If it is true that the Straits-born Chinese wife has too much her own way in the family it is only another argument in favour of a better education for her . . . . Rest assured that the education will make them better daughters and more obedient wives . . . . If you do not approve of female education then keep your family folk at home. If you decide to let them go abroad in public, then in fairness prepare them for such a life so that they may be an honour to you.[7]

Girls' schools, then, were not supposed to displace the primacy of domestic roles for women or change the fact that women were chiefly defined in terms of their relationships to the men in their lives. Rather, an education that drew from Western knowledge while also being rooted in Chinese language and morality would create more up-to-date wives and mothers.

The "Nyonya problem" is a variation of the "woman problem" or "woman question" that preoccupied many nations at the turn of the twentieth century. Here it also had the added complications of hybrid ethno-cultural identity, diasporic history, and colonial subjecthood. This so-called problem can be read two ways. One is in the context of its time and from the male elite perspective. To reformist Straits Chinese, an urgent task was to thoroughly transform an embarrassing embodiment of backwardness in their community. Another is from the perspective of the Nyonya herself. What aspects of this education project did she internalize, and how did it shape her sense of being modern? Did schooling of the sort offered by SCGS equip her to confront the challenges of the early twentieth century?

While many modernizing states around the world were pursuing similar projects in female education, the Straits Chinese case was distinct. In the first place, the Straits Chinese did not stand on solid political or ethno-cultural ground. They were not exclusively British subjects, Chinese immigrants, or indigenous Malayans or Singaporeans, but some combination of these. The modernity they aimed to express through their women had to account for influences from all of these categories. Second, it was not only modernity that they sought but also its apparent opposite: a sense of ethno-cultural, and hence traditional, authenticity. In an age when few societies celebrated hybridity and multiculturalism, the Straits Chinese wished to assert leadership of the ethnic Chinese community in Malaya and Singapore, in a British-ruled colony.[8] But this leadership had to counter skepticism of their qualifications to represent an immigrant group defined by its ethno-cultural and national origins. What could the Peranakan do to claim a coherent and authentic Chinese identity, and hence a sort of moral authority, when their community was defined by hybridity? Was this search for authenticity merely a means to an end, to reclaiming their erstwhile sociocultural status, or was it a genuinely creative new move in Straits Chinese self-perception?

Two sources, the *Straits Chinese Magazine* and the archives of the Singapore Chinese Girls' School, provide valuable insight into the Peranakan pursuit of modern female education. The magazine, an English-language journal published in Singapore between 1898 and 1907, circulated Peranakan elite visions for ethno-cultural renewal. The school, founded in 1899, was an institution aimed at realizing one key component of that vision: creating an educated Straits Chinese female class. Taken together, these two endeavors show that the female education project was an integral part of a multicultural group's effort to secure a stronger position in a world increasingly divided along racial and national lines. As cultural cosmopolitanism became a double-edged sword, Straits Chinese male elites used a gendered discourse of modernization to cope with the pressures of rising Chinese immigration and the demands of Westernization in colonial Southeast Asia. For those educated Straits Chinese women whose views were captured in contemporary print media publications or in oral histories collected later in the twentieth century, there was a different set of concerns. By the 1930s and 1940s, literate Nyonyas began to express their dissatisfaction with the traditional domesticity that male elites still expected of them and to explore new avenues for being modern through professional and other means.

BETWEEN DIASPORA AND EMPIRE: THE STRAITS CHINESE

The freighted task of defining "Straits Chinese" and "Peranakan" is a political act in and of itself. Commentators from past and present often use the two terms interchangeably, since they both refer to the same group of people, but scholars argue that they each carry different political and historical resonances. In present-day Malaysia and Singapore, the broadest and most generally accepted definition of this community is that they are descendants of Chinese (typically Fujianese) males and local Malay females, who resided primarily in the former Straits Settlements of Penang, Singapore, and Melaka—hence, the "Straits Chinese." Their culture integrated Chinese and Malay language, dress, and foodways. With the advent of British colonialism in the Malay world during the late eighteenth century, Straits Chinese culture took on an Anglicized dimension, embracing the English language and Western intellectual ideas, and adopting Western European dress and leisure activities. Women typically wore Malay clothing, as in the case of the Peranakan schoolgirls who first attended SCGS. Many men wore Chinese clothing and even sported the Manchu-mandated queue until the popularity of Western dress took over. Families lived in houses adorned with Chinese and European architectural features, practiced a blend of Chinese patrilineal kinship and Malay worship of sacred sites and spirits, ate food that was spiced with local ingredients, and spoke a creole language of Malay and Fujianese dialects.[9] Even as Chinese-Malay intermarriage most likely did not extend beyond the earliest generations, as Straits Chinese in later years tended to marry among themselves or with new immigrants from China, the distinctively hybrid nature of their cultural practices endured.[10] Over time, the term expanded to include the locally born descendants of Chinese who were born in China but migrated to the Straits Settlements, especially if they married into Peranakan families or adopted their cultural attributes.[11]

The term "Straits Chinese" is open to debate and criticism. Given its geographic association, it technically refers to place of birth rather than ethnocultural roots. Also, Straits Chinese groups were not all alike across each of the three Straits Settlements, with variations in whether the Chinese or Malay elements of their culture dominated, and whether their language and customs drew on yet other influences from neighboring states in Southeast Asia.[12] Some even argue that the Straits Chinese are better understood as a social and economic merchant elite that was dependent on neither place of birth nor ethnic origin.[13] Furthermore, present-day scholars charge that the term perpetuates racial categories that were created by the British imperial regime.[14] For example, colonial authorities included the category of "Straits-born Chinese" in the 1891, 1901, and 1911 censuses of the Straits Settlements but omitted it thereafter. As such, the argument goes, it is best used in a strictly historical context, to refer to the group as it saw itself when the Straits Settlements were still in existence. Acknowledging the importance of these nuances, the terms "Straits Chinese" and "Peranakan" are used interchangeably in this discussion, but rely more heavily on the term Peranakan for the postcolonial period.

The term "Peranakan" also carries a wealth of references and meanings. It generally denotes heritage from intermarriage between a non-local male and an indigenous female and can therefore refer to many types of mixed-race populations in present-day Southeast Asia, such as in Indonesia, Thailand, and the Philippines.[15] The terms for Peranakan men and women were "Baba" and "Nyonya," respectively: the former derived from a Hindustani honorific for males, and the latter was a Malay form of address for non-Malay married women of standing which some etymologists have linked to a Portuguese word for "grandmother."[16] Because these designations are less bound to colonial time and place, they are more commonly used today by members of the community to describe themselves. Like the term Peranakan, these descriptors can also apply to Chinese-Malay creoles in other Southeast Asian venues.[17] In short, the tangle of cultural and political meanings in nomenclature surrounding the Straits Chinese/Peranakan community reflects the complexity of their history and identity formation. This genealogy of influences matters when considering how Straits Chinese male elites sought to re-make their women through an education that struggled to merge Chinese, Southeast Asian, and British visions of modernity.

Under colonial rule in Malaya and Singapore, the Straits Chinese occupied a favorable socioeconomic position.[18] Community leadership was in the hands of merchant-entrepreneurs and intellectual literati, whom the British also relied on to mediate relations with and among the more recently arrived immigrant Chinese.[19] These leaders included the Melaka-born Tan Tock Seng (1798–1850), a renowned philanthropist and the first Asian in Singapore to be appointed a justice of the peace by British authorities in 1846; Song Ong Siang (1871–1941), scion of a prominent Christian Straits Chinese family who studied law at Cambridge University, was called to the English bar in 1893, and was created Knight Commander of the Order of the British Empire in 1936; and Lim Boon Keng (1869–1957), an Anglicized and Anglophone doctor educated at Edinburgh University, also the leader of a Confucianist revival and a local branch of the Chinese anti-Manchu party, the Tongmenghui.[20] Song and Lim were among a generation of Straits Chinese who deliberately chose English-medium education and who began to shift their focus from business to the professions.[21] For example, in 1900, Lim co-founded the Straits Chinese British Association "to represent the minority interests of English-educated professionals and entrepreneurs within the Baba population."[22] These "King's Chinese" had closer affinities with the British than other ethnic Chinese in the region, and up to the early twentieth century, their influence was greater than their numbers suggested. In Singapore, Babas were only an estimated 2.5 percent of the ethnic Chinese population in 1848, and 9.5 percent in 1881.[23] In the Straits Settlements as a whole, the Straits Chinese were approximately 14.5 percent of the ethnic Chinese population in 1881 and 15 percent in 1891.[24]

In the 1890s, however, the Straits Chinese socioeconomic advantage began to erode. Several decades of new immigration from China had brought in waves of laborers and merchants with distinct notions of Chinese identity, and with new capital and leverage with which to negotiate directly with the British authorities. In 1891, approximately 50,000 Peranakan in the Straits Settlements were outnumbered by 175,000 newcomers from China, and by 1931, approximately 68 percent of ethnic Chinese in Peninsular Malaya were China-born.[25] As the number of new adult migrants increased, so, too, did the number of non-Peranakan children. Census reports show that in 1891 Straits-born girls accounted for 7,759 out of 13,026 Chinese females below the age of fifteen, but by 1901 this proportion had dropped to 9,969 out of 19,273.[26] Newer Chinese immigrants to these colonies, because of their more recent experiences living in China and their more direct familial and sentimental ties to their native places, felt a stronger connection to the language and culture of their homeland. They were hence more desirous of having their children educated in those traditions and less inclined to assimilate into British colonial culture. The Peranakan and later Chinese immigrants were also separated by a significant socioeconomic gap. An 1848 estimate found that of approximately 1,000 Babas in Melaka, the majority were merchants, shopkeepers, petty traders, or farmers, and virtually none were physical laborers.[27] This is not to overstate the bifurcation between the two types of Chinese immigrants, the long-settled and locally born versus the newly arrived and supposedly more arriviste. There was more overlap and interaction between these groups than previously thought, especially in the late nineteenth century.[28] Nonetheless, perceived or real, these dividing lines were perpetuated by observers and by the Peranakan themselves.

The Peranakan elite found themselves in a crisis of confidence about their position in the British colonies. They feared that Malaya and Singapore might follow the trend of the neighboring Dutch East Indies, where the Peranakan community was divested of valuable trade monopolies and given a new official designation—"Foreign Orientals"—that placed them in a lower social position, closer to the indigenous locals than to their European masters.[29] Their role as favored intermediaries between the overseas Chinese community and the British administration was no longer secure, as the more recently arrived Chinese began to supplant Peranakan ownership and influence of business interests in Southeast Asia. Newer migrants could also lay stronger claim to Chinese government protection and private connections, to the benefit of their business enterprises and social status.

Some Peranakan saw themselves as superior to more newly arrived Chinese immigrants due to their affinity with British language and culture. These commentators were the self-defined "enlightened and thoughtful Babas," who were also portrayed by the British as a "better class of Chinese."[30] They were self-conscious about their position as "British

Chinese" and were preoccupied with the role of their women in helping to perpetuate their distinct communal identity. Unions between Peranakan women and new immigrant Chinese men were considered intermarriage between two different types of people.[31] Public discussion fretted over the skewed gender ratio between Nyonyas and Babas, with the former beginning to outnumber the latter due to the outmigration of Babas seeking better job opportunities overseas. Some ventured that this would lead to increasing numbers of intermarriages, which could be beneficial "as the means of infusing a new spirit of enterprise and adventure into the lethargic blood of the Straits-born Chinese."[32] But Baba elites also feared that Nyonyas would find themselves in the unenviable position of a concubine, or that, unable to make as good a marriage as they would like, these disappointed women would be vulnerable to "scheming and unscrupulous persons who lead them away from the paths of virtue and honour."[33] Fusion of the Peranakan and new immigrant Chinese was thus neither easy nor entirely positive.

Straits Chinese leaders Song Ong Siang and Lim Boon Keng decided that an intervention was necessary. Both were English-educated and eminently successful at navigating the colonial system in Singapore. Song led various Christian and legal associations and was the first Chinese in Malaya or Singapore to be awarded a knighthood for his efforts in public service. Lim was an active social reformer and legislator, and a third-generation Peranakan who had learned the Chinese language as an adult, whereupon he became an ardent promoter of Confucian learning and a supporter of the late Qing reformer Kang Youwei.[34] Both Song and Lim were clearly aware of the benefits that a carefully managed affiliation with Chinese influences could bring to a Straits Chinese population at risk of decline. Conversant with but not solely grounded in Chinese, Malay, or British culture, they felt that launching a cultural reform movement that included the modernization of their women was essential for the Straits Chinese. Female education, then, would be an important part of the solution to their community's quest to regain prestige and relevance.

LET US LOOK AFTER OUR WOMEN: THE CONFUCIANIST REVIVAL, THE *STRAITS CHINESE MAGAZINE*, AND THE NYONYA PROBLEM

At the turn of the century, Straits Chinese male elites seeking to redefine their community identity were caught in an uncomfortable bind. They wished to retain a comfortable association with and the esteem of the

British, whom they associated with the civilization and modernity that they sought. However, they were acutely aware of the Chinese and local dimensions of their heritage, and with the rise of Chinese immigration and Southeast Asian nationalisms in the early twentieth century, they did not wish to lose all elements of "Chineseness" entirely.

From approximately 1895 to 1910, the latter impulse was expressed in a Straits Chinese cultural reform movement, sometimes also called a Confucianist revival, spearheaded by Lim Boon Keng and a cohort of fellow male elites. This movement was strongly influenced by the reformist trend that was sweeping across China at this time, led by Kang Youwei, who visited Singapore in 1900 and made direct contact with local Chinese leaders. Despite being steeped in British education, language, and societal norms, Lim also wished to resuscitate certain Chinese traditions to preserve a distinctive Straits Chinese identity that could withstand colonial, Chinese nationalist, or local political change. Through their publications, associations, and schools, Straits Chinese leaders promoted the study of Chinese language and classical literature and of Confucianism as a moral and social ideology.[35] However, these efforts were not wholly China-oriented, as these leaders also critiqued traditional Chinese habits of mind and behavior that they considered retrograde, such as superstition or excessive spending on rituals and ceremonies.[36] This cultural reform movement was hence a deliberate effort to assert a distinct Straits Chinese ethno-cultural identity—one that was not wholly dependent on either British or Chinese influences. It was also not universally popular. Older generations of more conservative Straits Chinese resented, or simply ignored, these calls to overhaul their identities.[37]

In 1897, Lim Boon Keng and Song Ong Siang became the founders and editors of the *Straits Chinese Magazine: A Quarterly Journal of Oriental and Occidental Culture* (*SCM*). Nominally multilingual in English, Chinese, and Malay, though primarily English in practice, this journal ran from 1897 to 1907 and had distributors in British Malaya, Singapore, Borneo, the Dutch East Indies, Vietnam, and Japan.[38] Though short-lived, the *SCM* was a major channel for circulating Peranakan elite visions for cultural reform and aimed at unifying literate Chinese under the banner of Straits Chinese leadership. In the inaugural issue, Lim declared that the main object of the publication was "to guide the present chaotic state of public opinion among [the Straits-born people] to some definite end"—that is, to discipline and mold diverse cultural orientations among the Straits Chinese into a stronger and more coherent group identity.[39]

In every issue of the *SCM*, the epigraph on the front cover was a Confucian quote: "If you have faults, do not fear to abandon them." Self-improvement was the watchword of the publication. Peranakan contributors to the *SCM* invoked elements from Chinese tradition to show the connection between culture, literacy, and moral repair. In his writings, Lim Boon Keng attributed the ability of Chinese Babas "to maintain their integrity as a people" to the fact that their forefathers had remained in touch with their roots in "a land of culture," "spoke their truly 'mother tongue,' read, studied and enjoyed . . . those immortal *Shoos* and *Kings* [Chinese classics] which proclaim peace and happiness to the righteous and virtuous . . . extending . . . their intellectual and moral powers."[40] He further urged that Peranakan children learn both Chinese and English, and be instructed in moral lessons drawn from Chinese tradition.[41] Song Ong Siang, too, saw the benefit of incorporating Chinese texts and traditions wherever necessary, suggesting that for female education, "in Christian schools, the Bible is and will continue to be read and taught, but in . . . other schools, general rules of morality or the Confucian ethics must be taught and explained."[42] This eagerness to fuse the best of Chinese and Western practices appeared regularly in *SCM* articles that sought to educate the reader on the basics of traditional Chinese literature and history, such as "Some Genuine Chinese Authors," a literary analysis of classical Chinese poetry.[43] This invocation of classical Chinese philosophy, ethics, and literature would help the Peranakan find a balance between cosmopolitanism and authenticity, using tools from multiple nations and cultures.[44]

Yet many Perakanan related to traditional Chinese culture as outsiders looking in, and the cultural reform movement was a complicated effort at "re-sinification." As founder and champion of this movement, which he hoped would reach all ethnic Chinese in Singapore, Lim Boon Keng faced skepticism in certain quarters about his suitability for leadership. One major reason was his lack of fluency in Mandarin Chinese, which he had only begun to learn as an adult, after a visit to China.[45] Furthermore, his vision was not what he considered a reactionary return to Chinese traditions of old but rather an invention of a new and progressive Chinese identity.[46] In this picture, Western elements such as Christianity and the rejection of ancestor worship were a matter of course. Lim and other *SCM* authors adopted the perspective taken by Western critics of Chinese culture, as if to make Peranakan readers aware of others' negative opinions of them. Their targets ranged from marriage customs to physical appearance to moral standards in the Chinese community. Their tone was often at best Eurocentric and at worst supercilious. In a somber address to the Chinese Philomathic Society in 1897, which was printed in the *SCM*, Lim expressed his distaste for certain traditions that the Peranakan had been unable to discard. Even though they were able to "salute one another in European fashion" and "highly appreciate European dinners and drink," when it came to wedding celebrations, "the horrid red table cloth replaces the pleasing snowy cover that speaks at once of good taste and cleanliness."[47] During funerals, "an excellent house elaborately furnished with the choice products of European and Asiatic art, is transformed as by the magic of Aladdin, into a prehistoric abode of the dead, where intentional carelessness allows every rubbish to accumulate."[48]

Even more damning were articles written by British contributors, most likely selected by editors such as Song himself to demonstrate to readers the low esteem in which the Straits Chinese were held by their colonial rulers. One example is W. M. Burbidge's discourse titled "The Present State of Morality amongst the Straits Chinese," an account of the "peculiar moral defects" and "moral cancer" spreading through the Chinese community in the British colonies.[49] These "defects" included gambling, womanizing, opium-smoking, and drinking—vices that Burbidge acknowledged were not unique to the Chinese, but that he suggested were entered into by them "with a zest that seems to be innate, i.e., they seem to consider these degrading vices as natural," and that would require significant efforts to be stamped out so that the Chinese might reform themselves "in keeping with Western civilization and moral culture."[50] The only rejoinder to this sweeping indictment of Chinese character was an editorial footnote correcting Burbidge's statement that the Chinese had "no moral standard whereby they can correct their failings." They did have one, the SCM editors protested weakly, most likely referring to Confucianism, but the majority either disregarded or ignored it. If there seems to be a whiff of self-flagellation about this, one must bear in mind that such language was similar to the discourse in China, India, or any number of countries struggling with political and social reform while fending off Western incursions at the time. In China, for example, early twentieth-century satirist Lu Xun's short stories lacerated fellow Chinese who were too selfish, hidebound, or ignorant to contribute to the vital task of rebuilding their nation.

In general, this self-critique applied to both sexes. Neither men nor women were solely responsible for the community's failings. However, most negative aspects of Peranakan social life were linked to traditional cultural practices and domestic rituals, as in the case of the weddings and funerals, which were typically associated with women. When specific criticisms of Peranakan women did appear, they were pointed and emphatic, occasionally self-contradicting, and at times gratuitous. Commentators fretted that Nyonyas were insufficiently modern and enlightened, yet also lacking as traditional wives and mothers; that they were so ignorant as to be superstitious, yet also worldly enough to be at risk of moral corruption;

and even that they were physically ugly to behold. Given the frequency and intensity with which the "Nyonya problem" was discussed in the pages of the *SCM*, it is fair to say that Straits Chinese women were a lightning rod for the cultural insecurities of the male elite and a ready target for modernizing activism.

Articles specifically aimed at Nyonyas were common from the *SCM's* early days. Some were measured, such as general essays describing "Chinese Women" and the complexity of their roles in traditional Chinese society. Even so, such articles took pains to point out the "ignorant and illiterate" state of females, and the loss sustained by the nation through this "defect."[51] Others were more strongly worded, even scolding in tone. In "Straits Chinese Mothers," regular contributor Lew See Fah penned an open letter to the women of his community regarding their ineptitude as mothers, aware that illiteracy would keep most of them from reading it themselves, but urging fathers and husbands to convey his message to them:

> It is not my purpose to find fault with you, the Straits Chinese grandmothers and mothers. I am conscious that you are more to be pitied than blamed . . . . [But] your ignorance of letters effectively prevents you from drawing upon the experience of abler and wiser counsellors on the subject of how to take proper care of your little ones. When these little folks [are ill], how helpless you are! . . . You do not understand the elements of nursing.[52]

Lew later turned his attention to the younger generation of Peranakan Chinese women, writing a similar letter to "Straits Chinese Maidens" and their parents. He argued that being ignorant and overly sheltered made Nyonya girls susceptible to temptation and vice.[53]

For the further edification of Nyonyas, there was also a running series of "Select Anecdotes from the Records of Famous Women." This column featured excerpts from the "Biographies of Heroic Women" (*Lienü Zhuan*), a text dating back to the Han dynasty and the earliest extant didactic book on feminine moral behavior. The collection of stories included legends of chaste, wise, and heroic women in Chinese mythology, which, according to the *SCM* contributor who edited the series, could be "taken advantage of by the social reformer who is working for the emancipation of the modern Chinese women from the thralldom of ignorance."[54] Several of these tales featured heroines who were intelligent, witty, and even educated, such that they were able to engage intellectually with their husbands.[55] Of course, these exceptional women also adhered to traditional Confucian norms in many important ways. They put the preservation of their chastity before their lives and valued the welfare of their parents and husbands above their own—an outlook that modernity and female enlightenment was supposed to help overturn.[56] This series of stories mirrored efforts of contemporary reformers in China who were using traditional women's biographies to promote self-contradicting ideals of female virtue and epic heroism.[57] The irony of such a series is that few Nyonyas would have had the requisite education to read these articles themselves. One might imagine, then, that the beneficiaries of these tales with female moral exemplars were Babas themselves.

Worse than simple ignorance or an embarrassing adherence to outmoded traditions was the sin of gambling, which was supposedly an endemic problem among Nyonyas. The *SCM* carried articles and short stories condemning the activity and the shame brought upon the community by Peranakan women who were unable to tear themselves away from the gaming table. Babas rebuked Nyonyas for breaching propriety, frittering away their families' money, forgetting their domestic duties, and even selling their jewelry to fund their habits.[58] According to Straits Chinese reformers, education for these women would solve the problem. However, the very few Nyonya voices that made themselves heard in the pages of the *SCM* took a different position on the gambling issue. One female contributor wrote an article on "Gambling amongst Our Nyonyas," suggesting that inattentive and unloving husbands were at fault for neglecting their families and causing their dissatisfied wives to seek diversion elsewhere.[59] Her proposed solution was not simply education, which might lead Nyonyas to "[follow] Western ideas . . . [and] resent the neglect of their husbands and take to something worse than gambling." Rather, "true love and affection" between husbands and wives would lead Nyonyas to prioritze the welfare of their families and households, and abstain from this "gambling poison."[60]

The "leaders and the lights of the Straits-born Chinese community," as Song Ong Siang put it, were obliged to improve the status of their women, whose condition "does not tend to reflect credit on the taste and higher qualities" of their people.[61] Recalling reports he had read of women in China successfully superintending the education of their children, Song concluded that the Peranakan were not even keeping up with their brethren who remained in the ancestral homeland or who had more recently arrived in Southeast Asia:

> This [account] therefore places the social status of the women in China on a much higher plane than that of their sisters in Singapore . . . . What a standing rebuke the degraded social status of the Nyonyas is to the boasted superiority of the Straits-born Chinese over their fellow-countrymen from China![62]

However, writers warned that Western-style modernization of women should not be accepted incautiously, either. Rather than allow Westernization to overtake them, the Peranakan should regulate the process:

> In the West women enjoy great liberty of action. But they are educated and trained to live in public as well as to take their places as mothers in the privacy of their homes. I foresee a possible danger to family life in the Straits Settlements in this matter . . . . In my opinion it will be a great mistake if you let your wives and daughters follow European customs, unless you train and educate them first to take up such a position.[63]

The Peranakan fear that their women's backwardness would reflect poorly on their community was similar to a major concern in many nationalist projects during this time. In China, commentators labeled it "the woman problem" or "the woman question": how to manage the changing role of women in the process of creating a modern nation-state.[64] On the one hand, female education was a necessary attribute of modernity. As it was in Western nations such as England and the United States, where schooling for girls and women had been in place for decades, so, too, should it be in non-Western nations such as China and India. On the other hand, anxieties over losing one's ethno-cultural integrity by pursuing a Western ideal of modernization perpetuated an emphasis on feminine attributes that could help to preserve traditional identity. For example, Hindu men in South Asia were able to resolve the conflict between modernizing along Western lines and preserving a sense of local ethnic tradition that was being threatened by British imperialism, by investing women with the duty of preserving their cultural heritage within the domestic sphere.[65] Hence, for the early twentieth-century Chinese woman, expanded access to education and new socioeconomic roles did not automatically include ready access to the political process or general acceptance of public roles for women. The new Chinese woman might be educated and skilled, but this was primarily in service of being a better wife and mother—being mothers of citizens as opposed to being citizens.[66] Society was still patriarchal, and it expected women to embody traditional qualities associated with ideal Chinese womanhood: chastity, femininity, deference to elders and males, devotion to home and family. In this way, the soul of Chinese society would remain intact despite the ravages of Western modernization on cultural life and the body politic. The women who had to play this dual role struggled with the self-contradictory, paradoxical nature of being a modern woman in the new nation while being responsible for the survival of traditional values.

Consciously or otherwise, the Peranakan community adopted the discourse of the "woman problem," including its exhortations for female education. From its inception, the *SCM* carried articles advocating schooling for Peranakan women, if only to serve as a corrective for their supposedly retrograde tendencies and to train them to serve the cause of modernizing the community. In an 1896 speech to the Chinese Philomathic Society, printed in the *SCM* in 1897, Song Ong Siang argued that elevating women through schooling would elevate the status of the community as a whole:

> Are we not desirous that the Straits-born Chinese community shall be looked upon as an educated and enlightened people? Then let us look after our women, and help them all we can to be themselves more enlightened, more perfect, more noble in their thoughts and aspirations, and more fit to be the worthy mothers of the future citizens of this settlement.[67]

This speech titled "The Position of Chinese Women" detailed the problems with Peranakan women, the reasons for wanting to improve their condition, and a basic plan for girls' schooling. Song opined that female education would improve the behavior of Peranakan women, whom he charged with being ignorant, superstitious, idle, and addicted to gambling.[68] Song even went so far as to conflate lack of education and cultural inferiority with physical attractiveness, quoting an English writer on the appearance of Chinese women: "Females are shorter than those of the European races, pretty when young, but soon become ugly and repulsive."[69] Regarding this condemnation, Song felt he had no choice but to agree. In fact, he blamed his own people for keeping the "youthful beauty" of Nyonya women confined within the home "to bloom and languish and die unnoticed and unadmired"—an error that might yet be remedied by female education.[70] In Song's mind, sequestering women for the sake of moral propriety made the Peranakan literally and figuratively look bad. Hence he prescribed physical education in girls' schools, which would help to "drive away that unhealthy paleness which is seen on the features of so many Chinese girls, and fit them to perform more satisfactorily their duties of maternity, and enable them to preserve their youthful appearance for a longer space of time."[71] Song was invoking women's reproductive and ornamental value— two deeply traditional functions of womanhood in a patriarchal world—as building blocks for modern life.

Other contributors to the *SCM* chimed in with support. In 1899, Lim Boon Keng suggested that "in all our efforts for the reformation of our people, none appears to us more praiseworthy than the attempt to induce our people to take an interest in educating our girls."[72] In 1901, Lew See

Fah (whose chastisement of Straits Chinese women and girls were featured earlier) articulated how Peranakan women were failing, but could yet be trained, to redeem their people's reputation:

> How much do [your] children lose by your not being able to take your share in lifting them on to the first rung of the educational ladder? . . . You will not, I hope, feel offended by a little straight talk . . . . What are you mothers doing to instill in the minds of your little ones the duties of morality and religion? . . . Give your daughters the opportunity you have lost [and let them go to school].[73]

At this time, elite Peranakan males also began to distance themselves from the indigenous Malay component of their ethno-cultural heritage. This, too, was a gendered component of their re-invention. Although their origins were embedded in inter-racial marriages between Chinese men and local Malay women, the Straits Chinese sought to downplay or remove the "Malay accretions" in their culture.[74] Babas blamed Malay influence, and, by extension, Nyonyas, for weakening Peranakan moral fiber. These accusations were not subtle, charging that "[Straits Chinese] maternal blood in whatever degree of dilution has something to do with that spirit of independence and thriftlessness, apart from the love of gewgaws and hatred of continuous hard work," and that the presence of Malay blood meant that Peranakan families would inherit flaws such as "extravagant habits, vice, distaste for work, eccentricity, excesses, and recklessness."[75] At the same time, an uncritical turn to Western ways could also be damaging, as articles in the *SCM* cautioned against Nyonyas taking after the excessive individualism and neglect of maternal duties that many Western women espoused.[76] The influence of British colonial discourse in this line of argument, both with regard to race and gender, is clear.

Whereas negative elements of one's bloodline might be hard to erase immediately, the behavior and appearance of Nyonyas could be addressed through modern approaches to literacy and domesticity. This was where the Singapore Chinese Girls' School came in. Song proposed that girls' schooling could include arithmetic, basic reading and writing in English and Chinese, music, and art, as well as "sewing and embroidery work under competent Nyonya mistresses, Domestic and household management," hygiene, and nursing.[77] Cultural practices that incorporated Malay elements such as creole language or hybridized clothing and foodways might be permitted in the private, domestic sphere of the Nyonyas but were not included in the new program for female education, and they were certainly not held up as representative of the new Straits Chinese identity. If anything, these practices were depicted in the *SCM* as backward and embarrassing. As a pro-reform contributor to the journal declared, "We, Straits Chinese fathers, should . . . encourage our girls in every possible way to give up the Malay language and revert to the Chinese tongue."[78] This rejection of Malay ethno-cultural connections would resonate in the decades to come, as certain political factions in postcolonial Malaya and Singapore began to challenge the national belonging of local descendants of immigrant Chinese. For now, however, re-making the Straits Chinese girl according to reformists' vision of modernity would be a source of uplift for not just women, but their community as a whole.

THE SINGAPORE CHINESE GIRLS' SCHOOL SOLUTION

Although missionary groups had already been operating girls' schools in Malaya and Singapore for half a century, Lim wondered why the Straits Chinese "should . . . relegate our primary duties when we are quite able—if we only choose to do so—to look after our own house."[79] Published in the *SCM* in 1899, his argument for founding a girls' school in Singapore was a combination of idealism and pragmatism. Anticipating resistance from the general public, he stated:

> It is necessary to teach the girls such practical things as sewing, cooking and the ordinary household duties in order to convince our detractors that education does not make them less fit as housekeepers . . . . Usefulness before ornament is an important fact to bear in mind.[80]

To coax local Chinese girls and their parents into the school, Lim proposed to "guide [the students] slowly in the acquisition of our language and of things in general," and that "a sufficient amount of physical exercise will be gradually introduced so as not to shock conservative parents."[81] With these accommodations, Lim felt, a girls' school should be an entirely reasonable and even attractive proposition for local Chinese residents:

> We have done everything in our power to gratify the peculiar views of our people on this subject, and there is really no excuse now why any respectable and sensible Singapore Chinese should not give his daughters the chance of a decent education. Before long I hope that some sort of education will have a marketable value from a marriage point of view, and then perhaps even this poor schooling will not be reserved for those alone who are fortunate enough to have sensible parents.[82]

It was in this spirit that the Singapore Chinese Girls' School was launched in July 1899. Its main founders were Lim Boon Keng, Song Ong Siang, and a wealthy non-Peranakan Chinese named Khoo Seok Wan. Like many of its peer institutions, SCGS struggled for decades before reaching stability. Until 1927, its survival was precarious, despite the fact that the school had the backing of several prominent local Chinese, Peranakan and non-Peranakan, and the approval of the colonial administration. It had also taken pains to accommodate the interests of multiple parties. The key meeting that elected the SCGS' founding committee or board of directors was held at the Chinese consulate and included among its members a number of prominent non-Peranakan Chinese. The group acceded to the request of local British educators that they avoid naming the school "Chinese Girls' School," perhaps to preempt the appearance of pro-China factionalism.[83] In 1900, the colonial administration registered the school as Government Aided, and by 1901, a visit by the British Director of Public Instruction and a successful first government inspection had elicited favorable reports and a First Class Grant from the authorities.[84] With an Englishwoman as principal, SCGS had the basic attributes of a formal school. The institution offered the first five years of elementary education and a curriculum that included Malay and Chinese language, arithmetic, geography, music, and sewing. As a temporary measure to increase fee revenue, it also admitted some male students. It held an annual prize-giving ceremony, which parents and relatives of students could attend, and observed standardized school holidays, including both Western ones such as Christmas and Easter, and Chinese ones such as Chinese New Year and Confucius' Birthday. As part of the Confucianist revival's "Speak Mandarin Campaign," Lim Boon Keng's first wife, Margaret Wong Tuan Keng, took personal charge of teaching the Chinese-language classes, in which "the elder girls" were apparently "taking a great interest."[85] Student enrollment rose from approximately sixty in 1900 to more than 250 in 1921.[86] Song Ong Siang took a deep interest in the workings of the school, visiting classes, attending school ceremonies, and even administering tests.

However, SCGS suffered from lack of traction with the "sensible Singapore Chinese" who were supposed to come around to what Lim claimed were the obvious benefits of female education. Even before the school opened, Song noted with some bitterness that some senior members of the Straits Chinese community had refused to patronize the school or had decried the school's efforts as disrespectful toward social norms. Despite the increase in number of students over the years, it was clear that parents only wished to enroll their daughters for a few short years, withdrawing them from school in preparation for domestic life before they reached their early teens. As the editors of the *SCM* ruefully observed in 1903:

> Year after year the most promising girls in the School cease to attend for no other reason than that pernicious custom proclaims that they have attained the age when they must be condemned to zenana life [whereby women are confined to a sequestered area of the home].[87]

In 1907, eight years after the school's founding, the editor of the *SCM* fumed that thanks to the recalcitrance of an older, more conservative generation, "there is no more absolutely ignorant, prejudiced and superstitious class of people in the world than the Straits-born Chinese woman."[88]

The first two decades of the school's existence were marked by bleak financial circumstances that were barely remedied by repeated infusions of Straits Chinese philanthropic and government aid. In 1903, for example, the school's committee of directors issued a plea for donations, appealing to local Chinese pride by pointing out that ethnic Chinese in Batavia had "numerous schools for girls" with at least "two hundred pupils" in them, and that with additional funds, not only would SCGS be saved from collapse but would also be able to start teaching Chinese language, "one of the principal objects in establishing this school."[89] In 1906, the school had to relocate to smaller premises with cheaper rent, the previous rent of $76 per month having become unaffordable. The next several years witnessed more just-in-time, public-private financial arrangements. These included an agreement in 1908 between the government and the committee of directors that should the committee permanently invest $15,000 in an endowment fund, the government would provide the school with more land and a larger building. This agreement was replaced in 1924 by yet another arrangement that involved SCGS directors raising more than $77,000 to build a new, larger school on a piece of land worth $50,000 that was leased to the school by the government.[90] To support this expenditure, SCGS relied heavily on local Chinese patronage, within and beyond the Peranakan community, with the committee's continuing, dogged goal of building "the premier Chinese Girls' School in Singapore."[91] This patronage included donations ranging from $1,000 from local business leader Aw Boon Haw to $460 from the sale of Song's book *One Hundred Years of the Chinese in Singapore*.[92] Throughout these financial tribulations, it was the sustained interest of local Chinese elites and colonial support that allowed the school to stay open.

Then there were problems of staffing and teaching. In the first three decades of its existence, SCGS saw ten principals come and go; only one stayed longer than four years. During the 1900s, the teaching staff suffered frequent and sometimes complete turnover. At an annual prize-giving ceremony in 1921, Song read out a stern report from the British Inspector of Schools, which bemoaned how in just that one year, there had been four different headmistresses, and several experienced teachers had resigned, only to be replaced by inexperienced ones. According to the inspector, "the following needs are urgent: (a) a qualified European headmistress, (b) a qualified local staff, (c) a new school building."[93] In short, the inspector was pointing out insufficiencies in all the main components of a school. In stark comparison to the large sums of building and maintenance fees, teachers' salaries were $40 per month in 1912, and $1 for a day of relief teaching.[94] Teachers often left for better opportunities at other local schools, including the government-founded Raffles Girls' School. Those who stayed were often young and under-qualified, further compounding the problem of maintaining sound academic standards in instruction. Government inspection reports from this period observed that whereas SCGS was doing important work, some teachers were so young that they were "little girls" themselves, "unable to properly manage so many children, and the utmost confusion prevails."[95]

SCGS turned a corner in the late 1920s and early 1930s, with a move to new and larger premises and the arrival of a school principal whose tenure lasted more than two decades, well into the post–World War II era. Hailing from England, Jessie Geake made her largest impact in standardizing and formalizing the school following a Western model for female education. Changes ranged from outward appearances such as creating a standard school uniform, to introducing extra-curricular activities such as the Girl Guides and an annual Game Day, to instituting curricular reforms such as regular student report cards and building up enrollment in higher-level classes so as to be able to offer more advanced certification for students.[96] Cooking and domestic science became permanent parts of the syllabus. Although the Peranakan founders had intended that such home-making skills be taught from the outset, the school had been unable to implement the classes due to lack of funding for kitchen facilities. During a trip to England in 1936, Geake visited girls' schools to gain more firsthand knowledge of domestic science teaching, so that, as Song approvingly observed, SCGS students would be "equipped for their career as housewives and citizens of this country."[97] Teaching became more professionalized, as indicated by Geake's successful appeal to the government for the establishment of a Teachers' Provident Fund or pension fund in 1932.[98] Faculty and staff had subscriptions to English magazines such as *Teachers' World* and *London Illustrated* for pedagogical guidance and material. Teachers who could speak Chinese dialects were hired to facilitate communication with the youngest students who were new to English-language learning.

Already, the first local Chinese teachers had joined the faculty in 1916, and the first graduates of SCGS who had trained as teachers were returning to work for the school.[99]

Although a non-European was not hired as school principal until 1951, when Tan Swee Khin stepped into the role, Geake and other school leaders took pains to emphasize local involvement as well as Western leadership. This suggests the importance of the school's image as a hybrid, albeit ultimately British-oriented, venture. At the outset of her tenure, Geake declared that the students "are British Chinese, and their contribution to the Empire will be the more valuable if an appreciation of the excellence in things Chinese is maintained, as part of their education according to good British Standards."[100] Her view dovetailed neatly with the rhetoric of the Peranakan cultural reforms and British colonial concern that schools such as the SCGS should succeed in their quest to persuade "the better class of Chinese to send their girls . . . to school [as] it is impossible to overestimate the importance of this work to the future of the Colony."[101] An official school history points out that "Mrs. Geake was unusual in that she was a European willing to be employed by Chinese," although it is clear that these Chinese employers were highly Westernized to begin with, and that the school's development occurred along Western lines.[102] Much in the structure of the school relied on British ideas and customs, from the curriculum and textbooks, to a "House" system in which students were grouped under "House Captains" for sports and team spirit activities, to the school's Maypole around which students could dance as a form of appropriately decorous exercise for girls.[103]

SCGS schoolgirls, especially Nyonyas, undoubtedly experienced a broadening of their horizons, even if only partially or temporarily. Attending school enabled them to venture further out into the world than traditional restrictions on Nyonyas had previously allowed. Aside from academic and extra-curricular activities, students took folk-dancing classes and staged a dance concert for the school's first public fundraising event in 1924, dispensing with the taboo of Straits Chinese girls being seen outside their homes.[104] Even earlier, in 1921, the school held its annual prize-giving ceremony at Victoria Theatre, a large public venue near the commercial center of the island. (Of course, news coverage stressed the traditional elements of female education, observing that at the entrance to the theater was an exhibition of students' "needlework, knitting, and fancy work," which "demonstrated the cleverness of Chinese girls at needlework and the good instruction imparted in this useful line in the school.")[105] Students also took steps toward financial literacy when the school assisted them in opening post office savings accounts.[106] This was a far cry from the cloistered existence that some Peranakan women recalled struggling against. A Nyonya named Lim San Neo reflects that she was allowed to attend school at the age of eight only after "pleading [with] and persuading my father."[107] Her mother did not approve, believing that "girls should be kept at home and be trained in the rudiments of housekeeping."[108] Another Nyonya, Florence Chan, who was born in 1914, remembers that her mother pulled her out of school for fear that education and independence would lead Chan to "look for [her] own husband," rather than assenting to an arranged marriage.[109] Nonetheless, education up to the age of fourteen was enough to make Chan aware of changing times and new possibilities for her generation: "As we go to school, we learn more, and we say, 'What is this? So old-fashioned!' . . . We are educated, we know better. Why must we follow old-fashioned ways?"[110]

For Straits Chinese women who had the benefit of privileged family backgrounds and a modern education, formal literacy gave them confidence and motivation to advance their careers as well as the prospects of their fellow Nyonyas. For example, Mrs. Lee Choon Guan (1877–1978), neé Tan Teck Neo, was moved by her own experience receiving an education from Methodist missionaries and her father's advocacy of girls' schools to create scholarships for SCGS students.[111] Dr. Lee Choo Neo (1895–1947), educated at SCGS and Raffles Girls' School, was the first Straits Chinese girl to earn a Senior Cambridge certificate and became the first female medical doctor in Singapore.[112] She was also a member of the Chinese Ladies' Association, which was founded in 1915 by Mrs. Lee Choon Guan, Keng's second wife, Yin Pek Ha, and several other socially prominent Straits Chinese women. Although the initial mandate of this association was traditional, centered on needlework, cooking, and music, it was also progressive in creating a new alternative to the home for women's socialization. In short order, the association was also engaged in numerous social welfare projects, including public fundraising and political activism.[113] Although not all women from various socioeconomic levels could take advantage of such opportunities, the increasing visibility of these Nyonyas in the public arena showed what educated Straits Chinese women could potentially achieve. Even in less rarified social circles, more alumni from SCGS and other local girls' schools were working outside the home, many as teachers in the very institutions from which they graduated.

By the 1930s, new avenues appeared for educated Nyonyas to express themselves in the public sphere, primarily through print media. Periodicals such as the *Straits Chinese Monthly* and the *Malaya Tribune*, both sponsored in whole or in part by the Straits Chinese elite, published women's letters and essays in "Women's Corners" as well as articles discussing the emergence of "new women" throughout the world.[114] One particularly progressive feminine voice was that of Louis Kwan. Her articles in the *Straits Chinese Monthly* in the early 1930s echoed contemporary feminist activists in other countries by calling for financial independence, legal reform, and political involvement to bring about equality of the sexes. In a piece titled "Careers for Educated Chinese Girls," Kwan urged women to blaze the trail for future generations of girls and women by having careers of their own and suggested suitable professions such as teaching, nursing, and journalism.[115] From 1931 on, the *Malaya Tribune* printed writings by women in columns dedicated to women. Some of these articles reflected on the quest for gender equality in other Asian countries, such as India and the Philippines. Unlike Kwan's writing, however, some of these articles suggested that Asian women's pursuit of Western-style independence was unnatural and inappropriate and that neglecting the domestic sphere could result in personal loneliness and lack of fulfillment.[116] This tension between modernization and tradition was also well documented in Peranakan communities in neighboring Indonesia. There female education led to the publication of Peranakan women's writings on work, marriage, and equality from the late 1920s to the early 1940s, even as these same women had difficulty opposing social pressure to ultimately identify primarily as wives and mothers.[117]

The progress of SCGS stalled in the 1940s, but only because the same fate befell all schools in Singapore with the encroachment of World War II and Japanese invasion of the island in 1942. The school campus had to close after it sustained a direct hit from Japanese bombing in 1941 and was turned into a brothel for soldiers during the Japanese occupation from 1942 to 1945. Recovery from these traumas was halting in the immediate postwar years, but the school successfully regained its footing by the late 1940s, enrolling 370 female students in 1947 and 700 by 1950.[118] This surge in attendance was consistent with a general pattern of demand for schooling in the post–World War II era across Malaya and Singapore. With Geake's retirement in 1951 and the installation of SCGS' first Chinese principal, against the backdrop of Singapore's move toward political independence throughout the 1950s, the institution entered a new phase of educational development.

In the first half-century of its existence, the Singapore Chinese Girls' School both fulfilled and fell short of what its Peranakan founders had intended in 1899. Straits Chinese initiative, leadership, and money gave the SCGS its start and sustained it through its formative decades, ensuring a Straits Chinese ethno-cultural legacy. Student enrollment drew from Peranakan and non-Peranakan Chinese families, serving the founders' goal of extending their desired influence in female education and modernization among the ethnic Chinese population in Singapore. As girls' schools became more common and professionally run, the SCGS enjoyed a position of relative prestige and security in Singaporean society. That said, the institution was more akin to the missionary and colonial government-founded English-medium girls' schools than to a new kind of local, Western-Chinese model of female education, particularly in how it upheld European knowledge and norms. Chinese language was not a popular or widely taught subject at the school, so the original aim of a bilingual and culturally hybrid education was not attained. The Peranakan cultural reform movement quickly faded in the early decades of the twentieth century, due to the political risk involved in identifying too closely with Chinese nationalism. Straits Chinese anxiety shifted from intra-communal leadership, or asserting their progressiveness in relation to more newly arrived Chinese immigrants, to questions of local and national belonging. This change occurred as early as the 1910s, as Chinese-medium girls' schools arose as a distinct alternative to English-medium girls' schools.

The characterization of the "Nyonya problem" in the *Straits Chinese Magazine* at the turn of the twentieth century, and the proposed solution in the form of female education and the Singapore Chinese Girls' School, demonstrate how transnational groups could be swept up in trends that grew out of national priorities. As countries grappled with the problem of modernizing without losing their cultural traditions in this period, so, too, did non-national, diasporic groups such as the Straits Chinese. Peranakan male elites projected their fears about race, culture, and class status onto the minds and bodies of women in their communities and sought to assert control in part through the project of female education. As with women in the nation, Nyonyas in diaspora and empire were tasked with shedding the negative attributes of traditional femininity, such as ignorance and superstition, while continuing to embody the positive features of their cultural heritage, such as moral purity and housewifely competence. Educated Peranakan women in Malaya and Singapore had to bear the burden of proving their community's modernity in order to achieve some social and cultural parity with their Western rulers.

The discourse of gendered modernization in the nation filtered into efforts at identity construction on a global basis, even among transnational groups whose lives and affiliations had straddled multiple boundaries, sometimes for generations. For the Straits Chinese, their cosmopolitan heritage of migration, ethnic intermarriage, cultural assimilation, and social integration with British colonialism rendered their job of reclaiming Chinese cultural authenticity complicated and ambivalent. Their formerly advantageous multi-ethnic and multicultural heritage became a liability in an increasingly nationalistic world. Ironically, the quest to assert a more authentic and stable Straits Chinese identity involved the public erasure of their original Malay—and hence feminine—elements of their ethno-cultural heritage.[119] Westernized modernity in the form of female education seemed to be a strategically apt move, even as it aligned the Straits Chinese more clearly with British colonialism than with the Chinese and Malay nationalisms that would soon overtake European imperial dominance in Southeast Asia.

Throughout the first half of the twentieth century, the Peranakan were co-existing, collaborating, and competing with more recently arrived fellow Chinese. It is important not to overstate the division between these two groups. After all, Lim Boon Keng felt strongly enough about the importance of educating and uplifting all Chinese women that he also worked with the Chinese consulate, the local Hokkien (or Fujianese) dialect association, and a number of prominent Chinese businessmen to support the founding of local Chinese-medium girls' schools in the 1910s.[120] Yet, despite some common ground in angling for greater status and respectability in relation to the British and Chinese national authorities, the two groups had different attitudes toward national and cultural identity and had divergent approaches to female education and modernization. This division would be exacerbated by the growth of Chinese-language education. As the gap between the English- and Chinese-educated Chinese opened up, women were an integral part of this linguistic split, participating in and contributing to further struggles over cultural identity within the overseas Chinese community.

CHAPTER 4

Rare Flowers, Modern Girls, Good Citizens

Chinese Girls' Schools, 1900s–1950s

In December 1934, a major Chinese-language newspaper in Singapore announced that some "Rare Flowers of Overseas Chinese Education" ("Huaqiao jiaoyu zhi qipa"), also known as the senior class of the local Nanyang Girls' Upper Secondary School, had successfully graduated.[1] This was not an isolated instance of educated Chinese women being romanticized in such terms. In late nineteenth-century America, a Chinese female student was described by her classmates as "a sort of exotic blossom."[2] For the young women emerging from Chinese schools in colonial Malaya and Singapore, however, their self-image was less delicate or gauzy. Also in 1934, in Malaya, female students' essays in a commemorative graduation magazine for Kuen Cheng Girls' School focused on the gravity of the duties before them:

> We girls who have received an education and understand a little more of the greater situation . . . feel that the future of women in China is very dark. We are among the first in the world to know and feel this, [so we] must take up the responsibility of leadership.[3]

Indeed, beyond their school gates loomed the hurdles of finding jobs, securing economic independence, and overturning long-held prejudices about women in the public sphere. Without many precedents or role models before them, it was unclear that these "rare flowers" could take root and thrive. Even before graduation, they had already encountered obstacles in the form of contradictory messages throughout their education. Should they be the unconventional and modern women their teachers and curriculum had suggested they could be? Or should they, as part of a symbolic vanguard in the overseas Chinese community, uphold the classic virtues of domesticity, chastity, and deference to male leadership? How should they reconcile what they had learned about the importance of gainful employment, companionate marriage, and the right to a political voice, with school-sanctioned strictures about preserving their virtue and a traditionally feminine demeanor? Once they no longer had to abide by the idea that a woman's place was in the kitchen, where did they belong, particularly in a world where nation, empire, and fledgling new governments were competing for ascendancy?

Chinese-language girls' schools in diaspora echoed the tensions between modernization and conservatism that were emblematic of nation-building in the first half of the twentieth century. These schools originated in the drive to reform and regenerate the Chinese nation, a drive that extended to its overseas communities and that was at least partly predicated on the education of its women. In early twentieth-century China, "the national question" and "the woman problem" were closely intertwined. Factions ranging from conservative monarchists to radical revolutionaries debated the role of women in their prescriptions for China's future.[4] Many overseas Chinese communities established their own schools based on the Chinese national model, drawing from their structure, curricula, and even teaching personnel. Over time, even as these overseas Chinese schools adjusted to local conditions and developed a range of unique identities, observers associated these institutions with a powerful sense of ethno-nationalism that oriented itself toward the ancestral homeland.

In these girls' schools, new attitudes toward female education and citizenship in the Chinese nation acquired a unique saliency as Western imperialism made the task of protecting ethnic authenticity even more urgent. Chinese political modernization became associated with cultural conservatism, both of which were transmitted through overseas Chinese formal education. This association overshadowed the social modernization of women, whose diverse socioeconomic and cultural affiliations were subsumed by a dominant narrative of ethnic loyalism. Aside from this totalizing discourse, educated Chinese women also had to contend with various labels that others applied to them. Early on, they were unusual, exoticized, and largely benign (*qipa* 奇葩, "rare flowers"). Eventually, they became active participants in their ethnic communities (*xiandainüzi* 现代女子, "modern girls") or ancestral nation (*haogongmin* 好公民,

"good citizens").[5] The challenge for these women was to build their own political and cultural identifications, independent of the categories and stereotypes that others imposed on them. Careful excavation of female students' own writings and oral histories can reveal their deeply felt struggle to uphold their families' and communities' largely traditional expectations, while fulfilling the new dreams that their modern education had laid out before them.

One difficulty of hearing these women's voices is that the archives of Chinese schools in Southeast Asia are sparse and uneven, especially for the first half of the twentieth century. During the Japanese military occupation of Malaya and Singapore in World War II, many Chinese schools either lost their records or voluntarily destroyed them to keep Japanese forces from using the information to persecute members of the Chinese community. Nonetheless, historical information is still available in the form of publications such as school magazines and local newspapers, oral histories of former teachers and students in these institutions, and select school records that survived the war years. Educated Chinese women also aired their opinions in local newspapers, often in columns or sections for female readers.

These sources indicate that educated overseas Chinese girls received mixed messages about what society expected from them. To confuse matters further, they had to ask which society in particular they were beholden to: Chinese national, overseas Chinese, British imperial, Southeast Asian, or some combination of these. Political turmoil and modernization exposed them to new possibilities for action beyond the domestic sphere. Intellectuals, including those who came to Malaya and Singapore from China for the express purpose of becoming teachers in Chinese high schools, helped to spread messages of political and social reform among male and female students alike. Many graduates of these schools describe their parents as being enlightened in allowing their daughters to receive an education, and they credit their families with an intellectual progressiveness that enabled their own. However, conventional expectations of female roles and feminine propriety dogged educated overseas Chinese women, in school and beyond. Families, teachers, and the general public scrutinized the behavior and appearance of schoolgirls, monitoring them for signs of lost virtue or deviation from the ultimate goal of becoming wives and mothers. Graduates of Chinese girls' schools in Malaya and Singapore portray their alma maters as "very strict"; "very particular about chastity, forbidding us to have any relations with boys"; "[fussing] over how we should smooth down our skirts when sitting down and standing up"; "conservative"; and "like a nunnery."[6]

Like their counterparts in early twentieth-century China, overseas Chinese women found that formal education could constrain as much as it could liberate. They grappled with the paradoxical demands of being at once modern and traditional, and of acquiring new knowledge and political consciousness while being expected to uphold inherited norms of cultural and moral behavior. This phenomenon of "modernizing conservatism" was present in China and the Chinese community in Southeast Asia, as well as other twentieth-century nationalist projects.[7] Female education was hence both progressive and conservative, a theme that has become apparent not just in China but around the world.

A complicating dimension in the diaspora is that this tension, born of burgeoning nationalist consciousness in China, was situated in a transnational context. As the first generations of overseas Chinese women with substantial formal education began to emerge in public, their political and cultural loyalties were subject to scrutiny and criticism. Implicit in the language medium of their education—which, in almost all cases, had been chosen for them by their parents or guardians—was a pre-determined set of affiliations that shaped others' assumptions about their political orientation, despite the fact that these Chinese-educated women were not a monolithic group. More important, these women struggled in a variety of ways, with a variety of outcomes, to strike a balance among the opposing demands to which they had to respond. By absorbing, representing, and perpetuating Chinese language and culture abroad, were they also political representatives of the Chinese nation? Did they want to be? For those who wished to merge a Chinese cultural identity with British imperial subjecthood, or Malayan and Singaporean nationality, could they convince their non-Chinese places of settlement that they were committed to making Southeast Asia their home?

These dilemmas were not simply theoretical. The Asian nationalisms of the early to mid-twentieth century compelled individuals to make choices that could permanently change their and their families' lives. This chapter looks more closely at how Chinese-language girls' schools in colonial Malaya and Singapore operated as sites of modernization and politicization for overseas Chinese women while holding fast to certain socially conservative positions as a matter of preserving cultural identity. These schools introduced non-gender-specific curricula, notions of gender equality and women's work, and ideals of national citizenship. Far from being limited to promoting Chinese nationalism, these institutions opened up a new world of knowledge, discourse, and sociability that encompassed both national and transnational belonging for women. Arguably, Chinese schools may have done more to usher in modernity for girls and women than English schools in Malaya and Singapore at this time, challenging the received wisdom that modernizing change was a Western-driven movement.

However, modern education was inherently disruptive to a sense of continuity and tradition. Many Chinese associated modernization with Westernization, along with its attendant threats to Chinese cultural integrity and traditional values. These values were typically linked to the sacrosanct institution of the family and its domestic guardians, women. Hence, the ideal graduate from a Chinese girls' school had to contain multitudes. Her academic achievements would enable her to work outside the home, ideally as a teacher, but feminine propriety would also drive her to maintain a virtuous, and ultimately domestic, orientation. Her political awareness would lead her to support her nation (usually China, but sometimes also Malaya or Singapore) in its efforts to fight off invaders such as Japan and to build a modern economy, but her patriotic role was mostly limited to a supporting part in fundraising or education rather than political activism or being on the front lines. Her school-sanctioned modernity might be inspired by China's race to catch up with Western powers, but her appearance and behavior had to avoid casting doubt on her moral purity—an imperative that acquired an outsized symbolism and a greater longevity in a multi-ethnic, Western-dominated environment than in China itself.

HISTORICAL ORIGINS AND DEVELOPMENT OF OVERSEAS CHINESE GIRLS' SCHOOLS

Chinese girls' schools in Malaya and Singapore, from their inception in 1908, were shaped by the political and social events that transformed China at the turn of the twentieth century. In 1907, Qing imperial authorities promulgated the first official regulations for female education as part of a national modernization effort: "Zhouding nüzi shifan xuetang zhangcheng sanshiliu tiao" (Thirty-six Rules and Regulations for Girls' Normal Schools) and "Nüzi xiaoxue zhangcheng ershi tiao" (Twenty Rules and Regulations for Girls' Primary Schools).[8] Male elites from the late Qing into the Republican period debated whether educated women would be "citizens or mothers of citizens," revealing the conditional nature of female emancipation and holding up ideals for modern women that were alternately gender neutral and gender specific.[9] As reformers and revolutionaries began to cultivate the overseas Chinese as potential supporters for their political movements, they became involved in Southeast Asian Chinese efforts to promote education. In Singapore, Sun Yat-sen's influence was said to have contributed to the establishment of Chung Hwa Girls' School in 1911.[10] From 1919, the

May Fourth movement focused even more attention on gender equality and female education. In Southeast Asia, Chinese girls' schools, like their models and counterparts in Republican China, were mindful of their role in the promotion of ethnic and national strength through the training of girls and women, competing with Western missionaries for influence over the cultural orientation of their youth.[11]

The girls' schools that emerged during this time were considered "modern" by their founders in the sense of moving past the traditional Chinese approach to education. Instead of small, privately tutored groups that focused on memorization of classical texts, these institutions offered Western-based educational techniques and subjects. Their reformist character lay in their goal of spreading formal female education, itself a relatively new phenomenon; in their "scientific" (kexuehua) curriculum, which meant classes organized by academic subject areas instead of Confucian classics; and in their determination to guide Chinese women away from what was labeled ignorance and superstition, molding them into better wives, mothers, and citizens instead. In the new era of nationalist improvement, this modern female learning, encompassing topics from domestic science to physical education, would best prepare women for their mothering duties, which would in turn produce a superior nation of citizens overall.[12] Also, overseas Chinese schools, in which the language of instruction and curricular content were largely Mandarin Chinese, emphasized notions of nationality and citizenship. They were modeled on schools in Republican China, many of which stressed theoretical and practical training in concepts of civic action and citizenship.[13] They did so, however, in colonies where local nationalities and British subjecthood might have been more relevant than Chinese citizenship, and where local (Malayan or Singaporean) citizenship later became a sometimes elusive goal.

In British Malaya, the pioneering Chinese girls' institution was Kuen Cheng Girls' School, founded in Kuala Lumpur by an overseas Chinese community leader in 1908.[14] Its name, Kuen Cheng (Kuncheng 坤成), can be translated as "perfection of femininity." The school's founders were Wu Xuehua, a Chinese woman; Zhong Zhuojing, a Chinese man; and Watanabe Yoshiko, Zhong's Japanese wife. Zhong was also a local community leader and principal of the Confucian High School for boys. Zhong became Kuen Cheng's first principal, and Wu and Watanabe were its first teachers.[15] Interestingly, chronologies of the institution's history in school magazines published before the 1960s give the impression of Watanabe as peripheral, but accounts from later years identify her as one of the institution's cofounders. In 1953, Kuen Cheng's *Forty-fifth Anniversary Commemorative Magazine* simply names Watanabe as Zhong's wife and one of the teachers, whereas in 1968, the *Sixtieth Anniversary Commemorative Magazine* states that Wu and Watanabe "exerted the greatest effort to start" the school.[16] This discrepancy hints at a possible wariness on the part of a Chinese institution in ascribing its origins to a Japanese founder, due to Sino-Japanese antagonism. It also serves as a reminder that China nonetheless looked to Japan in the late nineteenth and early twentieth centuries as an example of successful modernization and educational reform, and that Chinese women traveled to Japan during this time to further their education.[17] To conservative Chinese nationalists, Japan's gender ideology of good wives and wise mothers who supported the new national project without being overly Westernized was a successful model of feminine modernity that China should emulate.[18]

Like the English-language girls' schools that preceded it by several decades, Kuen Cheng had a modest beginning. However, demand for formal education among the ethnic Chinese community had reached a level whereby Kuen Cheng, and many other Chinese girls' schools that came after it, eventually enjoyed steady growth. Initially, Kuen Cheng offered only primary level classes and in its first year enrolled just twenty students. Between 1915 and 1940, it established the country's first kindergarten, started lower and upper secondary classes, and set up a four-year teacher-training or Normal course to help meet the growing demand for certified teachers in Malaya. By 1933, the total number of students had jumped to approximately 400, and in 1956, total enrollment stood at 3,000.[19] Almost this entire period of growth was anchored by the long tenure of one principal, Sha Yuanru, from 1933 to 1951. By the late 1930s, there were approximately fifty Chinese girls' schools across Malaya. In Penang, Kuala Lumpur, and Melaka alone, more than 10,000 Chinese female students were enrolled. Their numbers in fact surpassed those of English girls' schools in the same areas, which had on their rolls an estimated 6,800 Chinese female students.[20] One possible reason for the higher enrollment in Chinese schools is that migration had surged in the late nineteenth and early twentieth centuries, bringing in more migrants with stronger ties to China.[21] Another is that school fees were comparatively lower than those of English girls' schools. In 1934, estimated annual fees for Chinese primary schools were between $5.00 and $10.00 versus $36.00 for English primary schools.[22] Consequently, students in Chinese schools also tended to come from a wider and more evenly distributed range of socioeconomic classes than those in English schools.

These institutions consciously and proudly identified themselves as overseas Chinese entities. In its name, Hua Ch'iao (*Huaqiao* 华侨) Girls' School, founded in 1911, used a common term for "sojourning Chinese."

Chung Hwa (*Zhonghua* 中华) Girls' School, founded in 1917, invoked the new Republic of China. Nanyang (*Nanyang* 南洋) and Nan Hwa (*Nanhua* 南华) Girls' Schools, both founded in 1917, located themselves in the "Seas South of China," using long-standing Chinese terminology referring to Southeast Asia.[23] Sponsors of these institutions ranged from private individuals to dialect-based associations to Western missionary societies. In Singapore, Chong Hock (*Chongfu* 崇福) Girls' School was founded in 1915 by the Inspector of Schools for the Hokkien Huay Kuan or Fujian native-place association, and classes were conducted in Fujianese ("Hokkien" and "Fukien" were local transliterations of "Fujian").[24] Kuen Cheng's school motto, *li yi lian chi* (礼义廉耻), meaning "propriety, righteousness, integrity, honor," drew upon traditional Confucian values that were still a significant part of Republican Chinese discourse in the 1910s. The Chinese identity of these schools was hence a foundational element to be prominently displayed.

Affinities with China went beyond the symbolic, as school structure and curricula in overseas Chinese schools were based on the modern school system in the mainland. Schooling had two stages, primary and secondary, each six years long. Children entered primary school at age six or seven. Secondary education was further divided into three years each of lower secondary and upper secondary. Upper secondary could be replaced by two to three years of Normal classes, or teacher training, after which a graduate was qualified to teach up to the highest levels of secondary school. This system was identical to the one formalized in China's National Education Plan of 1922. It was also an adapted version of systems that had existed since the early twentieth century, based on the American-influenced Federated Education Association of China.[25] Curricula were similar to what was taught in English-language schools, with some key differences. History, geography, and literature focused on China instead of Great Britain or Europe. With the exception of books for English-language classes, most textbooks were obtained from Chinese publishers such as Zhonghua and Shangwu publishing houses.[26] These two companies dominated the publishing scene in Shanghai during the 1910s and 1920s. With the standardization of the publishing industry by the Nationalist (KMT, or Kuomintang) government after 1927, many of the publications in these schools arguably reflected KMT perspectives.[27] School libraries stocked newspapers and magazines from China, such as the *Minguo Ribao* (Republican Daily Newspaper), published in Guangzhou.[28] Unlike English-language girls' schools, domestic science subjects were either not compulsory or not offered at all.

Chinese girls' schools faced the same problems as boys' schools of their time: low student enrollment in the beginning, financial difficulties, and shortages of teachers. However, they had to deal with them on a greater order of magnitude, and with additional obstacles.[29] Compared to the number of Chinese boys in school in the first half of the twentieth century, Chinese girls were still in the minority. They numbered only around a quarter of the entire school-going population in Malaya and Singapore, in both Chinese and English schools.[30] Before World War II, many overseas Chinese parents were still reluctant to send their daughters to school, and when they did, they demanded that certain gender-specific conditions be met. For example, many parents insisted on having female teachers only, which led to a continuous staffing problem as not enough trained Chinese female teachers were available in the colonies at this time.[31] A visitor and observer from China in the 1920s described the obstacles that had faced one Pei De (*Peide* 培德, "cultivating virtue") Girls' School:

> That Pei De Girls' School was really a cause for disappointment! After operating for a good several years, it only had a few students, giving it a "spirit is willing but flesh is weak" kind of appearance . . . . Later on they finally hired Madam Liu Yunqin as principal, and gradually [the situation] improved, [as she] often went before the parents of female students, connected with their feelings, made them aware of the benefits of girls receiving an education [and] enlightened their mood . . . hence Pei De Girls' School began to advance from day to day and year to year.[32]

Still, 25 percent of the entire student population was an impressive figure for institutions that had struggled mightily in their early years to raise funds, find classroom space, keep students from dropping out, and gain social acceptance. The relative success of female education in general, especially among the ethnic Chinese community, could be measured by the fact that from as early as the mid-1920s, Chinese girls comprised two-thirds of all school-going female children. In 1926, out of a total of 20,846 school-going children, 5,172 were girls, and 3,515 were Chinese girls.[33] Between 1926 and 1937, Chinese schools in the Straits Settlements saw a jump in female enrollment from 4,053 to 10,620, while English schools saw an increase in Chinese female enrollment between 1920 to 1939 from 2,548 to 7,254.[34] While the former increase was less than threefold and the latter increase more than threefold, the absolute number of Chinese girls enrolled in Chinese-language schools decisively surpassed the number in English-language schools. In 1937, for example, Chinese girls in Chinese-language schools numbered just over 10,000, while those in English-language schools numbered approximately 6,850.[35]

Rapid growth of Chinese schools slowed in the 1930s, when a worldwide economic depression drained the pocketbooks of businessmen and community leaders who would otherwise have funded these schools. Many Chinese migrants were unable to find or keep their jobs and returned to China, further reducing demand for Chinese education. The Japanese Occupation of 1941–45 halted the operations of Chinese schools entirely, but in the postwar years, growth accelerated once again. More people had become aware of the need to gain literacy and work skills through formal schooling, for boys and girls alike. Several years of school closures and wartime hardship had also created a pool of overage students who were eager to resume their studies and earn their degrees. Both Chinese and English schools quickly became overcrowded, and new institutions had to be rapidly set up to cope with demand.

All Chinese schools were private, or non-governmental, in their origins. Most began with small student enrollments, serving a narrow, often dialect-based community; the ones that survived the longest and most successfully often expanded their support base to increase enrollment and attract more financial backing. In the earliest years, most of these schools used the dialect of their founders or students, such as Hokkien or Cantonese. But after the May Fourth movement promoting vernacular Mandarin Chinese (*baihua*) in China, in order to make language and literature more accessible to the general public, many in the overseas Chinese community followed suit and the medium of instruction in these schools gradually switched to vernacular Mandarin.[36] In 1919, four members of the Hokkien Association in Penang proposed the founding of the Fukien Girls' School (*Fujian nüxiao* 福建女校), so named because its funding came in large part from surplus funds belonging to the Fukien Flood Relief Association. The school committee at the time comprised ninety-one members, reflecting an impressive level of participation. The school opened with a six-year primary school curriculum on March 8, 1920, March 8 also being International Women's Day. In 1951, the school changed its name to Penang Chinese Girls' High School (*Binhua nüzi zhongxue* 槟华女子中学), discarding its Fujianese identification in a gesture of cross-dialect group inclusiveness.[37] Like Kuen Cheng in Kuala Lumpur, Binhua became one of the largest and most highly regarded girls' schools in the region. Between 1928 and 1935, its enrollment doubled, from 400 to nearly 800 students, and the school had to offer two sessions daily, morning and afternoon, as well as set up a branch school to accommodate its population.[38] Another notable similarity with Kuen Cheng, and difference from many English-language schools such as the Singapore Chinese Girls' School, was the stability in its upper-level administration during a key period of growth. From 1934 to 1966, it had just one principal (or Supervisor), Zhu Yuehua. Zhu oversaw the school's expansion to include lower and upper secondary levels, a Normal or teacher training program, recovery after the devastation of Japanese occupation, and a rocky transition from British colonial to independent Malayan government policies concerning Chinese-language institutions.

Because a sense of nationalist pride was an important part of their institutional character, overseas Chinese-language girls' schools took a strong position against colonial intervention. By refusing to register with the British in exchange for financial assistance, these schools remained private and independent. As colonial concern grew over the political activism of Chinese schools, new regulations were introduced from 1920 onward that sought to control various aspects of Chinese education, ranging from the curriculum to the hiring of teachers, but their intended objects of regulation did not always comply. Only after the Communist revolution in 1949 did locally trained teachers and "Malayanized" textbooks begin to eclipse influence from China. At this time, the colonial administration recognized the approaching end of empire and began to cede control to local independence movements, giving preference to politically moderate locals over strongly anti-imperial activists.[39]

Between the late 1920s and 1940s, Chinese schools in Malaya and Singapore became infused with Republican and Communist Chinese politics. Many teachers and principals in these institutions came directly from or had received their educational training in China. In 1935, for example, out of twenty-three listed teaching staff in Singapore's Nanyang Girls' High School, sixteen graduated from universities or Normal programs in China, while the remaining seven graduated from local Singaporean or Japanese institutions.[40] In some cases, principals of these schools became particularly active in overseas Chinese politics and drew unwelcome attention to themselves from colonial authorities or other political groups. One example is Yu Peigao, the founding principal of Nanyang Girls' School in Singapore. When British authorities passed an ordinance in 1920 requiring the registration of all private schools, many Chinese schools protested against this perceived attempt at imperialistic interference. Yu Peigao was especially vocal in these protests and as a result was forced by the government to resign and leave Singapore for China permanently.[41] Another prominent principal of Nanyang was Liew Yuen Sien, who was the victim of the acid attack by Chinese radicals. One of Liew's major contributions to local Chinese education was spearheading an effort by local Chinese educators in 1930 to improve the quality of Chinese schools through a standardized common examination for primary school students. A few years after these examinations began, colonial authorities decided that these examinations touched on "politically sensitive" topics and took over the administration of these tests.[42] This colonial intervention was to become a recurring motif.

Through formal education, overseas Chinese women encountered a range of new ideas and activities, and engaged in an entirely new arena of interaction and expression beyond the traditional limits of the domestic sphere. Non-gender-specific curricula and educators with strong China connections promoted notions of gender equality and female citizenship. For example, a wide variety of extra-curricular activities and physical education was integrated into the curriculum, including sports such as basketball, volleyball, and soccer.[43] In China, similar introductions of Girl Scout groups and other supposedly Westernized activities were seen as inimical to the conveyance of feminine values to female students.[44] New opportunities for gaining literacy and vocational skills appeared, such as night classes for adults and after-school Chinese-language classes for English school students.[45] Students formed political organizations such as student unions and "underground" activist groups, engaged in wartime fundraising activities, and joined teachers' unions and alumni associations. For example, the Penang Chinese Girls' High School Alumni Association was established in 1940, and the Nanyang Girls' School's alumni association was established in 1945.[46] The idea that there were multiple accepted possibilities for non-domestic activity available to women from various socioeconomic classes stayed with graduates throughout their lives, in the form of continued participation or association with schools, and in their careers.

Modern Chinese girls' schools aimed to challenge or at least balance the seeming domination of Western-style modernization and education. Ironically, the development of modern Chinese female education owed much to Western influences in the first place. European and American missionaries had opened the first girls' schools in China during the late nineteenth century, and the first missionary-run and government-operated girls' schools pre-dated Chinese girls' schools in Malaya and Singapore by fifty years. Yet it was the curricula, practices, and ideologies of Chinese girls' schools that introduced radical notions of ethnic power, Chinese nationalism, and gender equality to their students and teachers. The process of modernization and change as brought about by Chinese-language female education was thus neither linear nor solely led by the West.

MODERNIZING CONSERVATISM IN OVERSEAS CHINESE GIRLS' SCHOOLS

Chinese-language girls' schools were agents of change in some areas and bastions of sociocultural conservatism in others. This dynamic was not particular to overseas Chinese female education. Indeed, its original appearance was within national boundaries, in East Asia and across the globe. The term "modernizing conservatism," coined to describe this pattern in late Qing and early Republican China, is applied here to an ethnic Chinese community in a transnational environment, where a similar dynamic unfolded in parallel time but with different results.[47] What was unique about the diasporic environment was when and how norms of culturally and politically dependent forms of femininity, developed in the nation, were transmitted by formal education to a group that had an ambivalent relationship with the nation. Women in early twentieth-century China were challenged, inspired, frustrated, and sometimes thwarted by the dual demands of traditional femininity and modern citizenship. For ethnic Chinese women of the same period who were born and spent their formative years or entire lives outside the Chinese nation, what was the impact of this dual burden? Did they feel more alienated from the political process than Chinese women in China, or, conversely, did they feel the pull of cultural and national belonging even more strongly?

As in China and as one would expect from any large group of diverse individuals, there was a wide range of responses. However, in terms of institutional attitudes in Chinese-language girls' schools, there was a detectable congruence with developments in China up to and slightly beyond 1949, at which point social conservatism regarding gender roles reasserted itself. During the Republican era, overseas Chinese girls' schools echoed ideals from China about modern education and women's emancipation, while simultaneously perpetuating traditional standards for feminine propriety. If anything, the pressure to project an image of virtuous and culturally authentic overseas Chinese women was stronger during a time when Western imperialism still held sway and Chinese nationalism fought for respect on the world stage. Hence the use of May Fourth and New Culture discourse was extended in the diaspora, even after such movements faded within China. After the Chinese Communist revolution and the beginning of decolonization, ethnic Chinese who had made Malaya and Singapore their homes feared that an overly aggressive pursuit of social change—including equality of the sexes—might jeopardize their acceptance in the newly independent Southeast Asian nation-states. As these overseas Chinese grappled with political and cultural adaptation in the mid-twentieth century, their girls' schools appeared to retrench their message of radical change and shift toward more gender stereotypical and locally oriented futures for their graduates. At the same time, in response to the literal and figurative dismantling of historical institutions in Communist China, many overseas Chinese adhered more closely to certain elements of Chinese culture. Even as overseas Chinese schools' direct connections to

China waned in the latter part of the twentieth century, the Republican-era approach to female education endured, preserved in an institution that had originated in an impulse for radical transformation.

Modernization for overseas Chinese women, then, was dependent on whether the change to their social roles and status would benefit their community in a political sense. Just as Straits Chinese women were "modernized" through education to boost the Peranakan community's standing, so, too, were students of Chinese-language girls' schools "modernized" in keeping with the changing priorities of Chinese nationalism and postcolonial local belonging. To be clear, this does not necessarily imply political opportunism. Rather, it shows the political limitations on the quest for modern female education and how educated overseas Chinese women labored under an additional set of constraints due to their contingent position in diaspora.

The modernizing impulse manifested itself in these schools in three major ways. First, unlike contemporary English girls' schools in Malaya and Singapore, Chinese girls' schools implemented curricula that were largely non-gender-specific. Second, they inculcated new ideas about gender equality and women's social roles. Finally, they encouraged political consciousness, even activism, among their students. However, there was also a simultaneous and divergent current of conservatism that actually grew stronger over time. Chinese girls' schools continued to uphold a number of conventions about Chinese womanhood, including girls' behavioral norms, familial and social duties, and roles in the preservation of Chinese culture. These impulses did not necessarily collide during day-to-day operations but did complicate the realities of work and life for educated Chinese women in a world that was not necessarily changing at the same pace as the schools from which they graduated.

Several of the earliest Chinese-language girls' schools followed the example of Republican Chinese girls' schools in seeking to eschew gender-specific curricula. In Singapore, Jingfang (*Jingfang* 静方, "Quiet and Upright") Girls' School stated in its official history that it was founded in 1928 due to demand for education for girls who had previously been studying at a boys' primary school, but who, at age twelve, were deemed too old to continue with co-educational classes and needed a dedicated all-girls' secondary institution.[48] Jingfang's mission was "to implement education that is appropriate for girls; to develop natural human talents; to mould moral nature; and to cultivate a healthy and whole character in girls."[49] Despite the fact that this was an institution designed specifically for girls, the curriculum for both primary and secondary levels in Jingfang did not include domestic science, as did English-language girls' schools. Instead, it covered Chinese language, citizenship studies, mathematics, English, geography, history, general knowledge, nature studies, music, physical education, art, and hygiene. The inclusion of physical education was in parallel with the curricula of late Qing and early Republican girls' schools, where modern, albeit gendered, ideas of health in citizens would lead to health in the body politic.[50]

For the teacher training program, there were classes such as "Introduction to Education," "Educational Psychology," "Primary School Teaching Materials and Methods," and "Primary School Administration."[51] This curriculum was more similar to what was being offered in local Chinese boys' schools than in local English girls' schools. Also in Singapore, the curriculum of Nanyang Girls' School in 1935 was largely the same as Jingfang's, with the addition of biology, chemistry, physics, sociology, and philosophy at the upper secondary and Normal levels. Nanyang did offer a subject called "domestic affairs" (*jiashi* 家事), but only at the secondary level, and even then as only one out of thirty-four units of classes per school term.[52] By 1948, the Advanced Normal course in Nanyang had eliminated domestic science as a required class.[53] In 1953, Kuen Cheng Girls' School in Kuala Lumpur did not include domestic science at either primary or secondary levels.[54]

This marginalization of domestic science in the 1930s and 1940s paralleled developments in Republican China, where the New Culture movement and its emphasis on gender equality had led schools to scale back training for girls in household skills such as home economics, gardening, and handicrafts.[55] Another likely reason is that many girls were already learning the practical basics of housework at home. Also, according to some overseas Chinese educators, domestic science as an academic subject originated from Western female education and did not translate well in the Chinese context. Mei Yulan, a teacher in the Penang Chinese Girls' High School during the 1940s, recalls that her school was well equipped with a classroom for sewing and cooking lessons, complete with twenty sewing machines and electric cooking appliances. But, as she pointed out, several factors undermined the success of home economics class: it was given very little time in the curriculum, and its teacher was an Englishwoman who "just taught how to bake cakes, Western-style biscuits, pork chops, steaks and other such Western dishes, which is quite impractical for Chinese people."[56] Mei also observed that "progress in sewing was so slow as to be pitiful; I have heard that at the point of graduation, some of the students could not even make a single piece of clothing."[57] In this area, Chinese girls' schools contrasted sharply with their English contemporaries, where needlework was at the forefront of the curriculum and a point of pride for teachers, students, and colonial school inspectors alike.

A second way in which Chinese girls' schools brought about modernizing change was their encouragement of new attitudes toward women's roles in society. Students learned about women's work beyond the home, companionate marriage (as opposed to arranged marriage), divorce, and individual self-fulfillment. Female students and teachers expressed these ideas in school magazines and local newspapers during the 1930s and 1940s, in language that mirrored that of May Fourth and 1930s Chinese intellectuals.[58] Of course, school magazines were official publications and could be seen as tools for homogenizing individual expression. All the same, these magazines captured the zeitgeist and demonstrated the politically correct expressions of these concerns. Also, they were the one major outlet for writings by female students themselves—the very individuals around whom so much public discussion swirled. Taken as a whole, they could be said to reflect the desired image of the educated female as conceived of by various parties. In contrast, school magazines in English girls' schools during the same era did not touch on these topics with the same frequency or intensity. This difference indicates a lesser degree of activism on this front, or, at least, that such issues were deemed inappropriate for discussion in official English school publications.

In their writings, Chinese students adopted certain prevailing notions about equality of the sexes and women's emancipation that were current among the Republican Chinese intellectual class. In 1934, the Kuen Cheng Girls' School annual magazine included essays with titles such as "Singlehood and Marriage" (*Dushen yu jiehun*), "Ambition" (*Zhi*), "Theories of Divorce" (*Lihun shuo*), and "Women [Told to] Get Back into the Kitchen" (*Funümen huidao chufang li qu*).[59] These topics were most likely assigned to students by teachers: each topic might have more than one essay on it featured in the magazine, suggesting that the published pieces were the best ones selected from an assignment given to an entire class. The topics were also nearly identical to those of essays and articles on women's issues that were being published in Republican China, such as "Freedom of Marriage and Democracy," "Women's Careers," "My View on the Issue of Divorce," and "The Great Inappropriateness of Women's Emancipation."[60] Some of the writers displayed a poignant combination of youthful naïveté and bleak pessimism. In an essay titled "Singlehood and Marriage," a student discusses the case against marriage in touchingly pragmatic detail:

There are two special reasons why women remain unmarried: (1) Fear of giving birth—This is something that every woman fears, because giving birth is a very painful business . . . . [B]efore giving birth, [one's] belly is so big that it is like carrying around a large drum, it really is ugly to look at . . . . [W]hen your friends see you,

you feel so embarrassed . . . and during and after pregnancy, if the man wants to beat you or love somebody else, there is nothing you can do about it . . . . (2) Fear of being deceived—The love of a man usually cannot last forever, he may truly love you at the present time, but later will have a change of heart . . . . [S]ome people are able to see this point, and are therefore willing to remain single; moreover, if one is able to be independent, why seek out so much trouble?[61]

As for women's motivations for getting married, the same student names three grim reasons: "(1) The family forces it . . . . (2) Some girls are used to being lazy . . . and rely on a man so they can pass their days in ease and idleness . . . . (3) Some girls are unable to live an independent life, and cannot not marry."[62] In this case, the student has decided that marriage and childbearing are not desirable goals, but her rationale is as much about fleeing a miserable future as it is an affirmative movement toward liberation. Regardless, it is a clear-eyed, if somewhat simplistic, re-examination of women's supposedly natural social roles.

Other essays in Kuen Cheng's school magazines focused attention on the public and patriotic aspects of women's roles in society. These writings detail the professional duties of educated women as teachers while seldom touching on the roles of wife and mother. One piece from the school's forty-fifth anniversary commemorative magazine in 1953, titled "Our Responsibility" (*Women de zeren*), called for educated girls and women to "render service to nation and country" by "throwing [them]selves into business and production organizations," so as not to let down their parents, teachers, country, and society.[63] In the same publication, when describing "The Life of a Normal School Student" in the teacher training program, one girl writes that the student's goal is to "take up the noble and sacred work of education," and that her life demands much sacrifice and "living seriously."[64] Similarly, when exhorting her Normal class colleagues to fulfill their calling as teachers, another student defined a woman's obligations as being useful to "self, school, children [i.e., students] and to society."[65] This sentiment was in keeping with the Republican educational program, which sought to prepare youth to participate in the industrial economy and citizenship in a public sphere that was distinct from the private family sphere.[66] It is difficult to ascertain how many of these opinions were developed independently, if at all, and how much was faithful repetition of what students had read and heard in school. Nonetheless, these writings indicate a widespread awareness among Chinese female students of issues surrounding the changing roles and images of women, and the fact that these schools created a physical and intellectual space for them to express their thoughts on the subject.

Feminist activists, teachers, and principals constantly reminded students that women's work and independence were important. In 1929, the well-known Nationalist revolutionary and feminist He Xiangning visited from China and gave a speech at Nanyang Girls' High School in Singapore in which she encouraged students to pursue education and gender equality.[67] On a symbolic level, official school songs such as that of Nan Hwa Girls' School in Singapore referenced "the feminine world" (*nüjie* 女界) and "women's rights" (*nüquan* 女权).[68] In her parting message to the graduates of Nan Hwa's 1949 Normal or teacher training class, principal Yang Ruichu exhorted her students to serve society by becoming teachers or by continuing their studies.[69] Teachers writing farewell messages addressed their students as "younger sisters" and, in envisioning the future for their charges, predicted that they would work in either education or in the commercial world, "deepening [their] knowledge and refining [their] professional skills."[70]

For female educators, their hopes and ambitions for the girls whom they had taught were expressed in terms of their roles outside the home rather than within it. Principal Yang was consistent over the years in her message to pursue education as far as possible and suggested that forgoing education or work outside the home was a loss. In a 1962 school magazine, her advice to graduates of the upper secondary class was to advance to higher education if possible. If this was not an option because of "difficult [financial] circumstances," then one should find a job and contribute to building a better society. If neither further schooling nor work outside the home was possible, and one was "restricted to the house," students should "not be discouraged, pessimistic or lose all hope," but rather seek self-improvement through life experience and correspondence courses.[71] This was markedly different from the social conservatism of contemporary English girls' schools, with their emphasis on home-making skills and domesticity, and from the educational agenda of the postcolonial government, which would make home economics a compulsory subject in girls' schools from the 1970s onward.

A third way in which Chinese girls' schools introduced new possibilities for educated women was through the creation of political identity options for Chinese women. For many overseas Chinese women, these schools were crucibles for politicization. Their awareness and activism began here, where they were frequently drawn into such activities as fundraising, volunteering, and joining organizations for political causes. School authorities provided an ethno-nationalist foundation for these activities by fostering a sense of connection with the mainland in statements that went beyond the symbolism of school names.

Both in and outside the classroom, these schools sought to instill in their students a strong sense of Chinese ethnicity, nationalism, and citizenship that was located in the public rather than the private domain. Chinese-language education in Malaya and Singapore thus became a highly politicized issue in the early twentieth century. British colonial authorities realized that these privately organized and financed institutions were becoming an alternative locus for social power and sought to exert more control over them.[72] Under siege, some schools and their students became even more determined to preserve Chinese culture and to maintain identification with the Chinese nation.

Educated overseas Chinese women actively participated in the political affairs of their local communities as well as on the larger national and international scene. Their ability to engage in political activities was often enabled by greater freedom of movement and less supervision outside the home, as they traveled to and from school and sometimes boarded in school hostels. From the late 1920s and into the 1930s, as Sino-Japanese military conflict escalated, overseas Chinese female students joined anti-Japanese boycotts and fundraising for the war effort. The events of World War II and China's Communist Revolution created an even wider range of possibilities for political action and identification. Female students variously identified with local Malayan or Singaporean anti-colonial nationalism, the Nationalists (KMT) or Communists, or local guerilla Communist groups.[73] Some schoolgirls were inspired to re-migrate to China in order to help rebuild the post-1949 nation, often running away from home, adopting new lives and career trajectories that departed dramatically from convention. When Chinese schools were being closely watched for possible Communist infiltration during the 1940s and 1950s, girls' schools did not escape monitoring, and some female students were arrested for their involvement in these activities. In the postcolonial period, girls and women who had studied and worked in Chinese girls' schools joined the movement to preserve vernacular Chinese education.

Political awareness and activism among Chinese schoolgirls was in part inspired by their teachers and school environments. Certainly, school authorities fostered a sense of deep connection to China. In her opening remarks of the 1936 Jingfang Girls' School magazine, principal Luo Yifang referred repeatedly to "[our] country's troubles," namely, China's struggle for political stability, and declared:

> Situated as we are at this juncture of survival or extinction for our country, how can we simply speak empty words? . . . The Overseas Chinese of the Southern Islands [i.e., Southeast Asia] number in the hundreds of thousands;

the importance of their education can hardly be ignored, and as for those teachers who bear the responsibility of carrying out this education, how especially important is their duty! . . . [They must] lead by example, cultivate the hearts and minds of children, develop the great spirit of our race . . . and hence complete the mission of education—to save our country.[74]

Female teachers, too, spoke their minds about overseas Chinese education and its connection to the mainland. In a piece titled "My View on Chinese Education in South Asia," a teacher from China named Huang Siou Chin who had been working at Nan Hwa Girls' School in Singapore for several years launched a scathing critique of local Chinese schools. She drew a direct link between overseas Chinese education and the well-being of China:

> As a teacher I take interest in the system of education of overseas Chinese in South[east] Asia. And from my survey I find that there is still room for much improvement . . . . Most of the school buildings . . . are housed not in proper buildings but in ordinary small shop houses . . . . The majority of teachers are . . . poorly paid. The shabby treatment of teachers and the harsh attitude adopted by principals towards them are very discouraging . . . . Schools . . . are run on the wrong lines by people who are ignorant of the true aims. They who are usually business-minded, regard them as business enterprises . . . . China's strength and unity depend on her educational system. Overseas Chinese likewise should not neglect this for there will come a day when they will have to return home and serve the Mother Country. Without sound education they would be a burden to the state. Whatever the Chinese do overseas will directly reflect on China.[75]

Interestingly, Huang wrote this essay in English. Her criticism of "business-minded" school administrators likely grew from observing that most private Chinese schools depended heavily on the financial support of local Chinese businesses and that donors would often be given places on school governing boards. Many Chinese merchants and philanthropists were cautious in displaying a sense of Chinese nationalism that might damage their business interests or their relationship with colonial British authorities. This attitude was not without reason, as overseas Chinese could not necessarily rely on the protection of the Chinese state, no matter what the political rhetoric of the season might say.

Interviewed about their experiences as students and teachers in these schools, overseas Chinese women recollect a charged political atmosphere. Tang Meijun, who attended Kuen Cheng and Hua Ch'iao in the late 1930s and early 1940s, stated that the latter school was "very progressive" because its vice-principal had been "sent over from China" and permitted the "infiltration" of many KMT teachers.[76] As Tang recalled, the degree of KMT influence was high enough that the British administration forced the school to remove this vice-principal and a number of other teachers for their activism. Another interviewee, Li Yue, was an activist teacher but with different political sympathies. She had been sent by the Communists to spread "progressive ideas" among Chinese youth abroad.[77] Both Republican and Communist supporters tended to use the term "progressive" to characterize the positive aspects of their political agendas. Li spent nine years in Malaya, from 1941 to 1950, teaching music at Kuen Cheng. Against school policy, she taught students revolutionary songs, such as the "Yan'an Anthem" (Yan'an song), celebrating the legendary stronghold of the Chinese Communist Party, and was suspended from teaching as a result. She remembers being criticized for doing this by some of the other teachers, who, in her estimation, had "probably [been] sent there by the Kuomintang." Asked about her students, she says that they were "very patriotic, except for the ones who were influenced by the running dogs of the British," and that when they expressed interest in re-migrating to China, she encouraged them and gave them advice on how to go about the journey.

Surrounded by these influences, Chinese schoolgirls internalized and acted on the ideals that their teachers and principals laid out for them, echoing sentiments of Chinese nationalism and organizing themselves for institutional and larger social causes. In their 1936 school magazines, when students wrote about "How to Be a Good Citizen" (Zenyang zuo yige hao gongmin) and discussed how best to "love [our] country" (aiguo), they were referring to China and not Malaya or Singapore.[78] That same year, the Jingfang Girls' School Student Association took the initiative to write an open letter to school authorities requesting the expansion of campus facilities, showing that female students were willing and able to advocate for their interests as a group in a public forum.[79]

The career of Ruth Ho, a pioneering Chinese-language teacher in Malaya and Singapore, is a different but equally illuminating example of how educated women found opportunities amid the political upheaval of this period. Born in 1910, Ruth Ho grew up in China with a Christian father who was headmaster of a Methodist school and ensured that his daughter received a modern education at home, in Methodist school, and at an American missionary university in Shanghai.[80] Inspired by Hu Shi's language reform movement to replace classical Mandarin with vernacular Mandarin, Ruth moved to Singapore and founded a Mandarin-language school for ethnic Chinese overseas. After a brief return to China from 1932 to 1937, during which time she married a lecturer in physiology from St. John's University in Shanghai and became Mrs. Ruth Lim, she relocated once again to Penang with her husband in tow. Once again, she started her own Mandarin-language school, offering afternoon classes for children and evening classes for adults. Her school had at least 150 students of all ages and socioeconomic classes. Ruth wrote her own textbooks, focusing on conversational Mandarin with phonetics to aid pronunciation. Her political engagement, which included organizing events for the China Relief Fund, was of such a high profile that she and her family fled south to Singapore upon the Japanese invasion of Penang in 1941, due to fears that she would be arrested for her pro-China activism. After World War II, Ruth resumed teaching Mandarin in Singapore, this time privately tutoring students from English-language institutions who did not have Chinese-language teachers in school and needed private classes. Her fluency in English and Chinese were particularly useful for moving easily between the two linguistic worlds.

While politicizing impulses coursed through Chinese girls' schools, other parties, within and without these institutions, wanted to ensure that certain traditional values would not be lost. Even as the focus on political awareness represented a break with the past for women, its basis in Chinese national and ethnic pride meant that it would be accompanied by a powerful strand of cultural conservatism. Chinese girls' schools, like almost all Chinese schools in British Malaya, were intended to preserve a sense of cohesive ethnic culture and identity among its overseas population, particularly by steeping younger generations in Chinese language, literature, and history. While the content of this education may not have been truly conservative in the political sense, as it often drew attention to China's suffering at the hands of Western powers over the previous century and to the rise of anti-imperialist sentiment, it did help to emphasize ethnic and cultural differences between the Chinese-educated overseas Chinese and the other peoples among whom they lived—including their English-educated fellow Chinese. An added layer of expectation existed regarding girls and women from Chinese schools and their roles in a patriarchal society. Educators, community leaders, and the printed press carefully monitored and remarked upon their appearance, comportment, femininity, and virtue, allowing traditional gender stereotypes to persist in these Chinese girls' schools.

Overseas Chinese female students were objects of a clear set of expectations about their appearance and propriety. These expectations were codified in long lists of institutional regulations that reflected fears of how schooling and work might expose girls to dangerous social influences. These paralleled contemporary concerns in Republican China over the ways in which female students exhibited transgressive behavior through their clothing and hairstyles.[81] Girls' schools had strict rules governing the ways their students dressed, with bans on makeup, jewelry, and artificially curled hair, and fines imposed for disobedience.[82] Report cards evaluated students on their demeanor, including their "Appearance and Attitude" (*rongmao taidu*), "Tone of Voice" (*shengyin*), and "Language" (*yanyu*).[83] At Nanyang Girls' School, the 1935 school magazine included a list of several hundred regulations, reminiscent of Kuomintang New Life regulations. A section of rules for primary school girls consisted of 120 items, including injunctions to "not eat on the street" (*zai lushang buke chidongxi*), "express appropriate gratitude when receiving gifts" (*shou renjia zengpin shi yao biaoshi xiangdangde ganxie*), and "be constantly glad in one's heart" (*xinli changchang huanxi*).[84] The secondary school section had thirty-five additional rules, including "not smoking, drinking alcohol or using opiates" (*wu xiyanjiu ji yongmazuipinde xiguan*) and the rather startling imperative of "keeping one's sexual organs clean and [having] the ability to control sexual desire" (*you baochi xinggong zhi qingjie de xiguan ji jiezhi xingyude nengli*).[85]

These strictures echoed similar rules regarding public decorum and character development in Republican Chinese middle schools. For example, in Jiangsu during the 1920s and 1930s, such school rules included such minutiae as "one's posture when sitting in the classroom must be upright and [one's attitude] serious," "do not pour out washing water on the ground at will," and "when going to meals do not talk and laugh loudly." They also ranged to the comparatively lofty, as at Zhenhua Girls' Middle School in Suzhou, where students were urged to "have a spirit of hard work and enduring hardship . . . obey the ideas of the majority . . . be able to transform society and not be transformed by it . . . [and] love society and the nation with zeal."[86] Such character development programs were commonplace in Jiangsu by the 1930s and undoubtedly served as a template for overseas Chinese girls' schools.[87]

Other concerns centered on how girls' schools might lead to the inappropriate presence of women in traditionally male spaces. Despite the fact that the movement for female emancipation in theory rejected the traditional sequestering of women, girls' schools at the secondary level—for students from age eleven or twelve onward—were mostly gender-segregated, as in the case of Jingfang Girls' School in Singapore. Heated debates over co-education did take place in Chinese newspapers, but proponents of the change were typically defeated on the grounds of immorality.[88] In 1920, an article in the Malayan *Penang Sin Pao* (*Bincheng Xinbao*) cautioned that women should not be "excessively" liberated or be allowed to participate in government.[89] These efforts at containment point to a persistent paradox in female education. Even as girls' schools prepared overseas Chinese women for work outside the home and conveyed the message that they would find personal fulfillment as well as serve the nation by doing so, political authorities and popular opinion continued to expect that educated women could only be modernized to the extent that they did not challenge traditional notions of feminine propriety. Educated girls and women received these messages from near and far, broadcast from China in some cases. In 1936, the *Sin Chew Jit Poh* (Singapore Daily Newspaper) reported on a speech given at Nan Hwa Girls' School by the Special Delegate from Guangdong Wu Zaimin, who remarked caustically on schoolgirls in China who considered themselves above the duties of cooking and sewing, only knowing "how to order servants around and spend money."[90]

Female students were acutely aware of the realities that they would confront upon emergence into a society still governed by patriarchal norms. They wrote essays and short stories about the difficulties that educated women faced in marrying freely and establishing careers. Parental pressure to focus on marriage before education was a continuing issue. One of the strongest indicators of this problem was student enrollment in the higher levels of girls' schools, which often peaked at the end of lower secondary, when students were typically fifteen years old, and fell rapidly thereafter. Upper secondary and Normal classes suffered the greatest attrition rate, and school authorities explicitly attributed this to girls dropping out to get married.[91] In this regard, Chinese girls' schools faced the same challenge as English girls' schools of this period. In the 1930s, school magazines contained student-authored fiction about girls who yearned to stay in school but were compelled by their parents to drop out and enter arranged marriages. In one tale, the protagonist met an unhappy end when she obeyed her parents, ended up in a miserable marriage, and went insane; in another, the protagonist was determined to control her own future and ran away from home to escape an arranged match.[92] The latter story draws to a gloomy close as women's liberation turns out to be an abstract ideal, touted by the protagonist's teachers but dismissed by her family, leaving her with no choice but to forsake her home to pursue a risky and uncertain dream:

> So life was in fact accursed, such that the cries of "women's liberation" and "equality of men and women," even though they had been unceasing for so many

years, ultimately could not be made into reality. The quest for learning had only produced privileged . . . young ladies, who, having obtained a university or secondary school degree . . . would imitate foreign women's fashions and dress, could this really be considered reaching the goal of liberation?[93]

Other students' voices echoed the intensely negative attitudes toward the "Modern Girl" who had emerged in East Asia as well as around the globe in the early 1920s and 1930s.[94] Their sentiments were heartfelt, but their language was formulaic, likely borrowed from elites in China. Both parties condemned "pseudo-modern" girls and women who adopted only superficial aspects of modernity such as a Westernized appearance, pursuit of material goods and hedonistic experiences, and sexual promiscuity.[95] In contrast to these fallen women, overseas Chinese schoolgirls saw themselves following in the footsteps of the "New Women" from the turn of the twentieth century: intellectually mature, politically engaged, and morally superior. In an essay called "What a Modern Girl Should Know" (*Xiandai nüzi yingyou de renshi*), a female student from Kuen Cheng critiqued the limited range of women's rights in her day, claimed the mantle of leadership in female emancipation for her generation, and denounced ersatz "liberated women" with a bourgeois or superficial sense of modernity. She decried "women with good intentions and high spirits who are tempted by bad influences in society to go down the wrong path."[96] In another essay titled "The Future," a student in teacher training at Jingfang cautioned that education did not exempt girls from being shallow, as they might use their literacy as just another tool for becoming Modern Girls with no sense of social or political duty:

> For many girls, their aim in going to school [is] they think that by studying and being literate, then they can consider themselves a girl with learning [*you xuewen de nüzi*], and are so-called girls with new minds [*xin tounao de nüzi*], able to marry men of the new age [*xin shidai de nanzi*]. They don't know how to struggle . . . they covet material goods and momentary pleasures, scarlet makeup, four-inch high-heeled leather shoes, *qipao* dresses that reach down to their toes . . . they are willing to be others' playthings. This is their future; this is all wrong![97]

Through dedicated sections for female contributors in local Chinese-language newspapers, members of the wider community joined the discussion. In *Sin Chew Jit Poh*'s "Funü yuandi" ("Women's World"), mothers fretted about their daughters' new attitudes toward love and marriage. Conversely, female students complained that girls' schools were simply becoming factories for wives and called on their peers to live up higher ideals in articles such as "A Small Hope that I Have for Intellectual Chinese Women in Malaya" and "A Word to Fellow Female Students in Kuala Lumpur."[98] Writers' appeals were to an elite of educated, intellectual women, and their exhortations were generally for women to be more socially and politically conscious, even as they faced challenges in finding jobs and attaining financial independence.

For educated overseas Chinese women, the greatest constraint to the ideals they had been taught lay beyond graduation. Social norms and economic conditions in the first half of the twentieth century limited career options for female graduates. Aside from a few professions, such as teaching, nursing, and clerical work, few career paths were open to women. A popular saying at the time was that "to graduate is to be unemployed" (biye ji shiye). Both teachers and students made reference to this saying, indicating that job security and financial independence—both considered essential for true emancipation—were elusive.[99] Where work was obtainable, the rationale for women having an education and a career was still drawn along traditional lines. Some students' writings showed the continuing influence of strongly gendered notions concerning women's work. Discussing the importance of female education, a student from Nan Hwa in 1949 invoked the "good wife, wise mother" ideology of decades before: "Children are the core of a family, and are the future masters of the country . . . . [W]omen cannot refuse to obtain a good education, so as to be able to teach and cultivate their children."[100] Others argued that certain "feminine qualities" made women especially fitted for certain jobs. A graduate from the Normal class of Kuen Cheng in 1953 stated, "Given their nature and [lack of] physical strength, girls are more suited to becoming teachers."[101] In 1960, a student from Nanyang continued to reinforce this image:

> Educated women will prove to be better housewives and can serve their countries in many other ways than just being parasites . . . . There [is] work which suits women better than men, such as nursing and teaching, for they possess the warmth and gentleness which the sick and young long for.[102]

These gender-stereotypical arguments often appeared side-by-side with fellow students' essays calling for women's liberation, equality of the sexes, and personal fulfillment through a career in service of the nation. They reveal the persistence of traditional attitudes toward femininity despite advances in social and economic options created by female education. These attitudes survived, sometimes more vigorously and for a longer period than in China, where the 1949 revolution inaugurated a society in which gender equality had been achieved—at least in theory. The tenacity of certain sociocultural ideals and rhetoric in the diaspora, beyond their life span in China, reflects the sometimes inconsistent nature of overseas Chinese nationalism and reformist impulses. Whereas efforts to mobilize the diaspora for the Republican cause were led by intellectuals who journeyed abroad specifically for that purpose, such as teachers, the diasporic communities in which they operated were often led by Chinese businessmen who had only partial affinities with such elite literati. Most of these businessmen, who were the primary sponsors of Chinese-language education, were "men of honor but not normally men of political enthusiasm."[103] In places, this led to an attenuated and partial transmission of Chinese nationalism. At the same time, the physical and political distance between China and colonial Southeast Asia meant that events in China might not have the same impact in Southeast Asia. For example, when KMT promotion of New Life gender traditionalism seeped into the curriculum and ethos of many girls' schools in China during the 1930s, teachers and students in Malayan and Singaporean Chinese girls' schools continued to use language that echoed May Fourth and New Culture radicalism from the early 1920s.[104] The stubborn afterlife of certain mainland Chinese sociopolitical trends among Chinese migrant communities could be due in part to the distinct role that Chinese schools played in the colonial diasporic setting—that of upholding Chinese sociocultural heritage, complete with its traditionalist and reformist contradictions. For KMT supporters, in China and abroad, the threat of leftist social radicalism may have led to greater entrenchment of social and cultural traditionalism as a hallmark of legitimate Chinese nationalism.

As educated Chinese girls left school, venturing into the world to work and/or take up their expected domestic roles, most of them claimed to suffer from few illusions about the realities of the society in which they lived. Many alumni of these schools, reflecting on their experiences from the vantage point of the present, state that they felt no sense of disjuncture between their academic and post-school lives.[105] They evince little surprise that patriarchal norms at home and in the workplace would limit their career choices; after all, this was simply the reality of the time. Yet there were others who wrestled strenuously with their consciousness of possible alternative frameworks that would accommodate the ambitions and talents of the new women they had been enjoined to become. These students argued that a meaningful life should include a professional career and were worried that this choice was often denied to women, well into the post–World War II period. "All people in the world should have a proper career, then only will their lives have meaning . . . [but] in this deficient society, the job opportunities that are given to girls are too few," observed one student in 1953.[106] Some even proposed new social arrangements, such as public child care for working mothers, which were based on developments in post-1949 Communist China:

> A progressive and civilized country must have various kinds of child care facilities, such that when parents go out to work, it will not lead to the children losing the nurturing that they should have, and this will also allow women to focus on their work without any worries, taking on important jobs together with men, obtaining similar results, and achieving a position of equality.[107]

Such far-reaching change came about only gradually, in part due to the countervailing forces of conservatism in Chinese girls' schools and wider society. At the same time, this change could not have transpired without the new ideas, activities, and spaces that educated Chinese women found in girls' schools, even if only for a while, to envision and practice being modern—whatever their interpretation of modernity might be.

In Chinese-language girls' schools across colonial Malaya and Singapore, female students grappled with gendered and politically defined visions of modernity. These institutions opened up a range of career and identity options that had not existed previously. They brought overseas Chinese girls and women in Malaya and Singapore into greater contact with one another as well as with transnational processes of modernization. Like their Republican Chinese counterparts, these women sought to reconcile the contradictions between modernization and tradition. They grew increasingly aware of their positions in the nation, even as the meaning of those positions was largely defined by people and circumstances beyond their control. In Republican China, women's roles were constrained by male political and intellectual elites, as well as Nationalist state imperatives.[108] In Malaya and Singapore, the increasingly polarized struggle between British colonial and Chinese nationalist visions of modernity shaped processes of female emancipation and identity construction.

In the late twentieth and early twenty-first centuries, scholars have re-interpreted Benedict Anderson's classic model of the "imagined community" as a potential framework for conceptualizing diaspora.[109] To the deservedly disputed extent that a dispersed collection of people in a variety of migrant situations might regard themselves part of a unified whole, this approach works. As with the social construction of national identity, a unified diasporic consciousness depends on a people's sense of shared languages and cultural practices, facilitated by greater political awareness, literacy, print capitalism, and other forms of media or organizations that cultivate common interests and identification. For the overseas Chinese and other migrant populations, the notion of a diasporic imagined community may also rely on the existence of a national imagined community, regardless of how closely tied they are to it in reality. However, the model becomes shaky when the unruly possibilities of imagination are considered. Nationalism was not the only political ideology available to educated overseas Chinese women in the early twentieth century. There was also feminism, democracy, socialism, and other new paradigms for political and socioeconomic organization during this time of transformation. Educated overseas Chinese women did indeed build new imagined communities based on the language medium of their schools, their alumni associations, and the broader population of women who had passed through the gates of these institutions. Perhaps the operative word here is "imagined"—not in terms of delusion or fantasy but rather in terms of the innovative, pathbreaking, yet at times tenuous quality of the identity that these schools created. That which is imagined is unfettered, but also inherently unstable and vulnerable to external intrusions.

Alternately praised and rebuked for their boldness in crossing boundaries that limited earlier generations of Chinese women, graduates of Chinese girls' schools were excited and confounded by the ever-shifting possibilities before them. Their movements were hampered by the weight of ethno-cultural symbolism that had been thrust upon them by Chinese nationalist and diasporic forces. The terminology and ideas in debates over their education largely mirrored those of Republican China, in no small part due to the influence of Chinese nationalism on these institutions. Yet this discourse masks the fact that educated Chinese women in diaspora faced unique circumstances and responded to them as individuals making their homes between nation and empire. Their situation was somewhat akin to their Nyonya sisters, but in a very different cultural and linguistic milieu, with distinct sociopolitical implications.

Amid these varied influences, overseas Chinese women's identities were caught in an eddy formed by powerful nationalist and anti-imperial currents. A small but significant minority among these Chinese-educated women made the drastic move of detaching from their diasporic situation altogether. They took the lessons of political consciousness and Chinese patriotism to heart and ran away to China in the 1940s and 1950s to help rebuild a motherland that they had never seen, returning to a place they had never left—an imagined homeland.

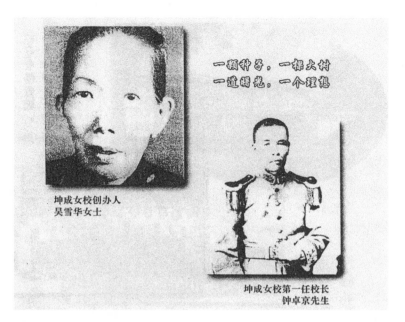

一颗种子，一棵大树
一道曙光，一个理想

坤成女校创办人
吴雪华女士

坤成女校第一任校长
钟卓京先生

Figure 11 Wu Xuehua and Zhong Zhuojing, founders of Kuen Cheng Girls' School in 1908, Kuala Lumpur. *Kuncheng nüxiao bashi zhounian jiniankan* (Kuen Cheng Girls' School Eightieth Anniversary Commemorative Magazine). Kuala Lumpur: 1993.

校　長

沙淵如先生

Figure 12 Sha Yuanru, Principal of Kuen Cheng Girls' School from 1933–51, Kuala Lumpur. *Kuncheng nüzhong chuzhong diqijie biye tekan* (Kuen Cheng Girls' School Lower Secondary Seventh Annual Graduation Special Commemorative Magazine). Kuala Lumpur: 1934.

1.	My Favourite Book	...	...	By	Fong Hon Meng
2.	The Rain	...	...	,,	Choy Ngan Ling
3.	The Kuala Lumpur Museum	...	...	,,	Loh Choon Khow
4.	Reflections of a Dog	...	...	,,	Lim Yueh Chan
5.	Slow and Steady Wins The Race	...	...	,,	Choy Ming Hoi
6.	The Best Indoor Game	...	...	,,	Lum Yuet Seam
7.	A Letter	...	...	,,	Yen Wah
8.	Basket Ball	...	...	,,	Leong Yuet Ying
9.	Not All The Same	...	...	,,	Oi Hong
10.	A Morning Walk	...	...	,,	Foo Sao Nam
11.	How I Spent Last Sunday	...	...	,,	Lim Yueh Oi
12.	Keep It A Secret	...	...	,,	Cho Chui May
13.	The Fox and The Grapes.	...	...	,,	Wong Wai Ying
14.	Good Saved and Bad Lost	...	...	,,	Wong Hui Lan
15.	Not At Home	...	...	,,	Yen Shui Lien
16.	Coconut Tree	...	...	,,	Loh Choon Khow
17.	Taking a Baby's Photo	...	...	,,	Fong Hon Meng
18.	The Monkey	...	...	,,	Choy Ngan Ling
19.	A Dream	...	...	,,	Lim Yueh Chan
20.	The Apple	...	...	,,	Choy Ming Hoi
21.	Holidays	...	...	,,	Loh Choon Khow
22.	The Crow And The Pitcher	...	...	,,	Choy Ngan Ling
23.	How I Would Spent Ten Dollars	...	...	,,	Lim Yueh Chan
24.	Reflections of an Old Tree	...	...	,,	Loh Choon Khow
25.	The British Empire	...	...	,,	Lim Yuet Seam
26.	The Crow and the Wind-Mill	...	...	,,	Ong Keng Sih
27.	A Letter	...	...	,,	Fong Hon Meng
28.	The Fox and The Crow	...	...	,,	Keng Ying
29.	The Apple	...	...	,,	Chang Swee Yueh

Figure 13 Excerpt from the table of contents for a collection of English essays by Kuen Cheng Girls' School students, 1935. *English Essays and Compositions by Junior Middle School Graduates (1935 Class) of the Kwan Seng [Kuen Cheng] Girls' School*. Kuala Lumpur: Union Press, 1935.

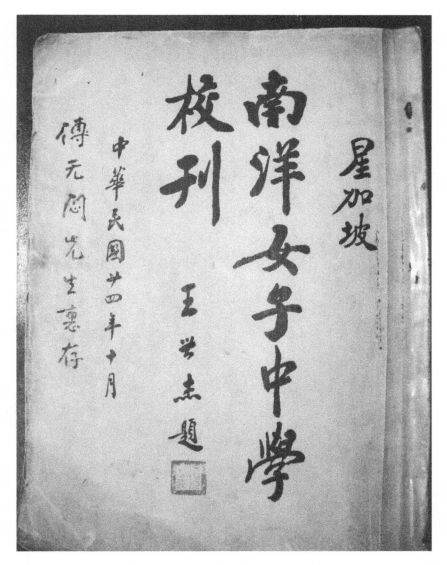

Figure 14 Cover of Nanyang Girls' High School Magazine, Singapore, 1935. The year of publication is rendered according to the calendar of China at the time, which numbered the years relative to the founding of the Chinese Republic in 1911 rather than according to the Western Gregorian system. *Nanyang nüzi zhongxue xiaokan* (Nanyang Girls' High School Magazine). Singapore: 1935.

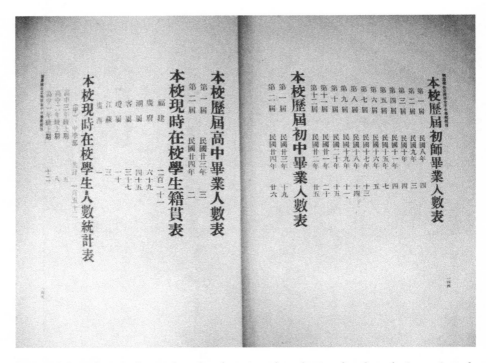

Figure 15 Lists showing the number of students in each graduating class from the Lower Secondary, Upper Secondary, and Teacher Training (or Normal) levels, as well as the Chinese dialect group or provincial origins of students, in Nanyang Girls' School, Singapore, 1935. *Nanyang nüzi zhongxue xiaokan* (Nanyang Girls' High School Magazine). Singapore: 1935.

Figure 16 School magazine photographs showing Nanyang female students engaged in a wide variety of sports-related and extra-curricular activities: (from top right clockwise) badminton, harmonica playing, guitar playing, swimming, calisthenics, cleaning school grounds and classrooms, volleyball, and being measured for height. Singapore, 1935. *Nanyang nüzi zhongxue xiaokan* (Nanyang Girls' High School Magazine). Singapore: 1935.

現 任 校 長

朱 月 華 先 生

Figure 17 Zhu Yuehua, Principal of Penang Chinese Girls' High School from 1935–66, Penang. *Bincheng Binhua xiaoyouhui qingzhu guangfu ershiyi zhounian, xinhuisuo luocheng jinian tekan* (Penang Chinese Girls' High School Alumni Association Special Commemorative Issue Celebrating the Twenty-First Anniversary of School Revival and Establishment of a New Center). Penang, Malaysia: Penang Chinese Girls' High School Alumni Association, March 1979.

Figure 18 Cover of Nanyang Girls' High School Magazine, Singapore, 1948. Note the more professional appearance of the magazine cover compared to the 1935 edition, with printed type, bilingual titles, and detailed publication information. The year of publication is now rendered in both Republican Chinese and Western formats. *Nanyang nüzi zhongxue xiaokan* (Nanyang Girls' High School Magazine). Singapore: 1948.

Figure 19 School magazine photographs showcasing the athletic accomplishments of Nanyang students, who are shown engaging in inter- and intra-school sports competitions, in events ranging from the javelin to shot put, from long jump to high jump, and in school Sports Day "group performances." Singapore, 1948. *Nanyang nüzi zhongxue xiaokan* (Nanyang Girls' High School Magazine). Singapore: 1948.

昔日猛將英姿

福友足球隊(一九四〇年)

前排左起：陳金片　林金包　李冬英
後排左起：孫真珠　傅育新　王月桃　謝友蘭　何淑媛
（此相片由傅育新同學提供）

福友籃球隊(一九四六年)

前排左起：謝友蘭　林姮心　黃美裳　尤平素　傅彩根　薛玉葉
後排左起：敎練林嘉揚　施依乖　陳春容　領隊翁素碧　陳金片　李冬英
財政戴秀蘭　（此相片由陳金片同學提供）

Figure 20 Penang Chinese Girls' High School soccer and basketball teams, from 1940 and 1946, respectively. *Bincheng Binhua xiaoyouhui qingzhu guangfu ershiyi zhounian, xinhuisuo luocheng jinian tekan* (Penang Chinese Girls' High School Alumni Association Special Commemorative Issue Celebrating the Twenty-First Anniversary of School Revival and Establishment of a New Center). Penang, Malaysia: Penang Chinese Girls' High School Alumni Association, March 1979.

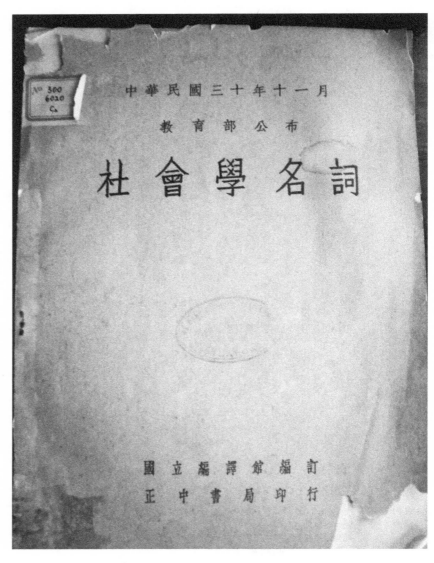

Figure 21 Cover page of *Shehuixue mingci* (Sociological Terminology), a text from Zhengzhong Shuju, a publisher in Republican China, and used by Nanyang Girls' High School. Singapore, 1941. Guoli bianyi guan (National Compilation and Translation Center), comp. *Shehuixue mingci* (Sociological Terminology). Nanjing: Zhengzhong shuju, November 1941.

266. Configuration of personality	人格的盎形	299. Convention	俗例
267. Conflict	衝突	300. Conventionalization	慣例化
268. Conflict situation	衝突情境	301. Convergence	湊合; 輻合
269. Congestion	擁擠	302. Conversion	突轉
270. Congregation	會合	303. Coöperation	合作
271. Conjugal relation	夫婦關係	304. Coöperative association	合作協會
272. Connubium	婚姻	305. Coöperative movement	合作運動
273. Conquest	征服	306. Coöperative society	合作社
274. Conquest of nature	征服自然	307. Coördination	調整
275. Consanguine family	血族家庭	308. Copper age	銅器時代
276. Consanguine marriage	血族婚姻	309. Corporate action	協同行動
277. Consanguinity	血親	310. Corporate interest	共同利益
278. Consensus of opinion	意見一致	311. Corporation	公司
279. Consciousness	意識	312. Correlation	相關; 聯繫
280. Consciousness of kind (Giddings)	同類意識	313. Cost of living	生活費
281. Consensus	一致; 協同	314. Counteraction	反抗行動
282. Conservation district	富源保存區	315. Counter-revolution	反革命; 反抗革命
283. Conservatism	保守主義	316. Counter-selection	反選擇; 反淘汰
284. Consistency	一貫; 先後一致	317. Courtship	求愛
		318. Cousin marriage	表親婚
285. Consolidation	聯結; 團結	319. Couvade	產翁; 產公 男子裝育俗
286. Continuity of germ-plasm	精質的綿續	320. Covenant	盟約
287. Constituent society (Giddings)	組成社會	321. Covert behavior	內在行為
288. Consummatory behavior	完成的行為	322. Coworker	同事; 同工
289. Content of culture	文化內容	323. Craze	時狂
290. Contraception	避姙	324. Creed	信條
291. Contract labor	契約勞工	325. Crescive institution (Sorokin)	自生的制度
292. Contract theory of society	社會契約說	326. Crime	罪; 犯罪
293. Contract rent	契約租金	327. Criminal	罪犯; 犯人
294. Contradiction	矛盾	328. Criminality	犯罪; 犯罪性
295. Contra-imitation	反模仿	329. Criminal type	犯罪型
296. Contra-suggestion	反暗示	330. Criminology	犯罪學
297. Contravention	違反	331. Crippled	殘廢者
298. Control	控制; 制裁; 統御; 約制	332. Crisis	危機
		333. Criteria of progress	進步標準

Figure 22 Chinese-English translations in *Shehuixue mingci* (Sociological Terminology). Guoli bianyi guan (National Compilation and Translation Center), comp. *Shehuixue mingci* (Sociological Terminology). Nanjing: Zhengzhong shuju, November 1941.

福建僑鄉報

1957年3月7日　星期四　農曆丁酉年二月初六

每月出6期　本期四版　第48期　社址：福州繁峰路32号
每份3分　每月1角8分　　　　訂報处：各地邮局

農業战綫上，侨屬女將多！

本省許多侨屬妇女荣獲劳动模范称号

【本报訊】誰說侨眷妇女"尖脚幼手"不会劳动？誰說侨眷妇女当不上劳动模范和生產能手？請看：

王淑卿　晋江縣泗鄉新星第二高級社的模范饲养員，晋江縣和全省農、林、漁、牧、水利模范代表会的代表。她饲养的母猪和小猪都很健壯，小猪成活率达100%。

（周玉湖、薛典元、潘松茂）

陈明地　龍岩縣田鄉農業社副社長。从1952年起，她就積極領導農民、侨眷參加互助合作运动。她不但自己積極学習農業生產技術，还教会許多侨眷妇女（如張秀娥、張五姑、張宝嬌、蔡嬌娥、黄零仔等等）学会犁田、插秧等耕作技術。因此，她曾被选为劳动模范，还得到幾張奖状。去年一月間，她參加了中國共產党。

（黃德光）

胡秀蓮　她是海澄縣新埗鄉的農業社員，曾經先后四次当选为劳动模范，还得到区委会的奖状和奖品。誰也想不到，她在1953年以前還是一个依靠侨匯生活、从未參加过劳动的家庭妇女。

（楊惠芳）

鄭月貞　和胡秀蓮一樣，她也是一向依靠侨匯生活，1953年才开始学習种田的。鄉里有人說她是"沒事討事做"，她却三年如一日地学会了各种生產技術。去年一年中，她挣了2,000个工分，分到30多担谷子，足夠全家7人一年的糧食。

珍为群众所爱戴的原因。去年春选时，她被选为副鄉長並侨屬工作委員会主任。（陳万里）

程金菊　閩侯荊溪鄉荊溪高級社副社長兼第一生產隊隊長。她的隊共34戶，其中有24戶是归侨侨眷。有人担心侨眷多不能搞好生產，結果：去年她的隊光早稻就收了43,801斤，超额完成社里規定的生產計划，晚稻也超額完成任务，得到社里的工分奖励。

1月19日，她被評为閩侯縣最优秀的侨眷先進生產者，得到縣人民委員会頒發的奖狀和奖品。

福建省人民代表、省農業劳动模范、鄉生產模范、丰產模范、劳动模范、工作模范、模范社員、信用社理事模范……这是龍溪縣侨眷林彩云几年來先后所獲得的光荣称号。

（維城、宝珍）

林彩云

余桃珠　她是个22歲的年輕姑娘。可是，別看她年纪小，她却是古田縣文洋鄉的生產模范、秋征模范和消滅四害模范，又是副鄉長。前年十月，她被吸收为中國共產党党員。她是1951年回國的華侨姑娘。

（陳占青）

黃秀华　她是个厦門姑娘——禾山区工農業社青年生產隊隊長，也是鄉人民代表。社里的人說："她是我們社里的劳动能手！"黃秀华說："'劳动是光荣，懶情是罪恶'，我去年离开了学校后就參加了農業生產劳动，我的四个姊妹也參加劳动。"

（黃增基）

她是个小学沒畢業的19歲姑娘，福

Figure 23 Front page of the *Fujian Qiaobao* (Fujian Overseas Chinese Newspaper). The cover story headline praises the contributions of re-migrant or *guiqiao* and *guiqiao*-related girls and women, declaring that "On the Frontlines of the Agricultural War, Many Are Overseas Chinese Female Soldiers!" Given the date of March 7, 1957, this item was likely intended to coincide with Women's Day on March 8. *Fujian Qiaoxiangbao* (Fujian Overseas Chinese Newspaper). March 7, 1957.

CHAPTER 5

Home Is That Which I Adore

Re-Migration to China, 1940s–1960s

Dearest Father and Mother:

Farewell, now nothing can stop me from [going to China and] taking up arms . . . . Before leaving, I am sorrowful beyond belief, and in every minute, multiple conflicts arise repeatedly within my heart. Home is that which I adore, my parents and brothers and sisters are those whom I love. But the broken ancestral homeland is even more that for which I feel passionate yearning and concern . . . . When the ancestral homeland is facing its moment of greatest danger is precisely when young people must rouse themselves and render service.[1]

The author of this letter, Bai Xueqiao, was part of a remarkable phenomenon that swept through Southeast Asia during the 1940s–'60s. During these decades, ethnic Chinese living outside China re-migrated to their ancestral homeland, escaping persecution in their lands of settlement or "returning" to a place that they had never seen in order to help build a nation to which they felt they belonged. Between 1949 and 1970, the ranks of these re-migrants swelled to an estimated half-million.[2] Initially hailed by the Chinese government as patriots and contributors to the post-1949 Communist society, returned overseas Chinese in later decades fell prey to growing hostility and persecution because of their so-called bourgeois backgrounds, links to foreign countries, and perceived lack of authentic Chineseness.[3]

Many educated overseas Chinese women in their teens and twenties who had been born and bred in British Malaya and Singapore joined this return migration movement with enthusiasm. As products of Chinese-language girls' schools, these women adopted ideals of political activism and ethno-national pride. They tapped into networks via their educational institutions to enable their physical and political movement across national borders. Yet they found themselves unable to reconcile these ideals with either the colonial or Chinese national environments in which they resided. The transnational circumstances of their upbringing and education rendered them, despite their best efforts, ineligible for authentic national belonging. This was a fate that was common to many Chinese re-migrants, but for women in particular, there were additional dimensions of marginalization that constrained their lives. These women's narratives of their experiences are varied: some are heroic, as in the case of Bai Xueqiao, and some have more poignant outcomes. But all are shot through with a strand of nationalism that has at once embraced Chinese women as vital elements of a greater political project and restricted the construction of their personal identities and recollections.

Chinese historical and popular discourse often refers to these re-migrants as "returning sojourners" (guiqiao 归侨). This label suggests, rather misleadingly, that these individuals were temporarily abroad and that China was a permanent homeland to which return was only natural. There are no perfectly accurate terms for describing this population. "Returnee" and "returned overseas Chinese" are problematic for the same reason as "returning sojourners." "Re-migrant" is not entirely accurate for those who were descended from migrants but who had not themselves migrated in the first place and who were often born and bred in their parents' or grandparents' land of settlement. The debate over this terminology reminds us that it was no simple thing to be an ethnic Chinese living outside China. There was an aura of permanent foreignness attached to this population by dint of their ethnicity and existing norms about national belonging, and this perpetual state of alienation clung to them even upon their "return" to the mainland. This chapter uses the term "re-migrant" as it captures, however imperfectly, the repeated cross-border movement of these historical actors' families, and the sense of homecoming for which they yearned. On occasion, the term guiqiao is also used to reflect re-migrants' self-perceived and externally imposed notion of an ineluctable belonging to China.

For women educated in overseas Chinese-language girls' schools, their youth was marked by traditional expectations and non-traditional freedoms. The message they received in school was that they should be modern, in the sense of acquiring skills and knowledge in a particular set of subjects, and also by developing a strongly ethno-cultural and nationalistic identity. At the same time, there were still clear rules of social propriety to obey and well-defined roles of wife and mother to fulfill. When the opportunity came for some of them to leave their homes and join a political cause, the fact that they breached convention to do so was at least somewhat ameliorated by their enrollment in schools in China—now a "proper" and socially acceptable occupation for young women. Re-migrant overseas Chinese women speak proudly of their tertiary degrees and qualifications, and the jobs that they held afterward: high school and university teachers, accountants, government officials. Both before and after their symbolic homecoming, these women found their road paved and protected by the institution of female education, even as it gave them a non-gendered framework within which they could situate their actions.

Bai Xueqiao was in her nineties when I met her in 2006, but she recalled with great clarity the moment when her adventures began back in 1939. At age twenty-five, prompted by letters from a male friend who was a poet in the province of Fujian, she ran away from her upper-middle-class home on the Malayan island of Penang to join the anti-Japanese war effort in China.[4] Since she knew her parents would never assent to her going, she secretly accumulated clothing and supplies in a friend's home while sign-ing up with the Overseas Chinese Engineer Corps. Eventually, there would be only three other women enlisted in this group of thousands. She also composed a farewell letter to her parents that was later published in a local Chinese-language newspaper. Its dramatic quality captured the imagination of readers throughout the region and it became so famous that it eventually made its way into the official archives of Guangdong province in China.[5] On the day of her departure, Bai's father, a merchant, discovered her plans and desperately sought to stop her. But he was unable to change her mind, and for several hours before her ship set sail, "father and daughter sat silently face-to-face, unable to speak for sorrow."[6] Several of her classmates from her alma mater, the Fukien Girls' School (later re-named the Penang Chinese Girls' High School), also showed up at the dock to speed her on her way.

The scene conjured up by this farewell recalls another moment of mar-itime departure by a group of revolutionary women depicted in radical activist Qiu Jin's short story, "Stones of the Jingwei Bird."[7] In that tale, which was unfinished at the time of Qiu's execution for treason in 1907, a sworn sisterhood of rebellious young women run away from their homes in China to pursue education in Japan. Leaving behind their traditionally minded families, rejecting the arranged marriages and male domination that would have hijacked their lives, these young women embody the spirit of optimism and adventure:

It is said that the girls boarded the ship, which set sail after the whistle was sounded three times. They stood at the railing holding hands and turned to look back at their distant homeland far away, engulfed in the evening clouds . . . . Facing the wind, they clapped their hands and chatted about their lives . . . . How great these girls' ambitions must have been to break through such barriers! They had gone 1000 *li* from home, and now they were traveling 10,000 *li* as fast as the wind. Everyone on board looked at them and thought, "The new learning will surely thrive. One day these girls will act as the bells of freedom and save the motherland."[8]

Although Bai was sailing toward and not away from China in 1939, she was, like these young women, embarking on a patriotic mission.

Upon arriving in China, Bai found that despite the political rhetoric urging young men and women alike to return from living overseas to their homeland, authorities were ill prepared for housing and placing female volunteers. At this time, the Sino-Japanese War had already begun, and conditions for work and travel were perilous. Bai traveled hundreds of miles over land, hoping to join the Communists at their base in Yan'an but was turned away with the advice that "one can fight the Japanese in many ways." Disappointed, she changed her plans and went back to school, graduating from university in 1943 and returning to Penang in 1946.

At home, Bai joined the Fukien Girls' School as a teacher but was fired for "anti-British activities." She then took a job as a principal at a smaller school. In 1949, from campus grounds, she caused an island-wide furor by becoming the first person in Penang to raise the red, five-starred flag of the new People's Republic of China. She had seen a picture of the flag in a newspaper and had secretly commissioned a tailor to make one. Blacklisted by the British colonial authorities for being a Communist insurgent, she was soon arrested and locked up in a prison camp where she was interrogated, in vain, every day for two months. She was detained throughout the next year, during which time she surreptitiously organized study sessions for fellow inmates.

In 1950, she and several other political undesirables were placed on a ship and unceremoniously deported to China, where her career and reputation flourished. This time, her departure from Southeast Asia was permanent. For the next several decades, she taught in prominent schools and colleges and worked at the Guangzhou Ministry of Culture, retiring at the age of seventy. Somewhere along the way, she changed the last character of her given name from the traditional and feminine *jiao* (娇), meaning tender, to the tougher, more masculine-sounding *qiao* (樵), meaning woodcutter.

After the Cultural Revolution of 1966–76, as China shifted into a new era of economic liberalization and eased restrictions on international travel, Bai recorded her thoughts about her life's journey in her diary:

> After these ten years of upheaval, someone asked me: do you regret having come back in the first place? I was pained; should one feel regret over returning to one's own homeland? After the breaking up of the "Gang of Four" [at the end of the Cultural Revolution], someone then asked me: are you leaving? Why [would I] leave, do they not know after that losing one's homeland or having one's homeland fall behind [other countries], then no matter where one goes, one can only be like a wandering orphan?[9]

The ties that bound the overseas Chinese to China, particularly in the decades following the Communist Revolution of 1949, are common themes in the historical narrative of twentieth-century China. Connections with China existed at multiple levels, from remittances for family or business reasons and wartime financial contributions; to voluntary and involuntary repatriation; to governmental efforts by the Qing at the turn of the twentieth century, the Kuomintang administration during the 1920s–'40s, and the Chinese Communist Party from 1949 onward.[10] In 1909, China introduced legislation based on the principle of *jus sanguinis*, whereby those born to a Chinese father or mother would be regarded as a Chinese national regardless of birthplace. For better and worse, these connections generated an image of ethnic Chinese overseas as being irrevocably linked to their ancestral homeland. Yet comparatively little is known about the gendered dimensions of these networks. Women tend to emerge mostly in the context of family, as wives and mothers left behind by a largely male emigrant population, or in fears and scandals over marital infidelity and illegitimate sons.[11] Compared to their well-studied male counterparts, female migrants, or re-migrants, are ciphers in the historical record. Who were these women who defied the gender conventions of their generation? How did they decide to re-migrate, and what were the consequences of their actions? Given that many of them seem to have been politically influenced by their experiences in overseas Chinese girls' schools, are they the ultimate success story for institutions seeking to inculcate diasporic nationalism, as politics trumped social conservatism to propel these women into radical activism? To date, few systematic attempts have been made to document the lives of these re-migrant women, whose narratives have often been submerged in more general accounts of returned overseas Chinese.[12] While they may not have been a large majority of the overseas Chinese female population, their actions show that there was greater diversity, depth, and ability to take political action among these women than previously realized, and that transnational female networks which sprang up around Chinese girls' schools facilitated vigorous movement of people and ideas.

The experiences and self-narratives of overseas Chinese women who re-migrated to China during the 1940s and 1950s highlight the complex effects of early twentieth-century Chinese nationalism as it acquired a transnational reach among a female constituency. Overseas Chinese girls' schools were instrumental in transmitting political ideology from the mainland to its diaspora, transforming the lives of ethnic Chinese women by giving them new options for configuring their ethnic, national, and gender identities, and politicizing some of them sufficiently to detach themselves from their natal homes in a quest for an ancestral home. Yet these options could not be exercised freely or simply. Identity was not just a matter of individual choice, and others' expectations of what it meant to be Chinese and female, whether outside or within China, continued to impinge on these women's lives. Recounted here, their stories draw from a series of interviews that I conducted with fifteen overseas Chinese women who re-migrated to China during the 1940s and 1950s. These interviews took place in the southeastern provinces of Fujian and Guangdong, from which many migrants to Malaya and Singapore originated.[13]

The history of these re-migrant women reveals some unanticipated and paradoxical dimensions of overseas Chinese female education. First, by attending girls' schools, these women learned to act and see themselves as non-gendered individuals. Despite having contravened a number of gender role expectations in overseas Chinese society—outwardly rejecting filiality and domesticity, for example—these women did not factor gender into their self-narratives, even as they acknowledged that they had engaged in a striking act of rebellion against social norms. In the process of breaking with tradition, re-migrant women found it more logical and justifiable to portray their actions as stemming from Chinese patriotic fervor rather than anything else, that is, using nationalism rather than gender as the "authorizing discourse" of their lives and identities.[14] Second, these women may have appeared to be rebelling against norms of politico-cultural identification according to certain overseas Chinese and British colonial strictures, but they were in fact conforming to norms of Chinese ethno-nationalism and sociopolitical revolution. In China, the Communist nation-state had become the dominant sphere within which it was acceptable for a woman to depart from conventional gender roles and to take on a new persona—that of national citizen. The fact that some Chinese women chose un-gendered citizenship over feminist identity as a means of claiming a greater voice in the nation is itself a gendered statement, pointing to potential for empowerment as well as the difficulties faced by women in joining a project in which the default category of citizenship was male. Educated overseas Chinese women were at once liberated and limited in their ability to construct their identities with the flexibility and hybridity that is often seen as a defining characteristic of the diaspora.

It is important to remember that individuals such as Bai Xueqiao were a minority in Malaya and Singapore. After more than 500 years of sojourning and settling in Southeast Asia, ethnic Chinese had formed communities that maintained cultural and sometimes political ties with their places of origin but that had also acculturated, assimilated, and rooted themselves in their places of settlement. Despite its ethno-cultural and frequently Chinese nationalist orientation, overseas Chinese education did not necessarily result in pro-China political thought. Many graduates of these schools identified culturally as Chinese but politically as British subjects, or, after the 1950s, as Malayan or Singaporean. Most did not even consider, let alone take, the extreme action of re-migration, even as postcolonial nationalism in post–World War II Southeast Asia began to destabilize the security of overseas Chinese communities.[15] There were nonetheless notable episodes of forced repatriation to China, such as the re-migration of more than 100,000 ethnic Chinese from Indonesia in 1959 in response to the introduction of anti-Chinese legislation.[16]

It may seem curious, then, to focus on a population that was a nonrepresentative minority. This is especially so when their story appears to confirm stereotypes of overseas Chinese as "essential outsiders," eternally loyal to the ancestral homeland, and whose efforts at cultural preservation, through Chinese-language education, perpetuate this sense of diasporic nationalism.[17] Yet a closer examination shows the over-simplified nature of that view. The politicization of overseas Chinese schools and some of its denizens was a reality. However, it was by no means evenly spread or complete. There were also unintended consequences and failures to bring this politicization to its desired conclusion, that is, inclusion in the "home" nation. Overseas Chinese nationalism was not uniformly distributed and much harder to put in practice than the rhetoric and laws of mid-twentieth-century political authorities—British, Chinese, Malayan, and Singaporean—would suggest. If anything, it appears that in their quest to reject marginalization and assert their Chineseness, the women in these stories exchanged one form of hegemonic identity for another.

One of the biggest obstacles to researching the history of re-migrant overseas Chinese women is the paucity of documentation about them. Present-day observers have to rely on newspaper reports and personal accounts to reconstruct their past. These sources are necessarily subjective. Public accounts reflect the ideological prejudices of the place, time, and state authority from which they originate, while oral histories are shaped by the vagaries of human memory and rationalization. Extant newspaper sources with information on returned overseas Chinese, such as the *Fujian Qiaoxiangbao* (Fujian Overseas Chinese Newspaper) and *Guangdong Qiaobao* (Guangdong Overseas Chinese Newspaper), only offer issues from the late 1950s and 1960s. Given their official mandate to promote a positive image of re-migrants, articles, some autobiographical, depicting the successful transformation of pampered overseas Chinese youth into patriotic, hardworking students or farmworkers must be interpreted cautiously.[18] Oral histories can help to compensate for this gap, but analyses of these histories must account for the subjective nature of personal narratives and the unavoidable impact that political situations and interviewer-interviewee interactions can have on these recollections.[19] At the same time, the value of this subjectivity is the insight that it gives us into individual perspectives and lived experiences, and the efforts that are made on a private rather than a state level to manage memories of the past.

YOU CAN'T GO HOME AGAIN: OVERSEAS CHINESE "RETURN" MIGRATION

Ethnic Chinese in Southeast Asia began to re-migrate to China in significant numbers during the early to mid-twentieth century. From the late Qing and early Republican period (1900s–1949) to the first decade of the People's Republic (1949–1959), a conscious effort by successive governments to harness the political loyalties and economic contributions of overseas Chinese attracted hundreds of thousands of re-migrants. Some of these re-migrants were sojourners who had made good abroad and wished to retire at home. Others were political and economic refugees. Still others simply sought a better life than they had found abroad. Republican and Communist governments alike welcomed them with dedicated policies and organizations such as the Kuomintang's Overseas Chinese Affairs Commission (established in 1928) and the Chinese Communist Party's Overseas Chinese Affairs Office (established in 1949).[20] Authorities created favorable provisions for returnees, such as work and housing assistance, educational privileges including reserved places at universities and the automatic addition of points in examination results, and even resettlement villages for overseas Chinese and their families.

Changes in the international political landscape either encouraged or forced such movement. The 1949 Communist revolution inspired some Chinese living abroad to re-migrate to partake of what seemed a hopeful new age, once the nation had overcome a century of foreign imperialism and socioeconomic chaos. In the British colonies of Southeast Asia, as the post–World War II era brought intimations of the end of empire, authorities struggled to contain the threat of Communist infiltration in their jurisdictions. The Malayan Emergency, which lasted from 1948 to 1960, was a state of emergency declared by the British in Malaya and Singapore as they battled an armed Communist insurgency that was primarily led by ethnic Chinese. During this period, the Chinese community was closely monitored, with policies such as forced relocation of low-income Chinese residents into guarded enclaves and tight supervision of activities in Chinese-language schools—including girls' schools. Between 1950 and 1952 alone, more than 15,000 overseas Chinese from Malaya re-migrated to China.[21]

Educated Chinese youth abroad were particularly affected by the return migration trend. Before 1949, Chinese schools abroad were already battle-grounds for the competing factions within China: reformists, revolutionaries, and, later on, Republicans and Communists. After its victory in 1949 and up to the mid-1950s, the Chinese Communist Party was keen to build up its population of educated youth in order to staff its industrial development program.[22] It actively courted Chinese school graduates in the British colonies of Malaya and Singapore, who were already facing uncertain futures as they struggled to compete with their English-educated peers for places in higher education and jobs in a British colony. Confronted with these obstacles, these graduates turned to China, where educational and work opportunities combined with a newfound sense of optimism in China's future. By 1958, official Chinese sources reported that 250,000 Chinese abroad had "returned," of which 20 percent were upper secondary and tertiary school students.[23] Official newspapers in China, for and about the overseas Chinese, trumpeted the success of return migration policies, with morale-boosting articles titled "Returned Overseas Chinese Students Everywhere Are Improving Greatly" and "Education Efforts for Overseas Chinese Should Be Taken Seriously and Encouraged."[24]

No reliable statistics are available as to how many of these *guiqiao* were women, but, in interviews, women from Malaya who attended Chinese girls' schools during this period recalled times when they would go to the train station almost every weekend to bid farewell to classmates leaving for China. "Some of these girls were leaving without their parents' knowledge and knew they would never be able to come back [to Malaya]," one woman reminisced. "We didn't dare to contact them after that . . . . [W]e never saw them again."[25] Several interviewees recounted experiences in their youth that spoke vividly of their idealism and activism, leading to their repatriation to China. One woman recalls that her determination to re-migrate was so strong that when her first few attempts to run away from home in Penang were foiled, she simply kept trying until she succeeded.[26] When another woman was detained in a prison camp in Malaya pending deportation by the British authorities on suspicion of Communist activities, she organized classes for the illiterate girls and women in her unit and led hunger strikes to demand better conditions for prisoners. She recalls with particular humor and relish how she faked death during one of the hunger strikes to terrify her wardens and sent political messages to compatriots using a code based on Romanized Chinese.[27] Notably, the girls and women who left for China were overwhelmingly from Chinese-language schools. For linguistic as well as political reasons, return migration to China was nearly unheard of among English-educated Chinese girls and women.

Many in China were suspicious about *guiqiao* motives, and their special privileges elicited resentment. Despite the fact that many of them had returned to China for patriotic reasons, or at least to join China's educational system, and some had even participated in Communist activity in Southeast Asia and China, returned overseas Chinese were considered "usable but not trustable" (*keyong bukexin*), a phrase used independently by a number of interviewees in separate conversations. This echoed a long-standing official attitude, entrenched since the fifteenth century, of negative views toward those Chinese who had seemingly deserted their homesteads to seek profit or engage in political mischief abroad and who would be troublemakers upon their return.[28] By the late 1950s, the tide of popular opinion turned even more strongly. Under the Second Five-Year Plan, China's economic focus shifted to intensive agricultural collectivization, undermining the rationale for importing more Chinese students from abroad. These same returnee youth, upon whom so many privileges had been lavished, were perceived to be wanting in their academic achievements and revolutionary ardor: needing remedial lessons in Chinese language, overly accustomed to material comforts, unwilling to shed their intellectual roles to labor alongside the peasantry. In 1957, official newspapers for and about the overseas Chinese began to air doubts about the scholarly ambitions of *guiqiao* students: "Returned Overseas Chinese Youth Discuss Whether Not Seeking Higher Education Means They Will Have No Future—If All Seek Higher Education, Who Will Engage in Production?"[29]

The 1960s saw a further emphasis on agricultural production and an even dimmer view of favorable treatment for re-migrants. Newspapers prominently featured articles such as "The Village Is Limitlessly Good," about the successful conversion of an overseas Chinese student into a farmworker, and "She Resolutely Refused to Ask For Special Treatment," about another such student who declined special privileges, focusing instead on sacrifice for and loyalty to the party.[30] In the mid-1960s, the Cultural Revolution swept many re-migrant overseas Chinese off to rural villages for their "incorrect class backgrounds" and ties to foreign countries. Some policies subjected *guiqiao* to labeling as landlords or capitalists, confiscation of property, and in the case of students, re-education or work assignments in the countryside. One interviewee possessed excellent revolutionary credentials: she had belonged to a Communist underground student organization in 1940s Singapore, married a man in the Malayan Communist Party, and returned to China shortly after 1949.[31] Nonetheless, she was "sent down" to labor in rural areas during the Cultural Revolution and endured multiple criticism sessions. Only in the 1980s were re-migrants like her considered rehabilitated and acknowledged as authentic revolutionaries. Some interviewees mentioned that they were eventually given the privilege of taking "veteran cadre retirement" (*lixiu*) instead of normal retirement (*tuixiu*) because they had returned to China to take part in revolution and nation-building. As a result, they enjoyed higher status and a better pension. But this privilege was conferred only after close government investigation into their pasts, reflecting a deep and ongoing suspicion of returned overseas Chinese.

In light of this history, Bai Xueqiao's story takes on new layers of meaning. Hers is an idealized narrative, one that has been polished by repeated telling and publication in government media, and that is congruent with state-approved images of returned overseas Chinese. Upon her death in 2014, state television in China broadcast a tribute that praised her love of country, featuring quotes from her now-famous letter of farewell to her parents.[32] Youthful patriotism, influence from mainland Chinese intellectuals, defiance of foreign imperialist authorities, and a fiery spirit that manifested itself through sacrificing the comforts of a bourgeois home in Southeast Asia for the unknown perils of wartime China—all the elements of an exemplary citizen's life story are present in this account. Other re-migrant overseas Chinese women who were not nearly as famous or fortunate as Bai had more complicated stories to tell. Before their so-called return to their ancestral homeland, their sense of being Chinese had been unambiguous. But after their return, their struggles to assimilate and to find acceptance among their fellow Chinese challenged this sense of ethno-cultural and national belonging. Their recollections of their experiences in repatriation reflect this tug-of-war between inclusion and alienation.

"YOUR DAUGHTER IS UNFILIAL": NARRATIVE, EXPERIENCE, AND INTERNAL CONFLICT

Few re-migrant overseas Chinese women led lives that were as closely documented by historical archives and official media as Bai Xueqiao's, but most of the women profiled here shared several traits with her. Now in their seventies and eighties, they were born and/or raised in Southeast Asia, typically in working- or middle-class families, were educated in overseas Chinese schools, and re-migrated to China during the 1940s and 1950s. Along with these biographical commonalities, there are also two major themes that recur in their stories: unanticipated difficulties in assimilating into Chinese society, and the dominance of nationalist over gender priorities in their self-narratives.

Reflecting on their experiences with re-migration, interviewees were generally upbeat, at least initially and superficially. Even though scholarly literature and oral histories indicate that decades of hardship were visited upon returnees from the 1950s up to the early 1980s, only one of the fifteen women whom I interviewed was openly bitter about having re-migrated to China. They were unanimous in their opinion that mainland Chinese women enjoy a great deal more social equality and female emancipation than their Southeast Asian Chinese counterparts. Most stated that they were very satisfied with their treatment by the government while in school and during their working years. When they were finally allowed to visit Malaysia and Singapore during the 1980s, some of their Southeast Asian friends and relatives asked if they felt any sorrow over the sacrifices they had made. As one woman defiantly declared, "I said to them, the word regret has never even floated across the ocean of my mind."[33] Few, if any, were as clear as Bai was in her farewell letter to her parents, in which she offered some words of self rebuke: "your daughter is unfilial."[34]

Official restrictions on my access to interviewees and the likelihood of self-censorship on their part meant that I simply might not have encountered individuals who could have spoken differently. Several of the interviews took place in group settings, with interpreters, family members, or colleagues present, which limited opportunities for frank expression of opinion. Ultimately, it is impossible to gauge with complete accuracy whether returned overseas Chinese women philosophically have no regrets about their youthful actions, are rationalizing them to justify lifetimes of sacrifice and struggle, are now masking their true feelings for the sake of political correctness, or, most likely, some combination of all of these factors.

Even with these restrictions on expression, some of these women were able to convey an ambivalence that belied their positive outlook. For example, no matter how strong the pull of the ancestral homeland, there was also no hiding the fact that families and friends were left behind in Southeast Asia, sometimes never to be seen again. There was also no eliding the widespread turbulence of the Cultural Revolution era. When asked about their lives in the 1960s, several interviewees blandly but clearly mentioned being "sent down" more than once, joining the estimated seventeen million urban educated youth who were relocated by government authorities to the countryside for work or ideological re-education. They also recalled that returned overseas Chinese were "severely investigated" and that they had no choice but to sever connections with their families and friends in Southeast Asia for a number of years. For those who had been especially bold in their revolutionary activities, there was a quiet but deep frustration that their service to the nation and the mistreatment they had endured had never gained official acknowledgment. In the three personal narratives below, which illustrate the diverse paths that could be taken to "return" to China, these themes recur with poignant frequency.

Cai Jianyu: "I Wished to Leave but Could Not, Wished to Return but Had No Way"

At the end of a group interview session in which she had said very little, Cai Jianyu came up to me and quietly slipped me a copy of a newspaper article she had written. "Mother, I Am Your Daughter!" was a first-person essay about the heartbreak of returning to Singapore after decades of not having been in contact with her mother, only to find that her mother had senile dementia and was completely unable to recognize her. In the article, she states that when her mother had lamented several years earlier that she should have returned to see her father before he died, "little did [Mother] know that her daughter wished to leave but could not, wished to return but had no way."[35]

Cai Jianyu is a third-generation Singaporean Chinese whose grandfather migrated to Southeast Asia in the late nineteenth century from Chaozhou, in Guangdong province. Born in Indonesia in 1929, she was seventy-seven years old at the time of our interview. Growing up in a family with eight sisters and five brothers, she remembers that her household was pervaded by a strong sense of boys being favored over girls. "My father felt that there were too many daughters," she says. Nonetheless, he was sufficiently influenced by contemporary social trends to allow some of his daughters to attend school. Cai, the fourth of nine girls, watched her older sisters attend primary school but either drop out before finishing or get married soon after.[36]

Cai recalls yearning for education and independence. "I was afraid of my father and wanted to escape his tyranny," she explains. She convinced him to send her and one of her sisters to Nanyang Girls' High School in Singapore, where she attended upper secondary classes. Just a year later, in 1949, she joined a group of classmates and went to China. She attributes her actions to the influence of her teachers and local organizations. Several male and female teachers at Nanyang Girls' School at this time were Chinese intellectuals, she recalls. There were also many groups and activities centered around the promotion of Chinese culture and politics, such as the Chinese Cultural Organization and Chinese Choral Group, in which she recalls singing "progressive songs."

Wishing to progress beyond secondary education, Cai applied to colleges in Hong Kong. "I wanted to learn a skill," she declares. She wrote a letter to her father appealing for support, and when he refused to provide it, she went on a hunger strike to plead her case. Interestingly, more than one interviewee mentioned the tactic of going on a hunger strike to protest her lack of access to education. Although they did not mention it, it is possible that they had learned of this tactic being used by British suffragettes in the 1900s and 1910s as a means of politicizing their bodies in a quest to win the right to vote.[37] Finally, an older brother agreed to give Cai financial support. However, the school in Hong Kong was closed because of political unrest, so she decided to try China instead.

Cai did not wish to elaborate on her life in China. All she would say was that she went to remedial tuition classes and did accounting work until 1976. At an unspecified time, she said that her daughter had been assigned to work in a rural village but suffered from ill health, so Cai volunteered to take her place. Now retired, she leads a quiet life. Her article, mentioned above, was published in 2004, perhaps during a window of time when state authorities had relaxed restrictions on recounting such stories publicly.

Yin Ling: The Treatment of Returned Overseas Chinese Was "Up to Fate"

A similar sense of ruefulness colors the recollections of another interviewee from Singapore, now living in Xiamen, whose revolutionary activities overseas did not translate into as much success as she had hoped in China. Although she smiled her way through our carefully worded one-on-one conversation, this woman would, after recounting a difficult experience, either lapse into a long silence or look me in the eye and ask earnestly, "Wouldn't you say that this was a pitiable situation?"[38]

Born in 1932 to migrants from Fujian, Yin Ling recalls that a family tradition of high educational attainment inspired her to attend Chinese schools in Singapore. Her strongest memories of her school years were of strict discipline, impressionable students, and little or no authorized contact with young people from other schools. "We secondary school students were muddle-headed. Fortunately our leaders had the right way of thinking," she states. Academic work did not make as deep an impression on her as did political activity. While at Nanyang, she joined an underground Communist organization whose leader was from Beijing. The organization maintained a system with only two to three members per cell to limit each member's knowledge about other members. Still, Yin had the sense that membership as a whole was large and included students from several other local Chinese schools, such as Hua Ch'iao Girls' School, Nan Ch'iao Girls' School, and Chinese Boys' High School. She even attended group meetings as a representative for her school. Reminiscing, she says, "I was only sixteen or seventeen at the time. I didn't know anything. I just thought political activity was fun!"

Shortly after the 1949 revolution, Yin left for China and never returned. She went to the Beijing Returned Overseas Chinese Association for help and managed to gain entrance to university. Her education was interrupted when she was "sent down" to a village in Sichuan for a year. She insists that she did not receive any special treatment because of her returnee status. "During this time, I only wrote to my parents—no one else. I didn't stay in touch with friends or classmates either," she remembers. She was "sent down" to rural areas a total of three times. "The farmers were kind to me," she laughs. "They only asked me to spread grain out in the sun to dry! But I was also criticized very harshly."

After the Cultural Revolution, Yin found work as a legal aide. In her career, she says that as long as she was accepting of things beyond her control, life was not unhappy. "Because I graduated from university, of course my salary was higher than average. But when [official] people came and told me that I should relinquish my job posting to someone else [for political reasons], then of course that's what I did. Could I have said no?" After a further few decades of work, Yin was able to take honorable retirement (*lixiu*), which confers better status and pension than regular retirement (*tuixiu*)—but not before the Chinese Communist Party conducted a strict investigation to verify that she was worthy. They had to confirm that she had truly been involved in underground Communist activities in Singapore and was therefore a genuine revolutionary. According to Yin, she had not been able to talk freely about these activities as "it was not a good thing in the 1950s and 1960s." Fortunately, her former cell group leader from Beijing was able to vouch for her.

Looking back on her past, Yin states that she made many decisions "in a muddle." Reflecting on the experiences of other re-migrant overseas Chinese, she states that those who were more simple and straightforward in their personalities had an easier time of things in China. "They were not calculating or particular, and accepted orders well." Her assessment seems to be that life was smoother if one did not fight the system too much, an approach that was particularly true of re-migrant Chinese. Nonetheless, she repeated a number of times that authorities would check returnee backgrounds very carefully, and that several re-migrants were "criticized harshly." "Ultimately, some *guiqiao* had good lives, some had unhappy lives. It was all up to fate," she says.

Tang Meijun: "We Could Be Used but Couldn't Be Trusted"

Yet another interviewee who had risked her life to fight against the Japanese and the British with the Communist Malayan People's Anti-Japanese Army, but who was poorly treated during the Cultural Revolution because of her "bourgeois" family background, openly declared that she was sorry she had returned at all. "It would have been better if I had never come back," says Tang Meijun grimly. "I was treated like a Rightist, and I didn't dare to have any contact with [family members] outside the country. Once upon a time I loved to talk [and express my opinions]; after that, I didn't say much anymore."[39]

Born in 1924, Tang developed her passion for political activism in her Chinese girls' school in Malaya. According to her, "Hua Ch'iao was very progressive [i.e., politically active]. Our deputy principal had been sent over from China. But he attracted too much attention [because of his politics] and was deported by the British from Malaya. My class teacher at the time was a Kuomintang person." Tang became caught up in this swirl of activity. "I felt very free to say whatever I wanted in school. I loved my country and wanted to fight the Japanese. I was brave. But I didn't realize the trouble that I was causing my family. Because I was caught carrying out illegal activities"—that is, participating in clandestine Communist groups—"I was expelled from school in 1941, just before the Japanese arrived."

During the Japanese Occupation, Tang threw herself into organizations that were actively resisting the invasion. For her efforts, she and some fellow students were arrested and detained for three months by the Japanese. "But we were still very young, so they let us go," she says. Upon her release, she promptly joined a guerilla force that was part of the Communist Malayan People's Anti-Japanese Army (MPAJA).[40] She recalls her fighting days with relish. "We had many perilous encounters. There were times when we were surrounded completely and were in grave danger, but somehow I always survived. Once I had to hide in the midst of a small bamboo grove while bullets were flying all around me. I had to make myself very thin!" she laughs. There were more men than women in the MPAJA, and the women often did more of the behind-the-lines work, such as cooking and conducting propaganda sessions. Very few women were in general combat, and she proudly points out that she was one of them.

When the war ended in 1945, Tang became a member of the MPAJA's peacetime incarnation, the Malayan Communist Party (MCP). "There was work to do," she explains. "The country was liberated from the Japanese, but not truly independent" because of British colonialism. She traveled all over the country to spread anti-imperialist ideology. In 1946, she was sent to Singapore, where she joined a rubber factory workers' movement. Two years later, alarmed by the surge of Communist activity in Malaya, the British declared a state of emergency; the factory where she was based was shut down, and she reports enduring "severe repression" by the colonial authorities at this time.

In 1949, she "returned" to China. "I had to deceive my parents in order to go," she confesses. "They would never have allowed me to do such a dangerous thing." Presumably, they had not been aware of the extent of her involvement with the MPAJA. Because of her experience fighting with the guerillas, the People's Liberation Army in China recruited her and assigned her to do "women's work," namely, managing grain supplies for the troops. After a short stint, she went back to school, acquired a degree in accounting, and worked for several decades before taking honorable retirement.

Tang's connections with her family and colleagues suffered greatly due to her decision to re-migrate to China. Her parents joined her in China in 1957, although they were deeply unhappy about how events had transpired. "My mother accused me of doing harm to the family," she recalls. Tang also did not dare to maintain contact with her erstwhile comrades from the MCP, as the group fell out of favor with the Chinese Communist Party.

By all accounts, Tang had an impeccable set of revolutionary credentials that marked her for praise or at least acceptance in Communist China. However, she feels strongly that she did not receive the treatment she deserved. More than any other woman whom I interviewed, Tang Sujuan was bitter. "People in China were suspicious of the overseas Chinese," she says with anger. "They didn't understand the situation in Malaya and assumed that we could be used but could not be trusted."

Despite the pressures of having to hew to state-sanctioned narratives of their life experiences, these three women found ways to express their disillusionment or regret. For Cai, Yin, and Tang, their decisions to re-migrate to China clearly had an impact, largely negative, on themselves and their family members. Their well-meaning efforts to gain full membership in Chinese society were often frustrated, if not outright rejected, by the very nation they were attempting to serve. They had made a bold attempt to assert their ethnic and political loyalty to China, only to find that they were trapped in a limbo between their overseas and their ancestral homes. To these re-migrant overseas Chinese, geography was not destiny. This was a painful irony, as their act of re-migration, portrayed as startling, irrational, or even disloyal by some of their peers and the various governments under whose authority they lived, did not so much reflect rebellion as it did a desire to belong.

"WE SPEAK LIKE MACHINE GUNS": GENDER AND NATIONALISM IN FEMALE RE-MIGRANT NARRATIVES

Even though it seemed that the Chinese nation had not always served them well, female re-migrants still viewed patriotism as the defining feature of their actions, over and above that of being women who had departed radically from gender role conventions of their time. Given that schools were a common incubator for their political beliefs and that the Chinese-language girls' schools they attended grew out of the Chinese movement to modernize women as part of the nationalist project, the absence of credit given to these factors in these women's narratives is striking. Most of them were arguably exposed to local and international politics to a greater extent than their non-school attending peers as a result of being students or teachers in Malayan and Singaporean Chinese schools. Furthermore, institutions of higher learning in China, such as universities in Fujian and Guangdong that were expressly set up by and for overseas Chinese students, provided young women who had left their families and homes with a ready-made niche into which they could fit upon their arrival in China. Female education was thus a bridge for re-migration on both sending and receiving ends.

Most interviewees agreed that having the opportunity to expand their intellectual and physical scope of activities was key in sparking their activism. Given that governments at the time were highly sensitive to the potential threat of a Chinese Fifth Column, teachers in Chinese schools were under close scrutiny and forbidden to bring politics into the classroom. Nonetheless, interviewees described a broad range of ways in which they became politically aware and active: acquaintance with a friendly teacher who would stay after school to chat with them about her experiences overseas; friendships with classmates in dormitories who would introduce them to clandestine Communist organizations; participation in youth groups and choirs that were fronts for activist newsletter publishing; and even having neighbors and friends who joined the Malayan Communist Party guerillas and who persuaded them to run messages and supplies between jungle hideouts and villages. One woman from Malaya recounted how she joined a political youth group and the Malayan Communist Party during the 1940s and was able to leave her house freely to participate in their activities by telling her parents that she was going to English-language classes.[41]

Some women fell into political activism for the excitement that it offered. Yin Ling, the interviewee who had joined an underground Communist organization in Singapore when she was a teenager, said that she did so because she thought "political activity was fun."[42] Others describe being swept up in a widespread social movement. Another interviewee recalled how, at the age of fourteen during World War II in Japanese-occupied Malaya, she would transmit written messages hidden in bundles of firewood from townspeople to guerilla fighters hiding in the jungle. "It was highly dangerous," she conceded, but the pressure to join the struggle against the Japanese came from all quarters, ranging from the guerillas to classmates to her own parents, "who hated the Japanese very much and were supportive of resisting them."[43] One must also remember that not all activists were engaged in Communist-related movements. Another interviewee, Chen Yiming, who became the director of the Overseas Chinese Museum in Xiamen, Fujian, described being deported from Singapore for being a Communist in 1953, even though she did not identify as such at the time. Her real crime, she said, was impulsively standing up to join a crowd in shouting "Down with the British imperialists!" at one of the night classes she was attending. At the time, she says, she was not so much pro-Chinese Communism as she was anti-Western colonialism.[44]

In all these accounts, overseas Chinese education formed some basis for these women's engagement with Chinese nationalism. The presence of teachers who supported that mission was an influential factor. Li Yue was one such teacher who went from China to Southeast Asia during the 1930s and 1940s to spread "progressive ideas" or Marxist ideology among Chinese youth abroad. Just before World War II broke out, she went to

Malaya with her husband, an ethnic Chinese who was originally from Malaya, and lived there for nine years. For one of those years, she taught music at Kuen Cheng Girls' High School in Kuala Lumpur.

"It was very strict and conservative," she recalled disapprovingly of this girls' school.[45] "Too nunnery-like. Teachers would line students up and sniff around them to see if any were wearing perfume! They [i.e., the teachers] were all reactionary. Not one was progressive." Asked about the students, she said that they were "quite good. Very patriotic, except for the ones who were influenced by the running dogs of the British."

Li offered an internally contradictory view of her work as a teacher in Malaya. On the one hand, she declared that she did not intend to spread ideology. "I was pure in intention," she insisted. "I only wanted to teach music. I was focusing on things like melody and tune. I didn't participate in political activities." On the other hand, she taught students Chinese revolutionary songs, such as the "Yan'an Anthem," celebrating the legendary stronghold of the Chinese Communist Party, and got into trouble for it. "It was a nice song, and students loved it, but because I taught the song I was immediately pulled out of class and suspended from teaching activities." She was criticized by some of the other teachers, "[who were] probably sent there by the Kuomintang." Yet other teachers advised her against staying at Kuen Cheng, as there was too much danger of her being arrested for being a leftist. Almost as an aside, she mentioned that she also encouraged some students to go back to China and gave them advice on how to go about the journey. In 1950, Li returned to China with the Chinese People's Cultural Work Group. After a few years of "doing cultural work," singing and dancing to help spread government propaganda, she became a music teacher for the rest of her career.

What do the inconsistencies in Li's narrative mean? The first and most obvious point would be the political sensitivities that likely placed limitations on all my interviews. At the same time, Li's almost willful denial of her political motives seemed to be as much for herself as for her audience. In our conversation, Li demonstrated a sharp mind, earnest beliefs, and a teacher's passion for music education. She did not strike me as confused, guarded, or disingenuous. On the way out from our interview, as we walked through the garden of her apartment complex with two of her friends, she merrily tried to enlist them in singing some Communist songs from their youth. It seemed that maintaining an upbeat attitude toward past and present required a narrative in which her political faction meant and did no harm. Although she was not a re-migrant in the same sense as the Southeast Asian Chinese women, her sojourn in their world involved her in the same political forces that exerted pressure on so many at the time. Li, too, had to practice self-preservation even as she served a cause greater than herself. By now, it is fairly well known within China that many re-migrants did not escape the Cultural Revolution era unscathed. Perhaps her inability to integrate her political loyalties with her actions in overseas Chinese schools was due to the fact that she took pride in both and had difficulty reconciling the idealism of the 1950s–'60s *guiqiao* movement with the harsh realities that followed.

Despite the common theme of female education in their self-narratives, almost all interviewees were uninterested in any feminist explanations for their actions during and beyond their school years. Although a few women voluntarily brought up gender equality in our conversations, they were not *guiqiao*. Rather, they were teachers and intellectuals from China, such as Li Yue. Most re-migrant women stated that their political activism and beliefs in the 1940s–'60s centered on patriotic and anti-Japanese sentiments instead of any notion of gender equality. Some declared that they had "passed the May Fourth moment" and were concerned with "more important things now," such as national survival in the face of Japanese military aggression during World War II. In the case of Bai Xueqiao, whose farewell letter to her parents in 1939 acquired such fame, when asked whether feminist ideals had played any part in her choices, she seemed nonplussed. She felt that gender equality was to be assumed in socialist China and was not part of her life's struggle.[46] It is no coincidence that these women's self-narratives parallel the discourse on revolutionary women in contemporary Chinese literature, in which protagonists are commonly portrayed as realizing socialist rather than feminist ideals.[47]

The term "feminist" has complex meanings in this situation. The specific context of Chinese historical experience in the twentieth century demands caution in the usage of Western terminology to describe the actions and attitudes of individuals in this society. With regard to the re-migrant overseas Chinese women, one must consider what feminism means in the Chinese social context and how the language or terminology of feminism was used in my interviews with these *guiqiao*.

Conceptions of feminism in China over the course of the twentieth century evolved along a unique path, such that Chinese women of a certain generation seem to be wary of feminist discourse.[48] At the turn of the twentieth century, Chinese intellectuals sought to lift women out of a benighted, feudal past through education, scientific domesticity, and contribution to the new nation. At the same time, male elites shied away from other dimensions of female emancipation and liberty, fearing that "excessive modernization" was a Western disease. This tension between male elite priorities, the demands of New Women, and the phenomenon of the Modern Girl colored the emergence of urban feminism.[49] During the

Republican period from 1911 to 1949, civic education in some secondary schools helped encourage new attitudes toward women's political participation. Many girls' schools in the lower Yangzi region during this period included civic training, "such as Scouting and self-government, designed to prepare all students for full civic participation," thus creating opportunities for female students to "draw on their education to perform public civic action for the sake of the nation and therefore claim the 'independent personhood' (*duli renge*) that [had been] identified as the basis of modern Chinese feminism."[50] As socialist thought gained strength in the first half of the twentieth century, such notions of independence and women's rights soon gave way to the prioritization of class struggle over individualism and seemingly factional emphases on gender attributes. Eventually, because ideology dictated that the successful establishment of a socialist system would automatically lead to the liberation of women, gender equality was considered a non-issue in the years after the Communist revolution of 1949. It was a goal that was already achieved, a topic that no longer needed discussion.[51]

In addition to these vagaries in the fortunes of feminist ideology, the definition of feminism in China was complicated by its constantly changing nature. Over the decades, it was condemned by political elites as something that was, if over-emphasized, inimical to the cause of socialist revolution. At the end of dynastic rule and the commencement of Republican statehood in 1911, feminism was initially used to refer to "the exclusive advocacy of women's rights." Later, it was nested within the larger context of social change, indicating "the women's movement which worked to forward the interests of its members within the context of the wider revolutionary movement." From the mid-1950s onward, it became "a term of abuse referring to those who exclusively pursue women's interests without regard for the forms which political and economic systems take."[52] In its original incarnation as one of the rights of an individual, feminism came into direct conflict with the dominant notions of class struggle and collectivism in the Chinese Communist polity. Scholars of China have commented on the vexed relationship between nationalism and feminism from the late imperial through the Republican and Communist regimes, with the former ultimately subsuming any attempts at promoting the latter.[53] What is notable in this situation is the transnational dimension of Chinese nationalism, with groups in China exerting their influence over Chinese women living well beyond their physical and political boundaries, and these women interpreting and acting on their understanding of this ideology.

As a result, one of my primary challenges in conducting interviews with re-migrant overseas Chinese women was choosing appropriate terms for discussing the issue of women's liberation. We talked about women's rights (*nüquan* 女权), gender equality (*nanü pingdeng* 男女平等), and openness (*kaifang* 开放), terms that some scholars have designated as especially problematic in translation because of their political significances in Chinese discourse.[54] In our conversations, interviewees seemed to be in agreement with me and one another about what these terms meant. However, they simply did not find them useful in describing themselves. In fact, many had strong views about the relative state of women and gender equality in China as opposed to Southeast Asia, often giving unsolicited opinions about the traditionalism of Chinese women outside China. More than one interviewee declared that women in China enjoyed far more equal status with men, that they received not only the same educational but also work opportunities, and even that in speech and mannerisms they were stronger and more assertive than their counterparts in Malaysia and Singapore. One interviewee proudly pointed out that while I, as a Chinese female who grew up in Malaysia and Singapore, spoke politely and gently (*jianghua hen wenrou*), they spoke rapidly and forcefully, "like machine guns" (*women jianghua haoxiang jiguanqiang*).[55] To their minds, feminism had progressed further in socialist China than in relatively tradition-bound Southeast Asian Chinese communities. Taken together with the historical presence, however complicated, of feminist ideology in Chinese society, these personal sentiments indicate that re-migrant overseas Chinese women were and are aware of women's liberation and gender equality as positive developments.

In essence, overseas Chinese girls' schools were channels for transmitting both Chinese nationalism and its eventual submergence of feminist discourse. The rhetoric of women's liberation was available to and used by educated overseas Chinese women in the decades leading up to the 1950s, as evidenced by female students' writings on feminist issues in school magazines of that period. Yet re-migrant women did not partake of it during the 1940s and 1950s when they left Southeast Asia for China, and this still seemed to be the case fifty years later when they were reflecting on their experiences. Both before and after settling in China, overseas Chinese women were assimilated into an ongoing trend within China itself, whereby "the prioritization of the nation as the most meaningful context for feminine self-definition [resulted] in the rejection of crucial social solidarities," such as feminism itself.[56] The absorption of young women and their nonconformist actions into this movement meant that the narratives of their lives would almost invariably be contained within the context of nationalism rather than any subgroup identity, leading them to de-emphasize the possibility of having acted as individuals and women.

Because of the subjugation of gender equality to socialist revolution, Chinese women's emergence into the public sphere, which would once have been considered a feminist act, became co-opted by the state. Although this dynamic had already been present under the Nationalist regime, the totalizing nature of the Communist state took it even further. As they learned to make sense of their lives within this unforgiving political discourse, re-migrant overseas Chinese women learned to use nationalism as a way to account for their acts of rebellion and non-conformity. It was a dominant ideology to which they had no choice but to subscribe. It was also an effective and widely acceptable way to justify or even valorize their departures from traditional family and community expectations. The Marxist revolution in China gave working Chinese women who reached adulthood in the 1950s a positive way to frame their work outside the home—something that was once considered shameful was now patriotic and glorious.[57] Similarly, Chinese nationalism and political activism gave overseas Chinese girls and women a way to cast their activities outside the safe confines of home in a righteous and triumphant light. They were not simply rebels or individualistic youth. Rather, they were patriots and nationalists who were empowered to act by education.

More than half a century after their re-migration, Bai and her fellow *guiqiao* have come to represent different things to different people. They are used as symbols of China's gravitational pull on its global diaspora; as cautionary tales of youthful idealism gone awry; and, as has often been the case in Southeast Asia, as stereotypical examples of how ethnic Chinese settled in other countries are never quite completely loyal to their new homes, even if they have been there for generations. The fact that educated women were part of this movement seems to give additional weight to the last notion, as even a part of the population that lacked significant political and social freedom was pulled into the orbit of Chinese socialism because of the influences they encountered in Chinese-language schools.

However, closer examination of the re-migrant experience reveals a number of ambiguities and paradoxes that not only deflate the "essential outsider" myth but also suggest different significances to the presence of women in this movement. Overseas Chinese in Malaya and Singapore have had to negotiate an ever-changing terrain of ethnic and political identity options, even as the outcome of their choices was not entirely up to them, both overseas and in the ancestral homeland. As an immigrant minority in a European colony, they were acutely aware of being Chinese in an ethnic sense; upon their "return" to China, it was not their ethnicity that was at issue, but whether they were sufficiently Chinese in a political sense. In the latter case, re-migrating to China was insufficient for the realization of authentic Chineseness. In fact, *guiqiao* were often marginalized and treated with suspicion, much as they had been in the overseas colonies where they had felt unable to express fully the extent of their ethno-cultural identity.

From the experiences and self-narratives of re-migrant women, it is apparent that ethno-nationalist female education played an important and complex role in their politicization, prompting them to make non-traditional choices for their gender while limiting the ways in which they could account for these actions. These educated overseas Chinese women sought to break out of the strictures imposed by traditional gender norms and perceived political suppression in a Western colony, imagining that the inclusive nature of their new national identities would afford them greater freedom—only to find themselves marginalized once again by new forms of gender and political categorizations.

It is by now a commonplace that processes of migration, settlement, and assimilation over hundreds of years have led to a range of complex and fluid identities among diasporic populations, particularly among the far-flung overseas Chinese community. However, there is an important constraint on this flexibility. An important and unavoidable aspect of identity construction is not just how one perceives oneself but also how one is perceived by others. Rightly or wrongly, the latter can overshadow the former and is often intolerant of ambiguity. This was a difficult lesson in the global classroom of ethno-national politics, learned at significant cost by female as well as male students whose formal education introduced a transnational idealism that nationalism could not accommodate.

Today, reflecting on their past, re-migrant overseas Chinese women recall their youthful initiative and daring with pride, but they acknowledge the sometimes painful burden that they and their families have had to bear for their decisions. Returning to Bai Xueqiao's farewell letter to her family: what does it mean to adore one's home? And is it reasonable to expect that home will love you back? For a diasporic people, perhaps the concept of home is more akin to the concept of identity: possessing a certain quality of being rooted, authentic, and pre-existing, but always subject to choice and change. As the personal stories here attest, the act of homecoming is sometimes more gratifying at the point of embarkation and on the journey than upon the arrival at one's destination.

Conclusion

The Domestic Citizen and Female Education in the Postcolonial Era

For all its innovations and wide-ranging impact, the female education movement among the overseas Chinese in late colonial Malaya and Singapore was not a straightforward revolution. Most founders of girls' schools in this period did not intend to overturn all traditional cultural norms. Most of these institutions had agendas that did not necessarily align with those of other schools. It may be tempting to see girls' schools as part of an upward trend leading to empowerment, enlightenment, and liberation for women. Yet these schools were established and run by largely conservative male-dominated organizations, such as the church, the government, or leaders in politics and industry. In a patriarchal society, home and family were still a woman's foremost priorities, which she neglected at the peril of the colony or nation she had to serve. To the extent that educated Chinese women could work outside the home or show an interest in politics, they did so within the framework of female citizenship, a gendered concept that privileged nation-building at the expense of women's individual freedoms for several decades in the early to mid-twentieth century.

As tertiary education institutions appeared in Malaya and Singapore, female students were not a significant constituency. Most jobs that female secondary school graduates took on, such as teacher or clerical worker, were typically lower-level jobs that men vacated in order to enter higher-ranking and better-paid positions. While ethnic Chinese and Europeans alike linked female education to modernization, educated women faced a reality complicated by clashing forces of cultural preservation, ethnic nationalism, and colonial power. Not until the post–World War II sociopolitical upheaval of the late 1950s could Chinese women in Malaya and Singapore agitate for locally based social change in an organized fashion.[1] However, during this era of national independence in the late 1950s and early 1960s, political rather than cultural priorities came to bear ever more strongly on female education. The curricula of girls' schools were standardized under new national governments, and the energies of the schools were harnessed to produce the kinds of citizens, workers, and mothers that the new nations required. The time was well past when patriarchal authorities accepted that lack of schooling or confinement within the home was beneficial for a girl, but they did introduce a new set of criteria, economic and domestic, for judging whether she was fulfilling her responsibilities to her family, community, and nation. Even as women's rights and options expanded over time due to feminist activism, traditional gender role expectations found extended longevity, sometimes in girls' schools themselves.

Social attitudes about girls' schools in colonial Malaya and Singapore did not evolve in a linear fashion. Despite the common assertion by the British colonial administration and overseas Chinese community leaders that girls' schools were a manifestation of social progressiveness, female education was just as frequently conservative in design and implementation. Founders and supervisors of girls' schools often sought to promote certain idealized images of Chinese womanhood and to preserve an authentic sense of feminine ethno-national identity in the face of rapid sociopolitical change. In the arena of female education, a persistent battle took place between British imperial and Chinese nationalist visions of women's roles in society, between national and transnational pulls on individuals' loyalties, and between domestic and public expressions of femininity and Chinese ethnic identity. While missionaries and British colonials advocated European notions of domesticity, the Straits Chinese male elite pursued a vision of Anglicized femininity to raise their social status, and Chinese nationalists introduced a brand of modernization that was tied up with cultural conservatism and ethno-nationalism. Educated overseas Chinese women emerged from girls' schools both armed with and hampered by these conflicting influences. Despite these pressures, and their own internalization of restrictions upon their gender, these women's responses and actions demonstrate that they were catalysts of change in the communities in which they lived and worked.

In a diasporic and multiracial milieu, tensions between Western-style modernization and Chinese cultural conservatism shaped the character of communally organized Chinese-language girls' schools. These institutions operated with greater latitude than schools tied directly to colonial and national authorities, such as missionary societies and the British government. However, they were still bound by a sense of common cause with the early twentieth-century drive in China to defend its ethno-cultural authenticity and political autonomy. Overseas Chinese-language girls' schools introduced non-gender-specific curricula and new options for social and political identities for women, arguably doing more than their English-language counterparts to promote female emancipation, and exposing Chinese girls and women to cultural, political, and social influences that lay beyond the colonial purview. Insofar as British colonial educational policies were made with Chinese women in mind, they placed greater emphasis on securing the political loyalty of the Chinese population, or at least obviating the leftist threat, particularly during the 1950s when the threat of Communist infiltration from China seemed imminent. Colonial gender ideologies therefore did not, or could not, influence Chinese girls' schools to the same extent they did in English girls' schools. Over the decades, Chinese-language girls' schools actually shifted along the spectrum in the direction of greater social conservatism, if only in the name of preserving a culturally defined sense of ethno-nationalism. These constraints on educated Chinese women suggest that national identities, ethnic categories, and patriarchal structures, while somewhat flexible, were enforced strictly by political and social elites to preserve a certain status quo. Creating social change, even through institutions that appear to embody them, proved to be difficult.

Nowhere was the conflict between modernity and ethno-national authenticity more pronounced than in the case of the re-migrants from Malaya and Singapore to communist China in the 1940s and 1950s. Their political activism and departure from traditional gender norms rendered them ultra-modern, even radical, in the eyes of their peers and authorities in the homes they left behind. But in their own view, they were conservatives in a literal sense, seeking to preserve or reconstruct a sense of ethno-national loyalty. Ultimately, and to their detriment, they were viewed as neither authentically Chinese nor sufficiently patriotic by the very nation they so desperately wished to serve. The poignant experiences of these overseas Chinese returnee women show that migrant or diasporic identities were not nearly as fluid and negotiable as these individuals had hoped. Rather, categorizations of national and ethnic loyalty could be rigid, persistent, and sometimes unforgiving.

Independence from British colonial rule in the late 1950s brought a host of challenges for the new governments in what became the new nations of Malaysia and Singapore. Formal education was a key channel for the state in socializing its citizens, creating a cohesive national identity for a multiplicity of ethnic, religious, and linguistic groups. While the political context was new, this period was not exactly a fresh start. The race and gender ideologies of the imperial age did not completely dissipate but rather gave way to a new and equally thorny world of race-based politics and unequal gender relations. The colonial inheritance would also make itself strongly felt in education, where the linguistically plural system of schools had become so entrenched that attempts to dismantle it became flashpoints for inter-racial conflicts between the Malays and Chinese.

Malaya achieved national independence in August 1957, while Singapore became a self-governing city-state in 1959. Initially drawn together by what were thought to be common economic and political objectives, the two states merged to form Malaysia in 1963, but the union was short-lived. Divergences between ethnic Malay leaders in Malaysia and the primarily Chinese leadership in Singapore led to the rancorous departure of Singapore from Malaysia in 1965 and its achievement, however involuntary, of sovereign statehood. Each nation had its own unique demographic patterns and sociopolitical challenges. In 1965, Malaysia's population of approximately 8.4 million was composed of an almost 50 percent majority of indigenous peoples (including but not limited to Malays), almost a third ethnic Chinese, a tenth from South Asia, and a small percentage of other ethnicities.[2] From the beginning, Malaysia had to contend with broad ethnic, religious, and cultural diversity, contained within a political system that had to be delicately balanced among all factions. At this time, Singapore's population of approximately 1.8 million was dominated by a two-thirds majority of ethnic Chinese, with slightly less than 15 percent of Malays and less than 10 percent South Asians and other ethnicities.[3] Although, like Malaysia, it had struggled with inter-ethnic tensions and even racial riots in the years prior to national independence, Singapore was able to achieve greater political stability at a faster pace than Malaysia because of its small size, highly centralized government, overwhelming majority of one ethnic group, and sense of needing to rally around the urgent cause of national survival. As a tiny city-state with no natural resources, surrounded by larger and mostly Malay-dominated countries such as Malaysia and Indonesia, Singapore feared for its economic and political security—a spur to what was to become an authoritarian and paternalistic governing structure.

One feature that both states had in common was the importance of education in their mission to create a unified sense of national identity. In Malaysia, the persistence of a Chinese-language school system well into the postcolonial era meant that many ethnic Chinese students remained potentially beyond the direct influence of the state, unlike students in English- or Malay-language schools.[4] In Singapore, the majority Chinese population was subjected to a new, state-mandated educational system in which vernacular schools were marginalized and eventually replaced by an English-language system.[5] To achieve stability and integration, Malaysia and Singapore would have to undergo several years of educational reform and controversial debate, balancing the demands of various ethnic groups to preserve the teaching of their vernacular languages and cultures with the state's imperative to mold citizens into a standardized national pattern. Part of this reform included the provision of education for all children, regardless of race or gender, and the revision of school curricula to equip youth with the economic skills and social outlooks that would best serve the nation's needs.

The different political circumstances in Malaysia and Singapore eventually led to divergences in educational policies for girls and women. The deep social control wielded by the more stable and authoritarian Singaporean state allowed a more comprehensive effort to engineer gender roles, while the more ethnically fractious political situation in Malaysia weakened its ability to foreground a gendered curriculum. In both states, however, there was a common tension between educating women as part of economic and social modernization and preserving their traditional roles as wives and mothers in the domestic sphere.

On the eve of national independence in the late 1950s, Malayan and Singaporean advocates for female education championed their cause in language and ideologies similar to those of their colonial predecessors. An important continuity between colonial and postcolonial times was embedded in the ranks of the political elites in both states, where the transition from colony to independent statehood had taken place relatively peacefully, with the reins of power passing from the British to their anointed inheritors. In Malaya, the majority indigenous Malays dominated the political ranks, even as the British had brokered a power-sharing agreement that included some Chinese and Indian representation in government; in Singapore, the upper echelons were populated by the majority Chinese. In both cases, however, political leadership was strongly influenced by a largely English-educated elite, whose social attitudes regarding women were not so different from those in preceding decades. For political leaders, the purpose of girls' education was cultivating a trained wife and mother who would more effectively and scientifically manage the domestic sphere and serve as an effective teacher to her children.[6] This state-mandated construction of femininity was not far removed from philosophies of girls' schooling at the turn of the twentieth century. In 1959, Malay political leader Onn bin Jaafar pointed out the utility of teaching domestic science in school to prepare women for their most important career:

> There should be education in child welfare and homecrafts for women. As the main contribution of women in this country is the running of homes . . . they must therefore be educated to fit them for the duty of making their homes happy and healthy.[7]

In Singapore, proponents of women's rights also called for increased attention to girls' schooling, although they were more likely to portray their mission in terms of women's emancipation. Their language echoed that of Peranakan Chinese elites such as Song Ong Siang and Lim Boon Keng, as they called for the enlightenment of their women and hence their community as a whole, relative to standards that they believed had been set by the Western world. As put forth by a women's rights activist associated with the Singapore Council of Women, a political organization created in 1952 to campaign for gender equality, "the only solution to the problem of backwardness of women in the East is to raise their standards of education," and "so long as women in Malaya remain ignorant and illiterate, all attempts at progress in health and social welfare will be handicapped."[8]

Local politicians, educators, and activists in the 1950s and 1960s largely agreed on the importance of female education in preparing women for their future careers and in remedying the "backwardness" embodied by the uneducated girl. This did not seem to be an area of contention or controversy during this period. Rather, problems of vernacular schools, interracial harmony, and economic improvement preoccupied the minds of policymakers. Universal and equal access to education for all children was enshrined in the law, and boys and girls alike were encouraged to participate in extra-curricular activities, including sports and games, which were thought to help promote physical health and positive character traits. The specific educational needs of girls took a temporary backseat to developing a unified, coherent, and widely accessible educational system, with one dominant language medium of instruction, that would meet the needs of the citizenry and the state.[9]

This is not to suggest that concerns about gender roles and the socioeconomic contributions of educated women did not exist, particularly in the case of Singapore. While recognizing the need to garner the productivity that a female labor force could contribute to the nation, especially in a small city-state with few natural resources and that was hence heavily dependent on its human capital, the patriarchal state also harbored a deeply conservative view of women's domestic roles. These roles were threatened by the expansion of women's participation in the workforce beyond the household. State discourse on women recognized the imperative for female equality and emancipation but also valued women's contributions in the home above all else, hence reinforcing a traditional bias toward female domesticity.[10]

Such ambivalence was reflected in aspects of education that aimed at nurturing certain ideal feminine traits in girls and women. By 1966, after the basic structure of universal education had been put in place, attention shifted to tailoring school curricula to the specific needs of female students, particularly as they reached adolescence. Despite a concerted effort to provide technical or vocational training to girls so that they might contribute to the nation's economic growth, there was still a keen desire that they not neglect their primary roles as wives and mothers. This period, from 1968 to 1979, was one of vacillating state intentions and mixed messages about gender roles. On the one hand, as a Singaporean government minister exhorted in a speech to St. Margaret's Secondary School, girls should "work as hard as the boys and become not just good housewives but economic assets as well."[11] That same year, the Singapore Ministry of Education revised the secondary school curriculum to include "technical studies," or workshop classes, for all boys and half of all girls and urged schools to channel female students toward the pursuit of "technical careers." At the same time, in 1969, domestic science—renamed home economics—became a compulsory subject for all girls in the first two years of their secondary education. This move suggested that it was the feminine-domestic training route, and not technical studies, that was more vital in preparing girls for their future vocation. Government-issued syllabi and textbooks had already been conveying this message since the late 1950s, when the ministry had stated that the goal of teaching female students practical domestic science skills in cooking, hand- and machine-sewing, laundry work, and hygiene, at both primary and secondary levels, was "to train a girl to look after herself and her home in a sensible and economical manner."[12] Textbooks from the late 1960s picked up on this theme, impressing upon their female readers the duties that fell upon their shoulders:

> It takes a woman with the necessary knowledge and know-how to transform a house into a home . . . . It is hoped that with a little guidance and practice

together with the inborn artistic ability, the present schoolgirls will grow up into a generation of house-proud and efficient housewives.[13]

Chinese-language girls' schools, previously notable for their lack of emphasis on domestic science studies compared to English-language girls' schools, became part of this trend. In 1971, Nan Hwa Girls' School in Singapore marked the inaugural establishment of dedicated home economics classrooms on its campus. In a souvenir magazine published to commemorate this occasion, the head of the school board of directors opined that these facilities were "a vital site for the training of new women (*xinfunü*) who would be suited for a new age and the building for a new nation," as today's secondary schoolgirls who would become tomorrow's housewives (*jiating zhufu*) prepared to assume the "heavy responsibility" of taking care of their households.[14] Some students internalized these values, as a Nanyang Girls' High School student writing in the school magazine in 1960 shows:

> As [for being] a housewife, an educated woman knows how to nurse her husband and children when they are ill. From books of interior decoration, she will beautify her home and learn how to make delicious and nourishing food from cookery books. Moreover she will be a better companion to her husband in discussing many subjects, such as politics and business. Definitely she is a better mother who will bring up her children healthy both in mind and body, because in a family the mother has more influence [on] her children than the father.[15]

Here, the student's language aligns with that of Chinese nationalists advocating for the "mothers of citizens" model some sixty years earlier.[16]

In comparison with the earlier colonial period, there was no claim that these domestic skills would have any industrial or larger economic application, as previously argued by British officials during the colonial period who had hoped that handiwork skills among Malay girls would allow them to participate in cottage industries. Rather, the focus was on what women could and should do within the home, as part of their expected domestic responsibility. The significance of this role only seemed to expand as, over the next decade, the number of girls enrolled in technical studies failed to grow at the rate the Singaporean Ministry of Education had projected, and principals of girls' schools came to expect that the vast majority of their students would opt for home economics if given the choice.[17]

Female teachers were also subjected to a continuing discourse on the importance of maintaining their domestic orientation even if they chose to work outside the home. In the periodical *Singapore Teacher*, which was aimed at the predominantly female teaching population, articles such as

"Kitchen a Place of Pride for a Smart Woman" and "It's Back to School for Asian Wives" accompanied others entitled "Technical and Vocational Education for Girls Too."[18] The gendered orientation of these articles and publications was based on the fact that teaching had, since the time of national independence, gradually become a feminized profession. Lower-level white-collar jobs taken up by local men under the colonial administration were vacated as more senior and lucrative jobs became available to them, leading to women taking over these men's erstwhile positions in secretarial, health, education, and social welfare fields.[19] While not unique to Singapore, this phenomenon highlighted the gender-based response of the government to the situation. Since the early 1960s, women had been actively encouraged by the state to free up men for other, more technical work by taking over their former occupations. Yet even as women stepped into the educational breach, state anxiety about the feminization of the teaching profession began to build.[20] By the late 1960s, the Singaporean Ministry of Education worried that the existing curriculum and attitudes in schools did not do enough to encourage "ruggedness," a masculine quality that was deemed necessary for a strong society and that might not be adequately supplied by a largely female teaching staff.[21] This sentiment was echoed by some senior personnel in the Malaysian educational administration. According to a former inspector of schools in 1960s Malaya, an excess of "lady teachers" across all language-medium schools meant a lack of male role models for boys, both in physical and moral terms:

> They say if you cannot run faster than the boy, you don't coach them. Now you
> have ladies in the school, they have to take the role of PE [physical education]
> teachers . . . . Boys should be taught by boys! Now discipline in schools [is declin-
> ing] . . . . [M]aybe there are too many women teachers in boys' schools.[22]

On this front, the supposedly innate qualities that suited women for the teaching profession were less compatible with the needs of the masculine postcolonial nation-state.

Far less academic research has been done on the topic of female education in postcolonial Malaysia than in Singapore, so it is more difficult to ascertain Malaysian state ideology on gendered curricula and the construction of femininity through girls' schools. However, in comparison with Singapore, there has not been as concerted an effort in Malaysia to make domestic science a compulsory subject in secondary girls' schools or as successful an attempt to promote an official agenda regarding the socioeconomic role of educated women with the totalizing reach of the Singaporean state. One possible reason for this is the difference in ethnic composition and racial politics between the two countries. With a diverse population nearly five times larger and a geographic spread more than 150 times greater than Singapore's, the Malaysian government had to contend with less centralized control and more balancing of power between various political factions. Faced with these challenges, Malaysian authorities were probably less able to devote time and resources to implementing a special program for girls' education. Still, social attitudes toward women across all ethnic groups continued for many years to privilege their roles in the domestic sphere. Formal classroom learning and centralized government policy were certainly not the only means for perpetuating traditional gender norms; family, religion, community practices, and general social mores have all played vital roles as well.

Considering the transformative potential of migration and diasporic life, the halting and politically fraught modernization of overseas Chinese women in postcolonial Malaysia and Singapore is striking. Female emancipation did not take an easy path, despite seismic changes in Chinese and Southeast Asian societies: Communist revolution in mainland China, the declaration of democratic and liberal principles in newly independent nation-states, and on the economic front, an urgent need for the mobilization of male and female labor alike that helped to narrow what had previously seemed an unbridgeable gap between the domestic and public spheres. Little more than a hundred years after the first successful girls' schools were established in Malaya and Singapore, after the political and economic circumstances of their environment had altered dramatically, the same fundamental question remained: what should a girl learn that would best prepare her for her adult life, and what could formal education do to help?

One answer, given by Lee Siow Mong, Singapore's director of education in 1959, shows how state policy in the 1960s drew from deeply traditional wellsprings. Lee argued that women's primary duties should remain within the home while men's duties lay outside it, and that this should not be seen as "separating the inferior from the superior, but rather as a division of a complete whole in home life."[23] His rationale was based on the "ancient Chinese classics," which, he said, stated clearly that "a woman's work is not only drawing and embroidering but should include spinning and the preparation of flavourings for cooking and a host of other things for making the home a comfortable place."[24] Here, Lee was prefiguring a "Confucianizing" movement that was to shape Singaporean gender politics two decades later. The year 1979 was a turning point of sorts in girls' education, when the Singaporean state imposed a one-third limit on the proportion of female students in the medical faculty of the national university.[25] The ruling was justified by the reasoning that female doctors, like many other educated women, would either short-change their professions, because they would be distracted by their domestic duties after marriage, or would neglect their roles as wives and mothers because of their jobs. This official reversal of equal opportunity in education occurred in the midst of a larger refocusing on social policy and public morality, in the form of so-called Asian values and Confucian ethics by the Singaporean government in the late 1970s and early 1980s.[26] Having secured political and economic stability by this time, the state began to concentrate on social engineering, attempting to counter the perceived negative influences of Western individualism and culture by introducing Confucian Studies as a subject in secondary schools and emphasizing the importance of moral education in building a strong and harmonious society.[27]

The Confucianizing movement eventually spread to such personal spheres as sexual reproduction, whereby the state projected its mingled anxieties about population control, racial balance, and economic competitiveness onto the bodies of women. In the 1980s, Singapore's founding prime minister Lee Kuan Yew observed that highly educated women had worryingly low birth rates, while less- or non-educated women had what his government considered disproportionately high birth rates. The explicit concern was that this demographic imbalance would hamper economic prosperity, with a larger population of the socioeconomically disadvantaged outnumbering those from wealthier and more highly educated backgrounds. The implicit coding was racial, as the "highly educated women" category was mostly ethnic Chinese, while the "less educated women" group was mostly Malay and Indian. Despite widespread criticism, the Singaporean government pushed ahead with propaganda and financial incentives to encourage certain demographic groups to procreate while urging others to "Stop at Two."[28] Once again, authorities viewed national well-being as built out of an interlocking matrix of gender, ethnicity, and class, in which educated women were as much of a problem for state management as they were individuals with equal claim to the freedoms and prerogatives of men. Postcolonial nationhood precipitated greater gender role conservatism, likely because the male elites who dominated the government were, despite their orientation toward political independence, also inheritors of social perspectives from the colonial or early Chinese national period.

The story of female education, whether as part of national, transnational, or diasporic development, does not seem to offer much refuge from the overwhelming experience of patriarchal domination. Those who would seek evidence of women's emancipation and a counter-narrative to the largely masculine accounts of political and economic history may find some of what they are looking for. But, like the students and teachers of girls' schools, they would also find the limits of patriarchal society hard to escape. In diasporic and transnational communities, where it would appear that the rules and conventions of the nation-state might be loosened or even overturned, people still felt the pressures of nationalism and its accompanying dogmas about the politics of ethno-cultural identity.

Still, attending to the personal stories of girls and women reveals the primacy of women and women's issues in this "man's world." Educated women saw a genuine expansion in their horizons, as they acquired a far greater range of knowledge, skills, social connections, economic opportunity, and identity options than those of generations before them. Their lived experiences offer a vivid corrective to overseas Chinese women's histories or many women's histories that have focused almost exclusively on an oppressed underclass or an exceptional elite. Highly educated or otherwise, in the nation or in diaspora, ethnic Chinese women were central in devising and living out ideals of twentieth-century modernity. Educated Chinese women also built for themselves and generations of women after them the physical and intellectual spaces of learning, sociability, paid employment, and politico-cultural expression that would become part of the national fabric in the postcolonial era. The story of female education and overseas Chinese women proves that the struggle for independence and belonging in diaspora was carried out by both sexes, and that the seeming absence of women in the overseas Chinese historical record can be remedied by stepping inside the gates of any number of girls' schools.

The global history of female education is as diverse and complex as the innumerable contexts in which girls' schools appeared throughout the late nineteenth and early twentieth centuries. One unifying theme, however, is how education for girls and women over the past century has been bound up with narratives of modernity, social improvement, cultural preservation, and techno-scientific advances in reproductive and domestic life. This discourse has not faded over time. Although single-sex institutions are no longer as common as they once were, there are still parts of the world where they are customary or even a prerequisite in order for girls to be able to attend school. In first-world countries, educational experiences of and opportunities for girls and women are still hotly debated topics. In the developing world, rates of female education are still markers of social and civilizational progress. In the past as in the present, formal education has brought women out of the home and into the world, but cultural and political agendas have constrained as well as expanded their possibilities. While struggles over the politics of female education continue at national and international levels, it is important to attend to their impact on the people whose welfare is at stake. It is, after all, on a quotidian and personal basis that individuals cobble and create, or don and discard, the identities that nation-states, religious authorities, ethnic communities, and family and friends demand of them. And it is on this universal level of the human quest for authentic identities and belonging that their stories offer their most urgent appeal.

NOTES

INTRODUCTION

1. Zheng Liangshu and Wei Weixian, eds., *Malaixiya, Xinjiapo huawen zhongxue tekan tiyao, fu xiaoshi* (Abstracts of Special Issue Magazines of Chinese High Schools in Malaysia and Singapore, with School Histories) (Malaysia: Chinese Studies Department, University of Malaya, 1975), 256.
2. Zheng and Wei, 256.
3. Zheng and Wei, 256.
4. Michael Macilwee, *The Liverpool Underworld: Crime in the City, 1750–1900* (Liverpool: Liverpool University Press, 2011), 132; and Thomas Hunter, John Smith, Archibald Swinton, and Scotland High Court of Justiciary, *Report of the trial of Thomas Hunter, Peter Hacket, Richard M'Neil, James Gibb, and William M'Lean: operative cotton-spinners in Glasgow, before the High court of justiciary, at Edinburgh, on Wednesday, January 3, 1838, and seven following days, for the crimes of illegal conspiracy and murder; with an appendix of documents and relative proceedings* (Edinburgh, Scotland: Thomas Clark, 1838), 66, 81, 87, 88, 151, 191, 192, 214, 246, 247, 260, 261, 283, 302, 320. http://books.google.com.tw/books?id=SGkNAAAAIAAJ&dq=%22throwing+vitriol%22&source=gbs_navlinks_s.
5. For example, see "Prisoners Awaiting Hearing: Throwing Vitriol. Garroting in Catharine-Street," *New York Times*, July 15, 1865, http://www.nytimes.com/1865/07/15/news/prisoners-awaiting-hearing-throwing-vitriol-garroting-in-catharine-street.html; and "Three Years for Throwing Vitriol," *New York Times*, November 14, 1884, http://query.nytimes.com/mem/archive-free/pdf?res=F60912F83F5B10738DDDAD0994D9415B8484F0D3.
6. Sharon Beijer, "Achieving Justice for the Survivors of Acid Violence in Cambodia," *Cambodia Law and Policy Journal* 1 (January 2014): 1–28, 1; and Jane Welsh, "'It Was Like Burning in Hell': A Comparative Exploration of Acid Attack Violence" (MA Thesis, Department of Anthropology, University of North Carolina-Chapel Hill, 2009), 1.
7. Adam McKeown, "Becoming Foreigners in Peru," in *Chinese Migrant Networks and Cultural Change: Peru, Chicago, Hawaii, 1900–1936* (Chicago: University of Chicago Press, 2001).
8. On China in the late nineteenth and early twentieth centuries, see Paul J. Bailey, *Gender and Education in China: Gender Discourses and Women's Schooling in the Early Twentieth Century* (London: Routledge, 2007); Joan Judge, *The Precious Raft of History: The Past, the West, and the Woman Question in China* (Stanford, CA: Stanford University Press, 2008); and Sarah Coles McElroy, "Forging a New

Role for Women: Zhili First Women's Normal School and the Growth of Women's Education in China, 1901–21," in *Education, Culture, and Identity in Twentieth-Century China*, ed. Glen Peterson, Ruth Hayhoe, and Yongling Liu (Ann Arbor: University of Michigan Press, 2001), 348–74. In the Southeast Asian field, some coverage can be found as part of larger works such as Norman Owen, ed., *The Routledge Handbook of Southeast Asian History* (London: Routledge, 2014); and in histories such as Runchana P. Suksod-Barger's *Religious Influences in Thai Female Education (1889–1931)* (Cambridge: James Clarke, 2014); and Chie Ikeya's *Refiguring Women, Colonialism, and Modernity in Burma* (Honolulu: University of Hawaii Press, 2011).

9. Ooi Yu-lin, *Pieces of Jade and Gold: Anecdotal History of the Singapore Chinese Girls' School, 1899–1999* (Singapore: Singapore Chinese Girls' School, 1999), 12.

10. For example, Hayden J. A. Bellenoit, *Missionary Education and Empire in Late Colonial India, 1860–1920* (London: Pickering and Chatto, 2007); and Clive Whitehead, *Colonial Educators: The British Indian and Colonial Education Service, 1858–1983* (London: I. B. Tauris, 2003).

11. For example, see Philip A. Kuhn, *Chinese among Others: Emigration in Modern Times* (Lanham, MD: Rowman and Littlefield, 2008); Anthony Reid, ed., *Sojourners and Settlers: Histories of Southeast Asia and the Chinese* (Sydney: Allen and Unwin, 1996); Elizabeth Sinn, *The Last Half Century of Chinese Overseas* (Hong Kong: Hong Kong University Press, 1998); Leo Suryadinata, *Migration, Indigenization, and Interaction: Chinese Overseas and Globalization* (Hackensack, NJ: World Scientific, 2011); Wang Gungwu, *The Chinese Overseas: From Earthbound China to the Quest for Autonomy* (Cambridge, MA: Harvard University Press, 2000); and Yan Qinghuang [Yen Ching-hwang], *The Chinese in Southeast Asia and Beyond: Socioeconomic and Political Dimensions Globalization* (Hackensack, NJ: World Scientific, 2008), to name a few.

12. For an overview of the term's history and role in contemporary diaspora studies, see Kim D. Butler, "Defining Diaspora: Refining a Discourse," *Diaspora: A Journal of Transnational Studies* 10, no. 2 (Fall 2001): 189–219. Without detouring into the many theoretical debates over this complex issue, I will note here that the difficulty of arriving at a commonly agreed-upon term for the population in question is itself an important indication of the challenges inherent in studying it, and that my use of the term is provisional.

13. Khoo, "Ethnic Structure," and Brenda S. A. Yeoh, *Contesting Space in Colonial Singapore: Power Relations and the Urban Built Environment* (Singapore: Singapore University Press, 2003), 38.

14. Eric Tagliacozzo and Wen-Chin Chang, eds., *Chinese Circulations: Capital, Commodities, and Networks in Southeast Asia* (Durham, NC: Duke University Press, 2011).

15. In the first half of the twentieth century, the Peninsular Malayan population was on average composed of approximately one-half indigenous Malays, more than one-third ethnic Chinese, one-tenth ethnic South Asian Indians, and a small percentage of other ethnicities. Malayan Census figures compiled by Khoo Boo Teik, "Ethnic Structure, Governance, and Inequality in the Public Sector: Malaysian Experiences," *Democracy, Governance and Human Rights Programme Paper 20* (December 2005), United Nations Research Institute for Social Development, 4.

16. Fan Ruolan, *Immigration, Gender and Overseas Chinese Society: Studies on the Chinese Women in Malaya (1929–1941)* (Beijing: Zhonghua Huaqiao Publishing,

2005), 111–14: and Lenore Manderson, "The Development and Direction of Female Education in Peninsular Malaysia," *Journal of the Malayan Branch of the Royal Asiatic Society* 51, no. 2 (December 1978): 100–22, 101–3.

17. Joyce Lebra and Joy Paulson, *Chinese Women in Southeast Asia* (Singapore: Times Books International, 1980), 6.

18. Lebra and Paulson, 6–7.

19. Lim Joo Hock, "Chinese Female Immigration into the Straits Settlements, 1860–1991," *South Seas Journal* 22 (1967): 99.

20. Joyce Ee, "Chinese Migration to Singapore, 1896–1941," *Journal of Southeast Asian History* 2, no. 1 (1961): 50. Together with the statistics on female migration in Lim Joo Hock's study, these numbers continue to form the basis for present-day studies into overseas Chinese women in colonial Malaya and Singapore.

21. Fan, 128–29.

22. Joan Judge, "Citizens or Mothers of Citizens? Gender and the Meaning of Modern Chinese Citizenship," in *Changing Meanings of Citizenship in Modern China*, ed. Merle Goldman and Elizabeth J. Perry (Cambridge, MA: Harvard University Press, 2002), 22–43; and Judge, *The Precious Raft*.

23. On overseas Chinese nationalism, see Wang Gungwu, *Community and Nation: Essays on Southeast Asia and the Chinese* (Singapore: Heinemann, 1981); and Leo Suryadinata, *Chinese and Nation-building in Southeast Asia*, 2nd ed. (Singapore: Marshall Cavendish, 2004). On Chinese women in Malaya and Singapore, see Lai Ah Eng, *Peasants, Proletarians and Prostitutes: A Preliminary Investigation into the Work of Chinese Women in Colonial Malaya* (Singapore: Institute of Southeast Asian Studies, 1986); Maria Jaschok and Suzanne Miers, eds., *Women and Chinese Patriarchy: Submission, Servitude and Escape* (Hong Kong: Hong Kong University Press, 1994); Tan Liok Ee, "A Century of Change: Education in the Lives of Four Generations of Chinese Women in Malaysia," in *Asian Migrants and Education: The Tensions of Education in Immigrant Societies and among Migrant Groups*, ed. Michael W. Charney, Brenda S. A. Yeoh, and Tong Chee Kiong (London: Kluwer Academic, 2003), 115–31; Tan Liok Ee, "Locating Chinese Women in Malaysian History," in *New Terrains in Southeast Asian History*, ed. Ahmad Abu Talib and Tan Liok Ee (Singapore: Singapore University Press, 2003); and Neil Jin Keong Khor and Khoo Keat Siew, *The Penang Po Leung Kuk: Chinese Women, Prostitution and a Welfare Organisation* (Malaysia: Malaysian Branch of the Royal Asiatic Society, 2004).

24. For examples, see Bao Jiemin, *Marital Acts: Gender, Sexuality, and Identity among the Chinese Thai Diaspora* (Honolulu: University of Hawaii Press, 2005); Agnes Khoo, *Life as the River Flows: Women in the Malayan Anti-Colonial Struggle* (Malaysia: Strategic Information Research Development, 2004); and James Warren, *Ah Ku and Karayuki-san: Prostitution in Singapore, 1870–1940* (Singapore: Oxford University Press, 2003).

25. Wang Gungwu, "Patterns of Chinese Migration in Historical Perspective," in *China and the Chinese Overseas* (Singapore: Times Academic Press, 1991), 3–21.

26. Lim Boon Keng, "Straits Chinese Reform—III. The Education of Children," in *Straits Chinese Magazine: A Quarterly Journal of Oriental and Occidental Culture* (September 1899): 102–5, 103.

27. Julia Clancy-Smith and Frances Gouda, eds., *Domesticating the Empire: Race, Gender and Family Life in French and Dutch Colonialism* (Charlottesville: University Press of Virginia, 1998); Elsbeth Locher-Scholten, *Women and the Colonial State: Essays on Gender and Modernity in the Netherlands Indies, 1900–1942*

(Amsterdam: Amsterdam University Press, 2000); and Ann Laura Stoler, *Carnal Knowledge and Imperial Power: Race and the Intimate in Colonial Rule* (Berkeley: University of California Press, 2002).

28. Charles F. Keyes, ed., *Reshaping Local Worlds: Formal Education and Cultural Change in Rural Southeast Asia* (New Haven, CT: Yale University Southeast Asia Studies, 1991), 2.

29. Christina K. Gilmartin et al., eds., *Engendering China: Women, Culture, and the State* (Cambridge, MA: Harvard University Press, 1994); and Christina K. Gilmartin, *Engendering the Chinese Revolution: Radical Women, Communist Politics, and Mass Movements in the 1920s* (Berkeley: University of California Press, 1995).

30. Tim Harper, "Globalism and the Pursuit of Authenticity: The Making of a Diasporic Public Sphere in Singapore," *Sojourn* 12, no. 2 (1997): 261–92. Also Prasenjit Duara, "Of Authenticity and Woman: Personal Narratives of Middle Class Women in Modern China," in *Becoming Chinese: Passages to Modernity and Beyond*, ed. Wen-Hsin Yeh (Berkeley: University of California Press, 2000), 342–64.

31. Some relevant discussions on these facets of modernity in postcolonial and global studies include Arjun Appadurai, *Modernity at Large: Cultural Dimensions of Globalization* (Minneapolis: University of Minnesota Press, 1996); Arif Dirlik, "Modernity as History: Post-Revolutionary China, Globalization and the Question of Modernity," *Social History* 27, no. 1 (2002): 16–39; and Bonnie Smith, ed., *Women's History in Global Perspective*, Volume 1 (Champaign: University of Illinois Press, 2004).

32. The foundational work in the scholarship on the Modern Girl is Alys Eve Weinbaum et al., eds., *The Modern Girl around the World: Consumption, Modernity, and Globalization* (Durham, NC: Duke University Press, 2008).

33. For an expanded discussion of modernity as a state of mind that invites self-doubt, see Steven Smith, *Modernity and Its Discontents: Making and Unmaking the Bourgeois from Machiavelli to Bellow* (New Haven, CT: Yale University Press, 2016).

34. Philip Fook Seng Loh, *Seeds of Separatism: Educational Policy in Malaya, 1874–1940* (Kuala Lumpur: Oxford University Press, 1975).

35. Sunil Amrith, *Migration and Diaspora in Modern Asia* (New York: Cambridge University Press, 2011).

36. Judge, *The Precious Raft*, and Bailey, *Gender and Education in China*.

37. Prasenjit Duara, "Embodying Civilization: Women and the Figure of Tradition within Modernity," in *Sovereignty and Authenticity: Manchukuo and the East Asian Modern* (Lanham, MD: Rowman and Littlefield, 2003), 131–69.

38. For some recent examples, see discussions of the Jewish diaspora in Howard Wettstein, ed., *Diasporas and Exiles: Varieties of Jewish Identity* (Berkeley: University of California Press, 2002); and of the Indian diaspora in Om Prakash Dwivedi, ed., *Tracing the New Indian Diaspora* (Leiden: Brill, 2014).

39. Daniel Chirot and Anthony Reid, eds., *Essential Outsiders: Chinese and Jews in the Modern Transformation of Southeast Asia and Central Europe* (Seattle: University of Washington Press, 1997).

CHAPTER 1

1. Standing Committee on Finance, "Training Course in the United Kingdom for Chinese Women Teachers," 1950, Federal Secretariat Files 13130/50, 1; "Supplementary Memorandum for submission to the Conference of Rulers,"

1950, Federal Secretariat Files 13130/50/6; and Commissioner-General's Office in Southeast Asia, Telegram to Secretary of State for the Colonies, September 12, 1950, Federal Secretariat Files 13130/50.

2. Draft Telegram to Secretary of State, "Women Teachers Training Course," November 1950, Federal Secretariat Files 13130/50.

3. *IJ Bukit Nanas, Kuala Lumpur School Annals—Book 1, 1899–1916*, Convent of the Holy Infant Archives. Examples on pp. 28 (September 1903), 80 (December 1909), and *passim*.

4. *Annual Report on Education in the Federated Malay States for the Year 1931*, 50–54.

5. Tan Liok Ee, *The Politics of Chinese Education in Malaya, 1945–1961* (Kuala Lumpur: Oxford University Press, 1997), 30.

6. Ann Laura Stoler, *Carnal Knowledge and Imperial Power: Race and the Intimate in Colonial Rule* (Berkeley: University of California Press, 2002); Julia Clancy-Smith and Frances Gouda, eds., *Domesticating the Empire: Race, Gender and Family Life in French and Dutch Colonialism* (Charlottesville: University Press of Virginia, 1998); and Frederick Cooper and Ann Laura Stoler, eds., *Tensions of Empire: Colonial Cultures in a Bourgeois World* (Berkeley: University of California Press, 1997).

7. Rajeswary Ampalavanar, *The Indian Minority and Political Change in Malaya, 1945–1957* (London: Oxford University Press, 1981).

8. Neil Jin Keong Khor and Khoo Keat Siew, *The Penang Po Leung Kuk: Chinese Women, Prostitution and a Welfare Organisation* (Malaysia: Malaysian Branch of the Royal Asiatic Society, 2004); and James F. Warren, *Ah Ku and Karayuki-San: Prostitution in Singapore 1880–1940* (Singapore: National University of Singapore Press, 2003).

9. Francis Wong Hoy Kee and Ee Tiang Hong, *Education in Malaya* (Singapore: Heinemann Educational Books, 1971).

10. Harold E. Wilson, *Social Engineering in Singapore: Educational Policies and Social Change* (Singapore: Singapore University Press, 1978), xi–xii.

11. D. D. Chelliah, *A History of the Educational Policy of the Straits Settlements, with Recommendations for a New System Based on Vernaculars* (Kuala Lumpur: Government Press, 1947), 16–20.

12. Wong and Ee, 11–16.

13. Lenore Manderson, "The Development and Direction of Female Education in Peninsular Malaysia," *Journal of the Malayan Branch of the Royal Asiatic Society* 51, no. 2 (December 1978): 100–22, 102.

14. Manderson, 102.

15. Manderson, 102.

16. Wong and Ee, 9.

17. Wong and Ee, 9.

18. Frank Swettenham, Resident of Perak, *Perak Annual Report*, 1890, 16, in Philip Fook Seng Loh, *Seeds of Separatism: Educational Policy in Malaya, 1874–1940* (Kuala Lumpur: Oxford University Press, 1975), 15.

19. H. B. Collinage, State Inspector of Schools of Perak, *Perak Government Gazette*, January 4, 1895, 4–7, in Loh, 16–17. Italics in original.

20. George Maxwell, Chief Secretary, *Report on Education for the Federation of Malay States*, 1920.

21. E. A. Blundell, Governor of the Straits Settlements, Report, *Letter Books*, Series R, Volume 27, Number 54. In Chelliah, 45.

22. Chelliah, 32.

23. *Straits Settlements Annual Report on Education for the Year 1924*.

24. Chelliah, 31–33.
25. Khor and Khoo, 20–22.
26. Khor and Khoo, 25.
27. Khor and Khoo, 31.
28. Warren, *Ah Ku and Karayuki-san*.
29. Wilson, xii–xiii.
30. Barbara Dennis and David Skilton, *Reform and Intellectual Debate in Victorian England* (New York: Croom Helm, 1987), 11–17.
31. Chelliah, 77.
32. *Straits Settlements Annual Report on Education for the Year 1924*.
33. Female Education in Kuala Lumpur, Letter from Inspector of Schools, April 9, 1895, *Selangor Secretariat Files, Education* 2009/95.
34. Frank W. Harris, Inspector of Schools in Selangor, Report on Government English School for Girls at Kuala Lumpur, September 2, 1896, *Selangor Secretariat Files* 4663/96.
35. Frank A. Swettenham, *The Real Malay* (London: John Lane, 1899), 272–73.
36. *Straits Settlements Annual Report on Education, 1906*, 73.
37. Chelliah, 52.
38. *Straits Settlements Annual Report on Education, 1918*, 597.
39. Lee Yoke Ming, *Great Is Thy Faithfulness: The Story of St. Margaret's School in Singapore* (Singapore: St. Margaret's School, 2002), 62; and Song Ong Siang, *One Hundred Years of the Chinese in Singapore* (London: John Murray, 1923), 86.
40. *Annual Report on Education in the Federated Malay States for the Year 1931, "Supplement to the F.M.S. Government Gazette," November 4, 1932*, 13.
41. *Annual Report on Education in the Federated Malay States for the Year 1931*, 13.
42. *Annual Report on Education in the Malayan Union for 1947*, 23.
43. *Annual Report on Education in the Malayan Union for 1947*, 6–7; *Annual Report on Education in the Malayan Union for the period 1st April 1946, to 31st December, 1946*, 80; and *Annual Report on Education in the Malayan Union for 1947*, 23.
44. *Annual Report on Education in the Malayan Union for 1947*, 5.
45. Frank W. Harris, Inspector of Schools in Selangor, "Suggests that the Government English Girls' Schools should become an Anglo Chinese School from January 1898," October 20, 1897, *Selangor Secretariat Files* 5008/97.
46. Presidential Address, Fifth Educational Conference of Malaya, Official Report of the Proceedings, [1939], 10–11.
47. Presidential Address, 9.
48. Presidential Address, 9.
49. [Note from Inspector of Schools for the Federated Malay States,] February 23, 1898, *Selangor Secretariat Files* 5008/97.
50. *Straits Settlements Annual Report on Education, 1911*, 285; and *Straits Settlements Annual Report on Education, 1929*, 896.
51. *Annual Report on Education in the Malayan Union for the period 1st April 1946, to 31st December, 1946*, 86.
52. Tan Liok Ee, "Chinese Independent Schools in West Malaysia: Varying Responses to Changing Demands," in *Changing Identities of the Southeast Asian Chinese since World War II*, ed. Jennifer W. Cushman and Wang Gungwu (Hong Kong: Hong Kong University Press, 1988), 354–84, 61.
53. "List of Books Used for Various Subjects in the Normal Class Department," in *Xingzhou Jingfang Nüxuexiao bazhounian jiniankan* (Singapore Jingfang Girls' School Eighth Anniversary Commemorative Magazine) (Singapore: 1936),

"School Administration," 6. Also *Kuncheng nüxiao sishiwu zhounian jiniankan* (Kuen Cheng Girls' School Forty-fifth Anniversary Commemorative Magazine) (Kuala Lumpur: 1953), 69–70.

54. Fan Ruolan, *Immigration, Gender and Overseas Chinese Society: Studies on the Chinese Women in Malaya (1929–1941)* (Beijing: Zhonghua Huaqiao Publishing, 2005), 129.

55. Tan, *The Politics of Chinese Education in Malaya*, 16.

56. Christine Inglis, "Chinese Schools in Malaya during the Colonial Period," in *Kabar Seberang, Sulating Maphilindo* 7 (1980): 82–93, 83.

57. Inglis, "Chinese Schools," 83–84.

58. Inglis, "Chinese Schools," 84.

59. "First Report of the Advisory Committee on Social Hygiene, 1925, Paper to be laid before the Legislative Council by Command of His Excellency the Officer Administering the Government, No. 48 of 1925," 4.

60. Loh, 40.

61. Annual Reports on Education for the Federated Malay States 1931–34, the Malayan Union 1946–47, and Federation of Malaya 1948–53, *passim*.

62. Female Education in Kuala Lumpur, Letter from Inspector of Schools, April 9, 1895, *Selangor Secretariat Files, Education* 2009/95.

63. Ann L. Stoler, *Race and the Education of Desire: Foucault's History of Sexuality and the Colonial Order of Things* (Durham, NC: Duke University Press, 1995), 122.

64. *Federation of Malaya Annual Report on Education for 1949*, 44; *Annual Report on Education in the Malayan Union for the period 1st April 1946, to 31st December, 1946*, 12; and *Federation of Malaya Annual Report on Education for 1949*, 99.

65. *Federation of Malaya Annual Report on Education for 1949*, 60; and *Federation of Malaya Annual Report on Education for 1948*, 98.

66. Colony of Singapore, *Annual Report of the Department of Education*, 1946, 28; and Colony of Singapore, *Annual Report of the Department of Education*, 1947, 56.

67. *Annual Report on Education in the Malayan Union for 1949*, 80.

68. Fang Jianyi, personal interview with author, Kuala Lumpur, Malaysia, 2005.

69. Christine Inglis, "The Feminisation of the Teaching Profession in Singapore," in *Women's Work and Women's Roles: Economics and Everyday Life in Indonesia, Malaysia and Singapore*, ed. Lenore Manderson (Canberra: Australian National University, 1983), 217–39.

CHAPTER 2

1. *The Charitable Mistresses of the Holy Infant Jesus, Known as the Dames de St Maur 1662, Published in the Mother Generalship of Reverend Mother Ste Marguerite-Marie Delbecq for the Missionary Exhibition Held at the Vatican December 25th, 1924* (Dornach (Haut-Rhin): Braun, 1925), 84. Other details here about the school's founding are also from this source.

2. *The Charitable Mistresses of the Holy Infant Jesus, Known as the Dames de St Maur 1662*, 86.

3. *Convents of the Infant Jesus (Nicolas Barre): Malaysia-Singapore, 1852–1981. Notes Compiled by Rev. Mother Charles DeLebarre, Provincial Superior Malaysia-Singapore, 1954–1970, from the Annals of the Communities of Malaysia-Singapore and Documents from the Archives of the Congregation, Paris*, Convent of the Holy Infant Archives, 3–5.

4. *The Charitable Mistresses of the Holy Infant Jesus, Known as the Dames de St Maur 1662*, 87.

5. *Convents of the Infant Jesus (Nicolas Barre): Malaysia-Singapore, 1852–1981,* 40.

6. *IJ Bukit Nanas, Kuala Lumpur School Annals—Book 1, 1899–1916,* Convent of the Holy Infant Archive, 16.

7. *Convents of the Infant Jesus (Nicolas Barre): Malaysia-Singapore, 1852–1981,* 40.

8. Walter Makepeace et al., eds., *One Hundred Years of Singapore,* Vol.1 (London: CM Turnbull, 1921), 443.

9. *The Charitable Mistresses of the Holy Infant Jesus, Known as the Dames de St Maur 1662,* 85.

10. Neil Jin Keong Khor and Khoo Keat Siew, *The Penang Po Leung Kuk: Chinese Women, Prostitution and a Welfare Organisation* (Malaysia: Malaysian Branch of the Royal Asiatic Society, 2004), 36.

11. Khor and Khoo, *The Penang Po Leung Kuk,* 40.

12. Khor and Khoo, *The Penang Po Leung Kuk,* 44.

13. Khor and Khoo, *The Penang Po Leung Kuk,* 45.

14. School History Exhibition, St. Margaret's Secondary School, Singapore (visited December 28, 2005).

15. Lee Yoke Ming, *Great Is Thy Faithfulness: The Story of St. Margaret's School in Singapore* (Singapore: St. Margaret's School, 2002), 40.

16. Ang Siok Hui, "Pioneer Female Mission Schools in Singapore, 1842–1942" (BA Honours Thesis, Department of History, National University of Singapore, 1993/94), 7.

17. Ang, 8.

18. Linda Lim, "Linda Lim's MGS Schooldays" (unpublished memoir, 2004), 1.

19. Sophia Blackmore, Report, *Methodist Message* (April 1899), cited in Lim, "Linda Lim's MGS Schooldays," 1.

20. See, for example, Felicity Hunt, *Gender and Policy in English Education: Schooling for Girls 1902–44* (Hertfordshire: Harvester Wheatsheaf, 1991); and Rita Smith Kipp, "Emancipating Each Other: Dutch Colonial Missionaries' Encounter with Karo Women in Sumatra, 1900–1942," in *Domesticating the Empire,* ed. Clancy-Smith and Gouda, 211–35.

21. Karen Graves, *Girls' Schooling during the Progressive Era: From Female Scholar to Domesticated Citizen* (New York: Garland, 1998).

22. Dorothy Ko, *Teachers of the Inner Chambers: Women and Culture in Seventeenth-Century China* (Stanford, CA: Stanford University Press, 1994); and Patricia Buckley Ebrey, *The Inner Quarters: Marriage and the Lives of Chinese Women in the Sung Period* (Berkeley: University of California Press, 1993).

23. Carrie F. Paechter, *Educating the Other: Gender, Power and Schooling* (London: Falmer Press, 1998), 13.

24. Paul J. Bailey, *Gender and Education in China: Gender Discourses and Women's Schooling in the Early Twentieth Century* (London: Routledge, 2007); and Sarah Coles McElroy, "Forging a New Role for Women: Zhili First Women's Normal School and the Growth of Women's Education in China, 1901–21," in *Education, Culture, and Identity in Twentieth-Century China,* ed. Glen Peterson, Ruth Hayhoe, and Yongling Liu (Ann Arbor: University of Michigan Press, 2001), 348–74.

25. Bailey, *Gender and Education in China,* 12–13.

26. Ye Weili, *Seeking Modernity in China's Name: Chinese Students in the United States, 1900–1927* (Stanford, CA: Stanford University Press, 2001), 131.

27. There is little other information about this school in the historical record, other than that it was situated in Love Lane, Penang.

28. Fan, *Immigration, Gender and Overseas Chinese Society,* 111–12. See also Chelliah, *A History of the Educational Policy of the Straits Settlements.*

29. Khor and Khoo, *The Penang Po Leung Kuk*, 73.
30. *IJ Bukit Nanas, Kuala Lumpur School Annals—Book 1*, 16.
31. J. M. Gullick, *Josephine Foss and the Pudu English School: A Pursuit of Excellence* (Selangor, Malaysia: Pelanduk, 1988), 33.
32. "Fete Week 1934: Event Proceedings," *Convent Light Street Penang Scrapbook 1: 1900–1930*, Convent of the Holy Infant Archives, 5.
33. *IJ Mission in Malaya, 1852–1945*, Convent of the Holy Infant Archives; and E. A. Blundell, Governor of the Straits Settlements, quoted in T. R. Doraisamy, ed., *150 Years of Education in Singapore* (Singapore: Teachers' Training College, 1969), 22.
34. Ang, 12.
35. *Convents of the Infant Jesus (Nicolas Barre): Malaysia-Singapore, 1852–1981*, 22.
36. Maria Yong, personal interview with author, Selangor, Malaysia, 2005.
37. *Annual Report on Education in the Federated Malay States for the Year 1931*, "Supplement to the F.M.S. Government Gazette," November 4, 1932, 7. For more details on these schools, see Lenore Manderson, "The Development and Direction of Female Education in Peninsular Malaysia," *Journal of the Malayan Branch of the Royal Asiatic Society* 51, no. 2 (December 1978): 100–22, 50–51.
38. *IJ Bukit Nanas, Kuala Lumpur School Annals—Book 1*, 28–30.
39. *IJ Bukit Nanas, Kuala Lumpur School Annals—Book 1*, 24–25.
40. *IJ Bukit Nanas, Kuala Lumpur School Annals—Book 1*, 23.
41. *Convents of the Infant Jesus (Nicolas Barre): Malaysia-Singapore, 1852–1981*, 51.
42. Ong Lay Fang, personal interview with author, Penang, Malaysia, 2006.
43. Rose Ong, personal interview with author, Penang, Malaysia, 2006.
44. Sister Enda Ryan, personal interview with author, Selangor, Malaysia, 2005.
45. *IJ Bukit Nanas, Kuala Lumpur, Book 8, Community Annals 1548–1946*, 12.
46. *Convents of the Infant Jesus (Nicolas Barre): Malaysia-Singapore, 1852–1981*, 28.
47. *Convents of the Infant Jesus (Nicolas Barre): Malaysia-Singapore, 1852–1981*, 6.
48. *Convents of the Infant Jesus (Nicolas Barre): Malaysia-Singapore, 1852–1981*, 19.
49. *Convents of the Infant Jesus (Nicolas Barre): Malaysia-Singapore, 1852–1981*, 19.
50. Tan, "A Century of Change," 125.
51. *Convent Light Street: 150 Years of Touching Hearts*, 1852–2002 (Penang, Malaysia: n.p., 2002), 50.
52. *Convent Light Street*, 51.
53. Ong Lay Fang, personal interview with author.
54. Rose Ong, personal interview with author.
55. Lee Yoke Ming, *Great Is Thy Faithfulness*, 38.
56. Khor and Khoo, 72.
57. *Convents of the Infant Jesus (Nicolas Barre): Malaysia-Singapore, 1852–1981*, 10 and 14.
58. *Convents of the Infant Jesus (Nicolas Barre)*, 16.
59. *Convents of the Infant Jesus (Nicolas Barre)*, 17.
60. *Convents of the Infant Jesus (Nicolas Barre)*, 26; and *IJ Bukit Nanas, Kuala Lumpur School Annals—Book 1*, 1 and 6.
61. *IJ Bukit Nanas, Kuala Lumpur School Annals—Book 1*, 21.
62. Philip A. Kuhn, *Chinese among Others: Emigration in Modern Times* (Lanham, MD: Rowman and Littlefield, 2008)
63. *IJ Bukit Nanas, Kuala Lumpur School Annals—Book 1*, 16, 103 and *passim*.
64. *Convents of the Infant Jesus (Nicolas Barre)*, 19.
65. *Convents of the Infant Jesus (Nicolas Barre)*, 46.

66. *Convent Bukit Nanas: 100 Years at the Top, 1899–1999* (Kuala Lumpur: Kamsiah Mohammad, 1998), 127.

67. Rose Ong, personal interview with author.

68. Lu Wei, personal interview with author, Selangor, Malaysia, 2006.

69. Lu Zhao, personal interview with author, Selangor, Malaysia, 2006.

70. Lu Wei, personal interview with author.

71. Lu Zhao, personal interview with author.

72. Rose Ong, personal interview with author.

73. Maria Yong, personal interview with author.

74. Chong Eu Ngoh, personal interview with author, Kuala Lumpur, Malaysia, 2005.

75. Maria Yong, personal interview with author.

76. Lau Wai Har, "Bridging the Gap between the Two Worlds: The Chinese-Educated and the English-Educated," in *Our Place in Time: Exploring Heritage and Memory in Singapore*, ed. Kwok Kian Woon et al. (Singapore: Singapore Heritage Society, 1999), 199–207; and Lim Chor Pee, "A White Rose at Midnight" (Singapore: s.n., 1964).

77. Lau, "Bridging the Gap," 201.

78. Lau, "Bridging the Gap," 201.

79. Kuen Cheng Girls' School alumni, personal interview with author, Kuala Lumpur, Malaysia, 2005.

80. Tan, "A Century of Change," 125–26.

81. Tan, "A Century of Change," 125–26.

82. Rose Ong, personal interview with author.

83. Margaret Chang, personal interview with author.

84. Maria Yong, personal interview with author.

85. Anonymous, personal interview with author, Kuala Lumpur, 2005.

86. Maria Yong, personal interview with author.

87. Margaret Chang, personal interview with author.

88. Loh, *Seeds of Separatism*, 124.

CHAPTER 3

1. Ooi Yu-lin, *Pieces of Jade and Gold: Anecdotal History of the Singapore Chinese Girls' School, 1899–1999* (Singapore: Singapore Chinese Girls' School, 1999), 12–20.

2. Ooi Yu-lin, *Pieces of Jade and Gold*, 12, 16.

3. Ooi Yu-lin, *Pieces of Jade and Gold*, 15.

4. Ooi Yu-lin, *Pieces of Jade and Gold*, 12.

5. Lim Boon Keng, "Straits Chinese Reform—III. The Education of Children," *Straits Chinese Magazine: A Quarterly Journal of Oriental and Occidental Culture* (September 1899): 102–5, 103.

6. Christine Doran, "The Chinese Cultural Reform Movement in Singapore: Singaporean Chinese Identities and Constructions of Gender," *Sojourn* 12, no. 1 (1997): 92–107, 95. For more on the Straits Chinese in other parts of the Straits Settlements, see Neil Jin Keong Khor, "Economic Change and the Emergence of the Straits-Chinese in Nineteenth-Century Penang," *Journal of the Malaysian Branch of the Royal Asiatic Society* 79, no. 2 (December 2006): 59–83.

7. Author unknown, *Straits Chinese Magazine*, 1897, 7–8.

8. For more on the complexities in Straits Chinese bilingualism, transculturalism, and identity self-fashioning, see Mark Ravinder Frost, "Transcultural

Diaspora: The Straits Chinese in Singapore, 1819–1918," Asia Research Institute Working Paper Series, No. 10, August 2003, www.ari.nus.edu.sg/pub/wps.htm.

9. Jean DeBernardi, *Rites of Belonging: Memory, Modernity, and Identity in a Malaysian Chinese Community* (Stanford, CA: Stanford University Press, 2004), 22.

10. Philip A. Kuhn, *Chinese among Others: Emigration in Modern Times* (Lanham, MD: Rowman and Littlefield, 2008), 71–72.

11. Kwok Kian Woon, "Singapore," in *The Encyclopedia of the Chinese Overseas*, ed. Lynn Pan (Singapore: Archipelago Press and Landmark Books, 1998), 202; and Frost, "Transcultural Diaspora."

12. Leo Suryadinata, "Peranakan Chinese Identities in Malaysia and Singapore: A Re-Examination," in *Ethnic Chinese in Singapore and Malaysia: A Dialogue between Tradition and Modernity*, ed. Leo Suryadinata (Singapore: Times Academic Press, 2002), 78; S. K. Yoong and A. N. Zainab, "The Straits Chinese Contribution to Malaysian Literary Heritage: Focus on Chinese Stories Translated in Baba Malay," *Journal of Educational Media and Library Sciences* 42, no. 2 (2004): 179–98, 180; and Tan Chee Beng, "Peranakan Chinese in Northeast Kelantan with Special Reference to Chinese Religion," *Journal of the Malaysian Branch of the Royal Asiatic Society* 55, no. 1 (1982): 26–52.

13. Karen Lee, "Between the 'King's Chinese' and 'Sons of Han': Fashioning Cultural Perfection in a Singaporean Chinese Status Group, 1890–1911" (MA Thesis, Harvard University, 2012), 2–5.

14. Suryadinata, "Peranakan Chinese Identities," 72–73; and Patricia Ann Hardwick, "'Neither Fish Nor Fowl': Constructing Peranakan Identity in Colonial and Post-Colonial Singapore," *Folklore Forum* 38, no. 1 (2008): 36–55, 38–39.

15. Charles A. Coppel, "Chinese Overseas: The Particular and the General," *Journal of Chinese Overseas* 8 (2012): 1–10, 1–2; and Suryadinata, "Peranakan Chinese Identities," 70.

16. Ooi Keat Gin, *Southeast Asia: A Historical Encyclopedia, from Angkor Wat to East Timor*, Volume 1 (Santa Barbara: ABC-CLIO, 2004), 198–99.

17. Suryadinata, "Peranakan Chinese Identities," 70; and Hardwick, 39–40.

18. Heng Pek Koon, "Peninsular Malaysia," in *The Encyclopedia of the Chinese Overseas*, ed. Lynn Pan (Singapore: Archipelago Press and Landmark Books, 1998), 172.

19. Heng, 173; and Mark Ravinder Frost, "Emporium in Imperio: Nanyang Networks and the Straits Chinese in Singapore, 1819–1914," *Journal of Southeast Asian Studies* 36, no. 1 (February 2005): 29–66, 40–41.

20. Kwok, 201–203, 205–206.

21. Kuhn, 178.

22. Heng, 174.

23. Kwok, 202.

24. Suryadinata, 75.

25. Kuhn, 250.

26. Tan, "A Century of Change," 120–21.

27. Seah Eu Chin, "The Chinese of Singapore," *Journal of the Indian Archipelago and Eastern Asia* 2 (1847): 283–90.

28. Frost, "Transcultural Diaspora," 33–35.

29. Kuhn, 251.

30. Chua Ai Lin, "Imperial Subjects, Straits Citizens," in *Paths Not Taken*, ed. Barr and Trocki, , 23; and Ooi Yu-lin, *Pieces of Jade and Gold*, 15. The latter quote is from the director of public instruction of the Straits Settlements, recorded on, November 24, 1903.

31. Song Ong Siang, "The Position of Chinese Women: A Lecture Delivered to the Chinese Philomathic Society and Subsequently to the Chinese Christian Association, in 1896," *Straits Chinese Magazine* 1 (September 1897), 16–23, 21.

32. Song, "The Position of Chinese Women," 20–21.

33. Song, "The Position of Chinese Women," 20–21.

34. Ooi Yu-lin, *Pieces of Jade and Gold*, 11–12; and Lee Guan Kin, *Responding to Eastern and Western Cultures in Singapore: A Comparative Study of Khoo Seok Wan, Lim Boon Keng and Song Ong Siang* (Hong Kong: University of Hong Kong, 1998).

35. Doran, 95.

36. Kuhn, 255.

37. Jurgen Rudolph, "The 'Speak Mandarin Campaign' of the Babas," *Commentary* 11, no. 1 (1993): 93–102, 96.

38. Mark Ravinder Frost, "*Emporium in Imperio*: Nanyang Networks and the Straits Chinese in Singapore, 1819–1914," *Journal of Southeast Asian Studies* 36, no. 1 (February 2005): 29–66, 53.

39. Lim Boon Keng, "Editorial," in *Straits Chinese Magazine: A Quarterly Journal of Oriental and Occidental Culture* (March 1897): 2.

40. Lim Boon Keng, "Our Enemies (Being the Presidential Address Delivered to the Chinese Philomathic Society in March 1897)," *Straits Chinese Magazine*, [1897], 52–58, 54.

41. Lim, "Our Enemies," 55; and Lim Boon Keng, "Straits Chinese Reform— III. The Education of Our Children," *Straits Chinese Magazine* (September 1899): 102–5, 102.

42. Song, "The Position of Chinese Women," 22–23.

43. Tan Tek Soon, "Some Genuine Chinese Authors," *Straits Chinese Magazine* (1898), 95–99.

44. Tim Harper, "Globalism and the Pursuit of Authenticity: The Making of a Diasporic Public Sphere in Singapore," *Sojourn* 12, no. 2 (1997): 261–92, 261–62. Also Su Lin Lewis, "Cosmopolitanism and the Modern Girl: A Cross-Cultural Discourse in 1930s Penang," *Modern Asian Studies* 43, no. 6 (2009): 1385–1419.

45. Frost, "Transcultural Diaspora," 21.

46. Frost, "Transcultural Diaspora," 26.

47. Lim, "Our Enemies," 56.

48. Lim, "Our Enemies," 56.

49. W. M. Burbidge, "The Present State of Morality Amongst the Straits Chinese," *Straits Chinese Magazine* (March 1899), 4–7, 5.

50. Burbidge, 5 and 7.

51. Lin Meng Cheng, "Chinese Women," *Straits Chinese Magazine* (March 1898), 154–58.

52. Lew See Fah, "Straits Chinese Mothers," *Straits Chinese Magazine* (June 1901), 112–14.

53. Lew See Fah, "Straits Chinese Maidens," *Straits Chinese Magazine* (March 1902), 43–46.

54. Lin Meng Ch'in, "Select Anecdotes from the Records of Famous Women," *Straits Chinese Magazine* 4 (December 1903), 132–33.

55. Seah Bee Leng, "Phoenix without Wings: The Negotiation of Modernity among Straits Chinese Women in Early Twentieth Century Singapore" (MA Thesis, Department of History, National University of Singapore, 2005), 38–39.

56. Philip Holden, "A Literary History of Race: Reading Singapore Literature in English in an Historical Frame," in *Race and Multiculturalism in Malaysia and Singapore*, ed. Daniel P. S. Goh et al. (London: Routledge, 2009), 19–35, 34.

57. Joan Judge, *The Precious Raft of History: China's Woman Question and the Politics of Time at the Turn of the Twentieth Century* (Stanford, CA: Stanford University Press, 2008).

58. For example, in Lew See Fah, "A Victim of Chap-Ji-Ki," *Straits Chinese Magazine* 6 (1898), 72; and Editor, "Nyonyas Gambling in Johore," *Straits Chinese Magazine* 4 (1903), 164.

59. Neo Puak Neo, "Gambling amongst Our Nyonyas," *Straits Chinese Magazine* 4 (1907), 153.

60. Neo Puak Neo, "Gambling amongst Our Nyonyas," 153.

61. Song, "The Position of Chinese Women," 18–19.

62. Song, "The Position of Chinese Women," 17.

63. Author unknown, *The Straits Chinese Magazine* (1897), 7–8.

64. See, for example, Paul J. Bailey, *Gender and Education in China: Gender Discourses and Women's Schooling in the Early Twentieth Century* (London: Routledge, 2007); Christina K. Gilmartin et al., eds., *Engendering China: Women, Culture, and the State* (Cambridge, MA: Harvard University Press, 1994); and Joan Judge, *The Precious Raft of History: The Past, the West, and the Woman Question in China* (Stanford, CA: Stanford University Press, 2008).

65. Partha Chatterjee, "The Nationalist Resolution of the Women's Question," in *Recasting Women: Essays in Indian Colonial History*, ed. Kumkum Sangari and Sudesh Vaid (New Brunswick, NJ: Rutgers University Press, 1999), 238–39.

66. Joan Judge, "Citizens or Mothers of Citizens? Gender and the Meaning of Modern Chinese Citizenship," in *Changing Meanings of Citizenship in Modern China*, ed. Merle Goldman and Elizabeth J. Perry (Cambridge, MA: Harvard University Press, 2002), 23–43.

67. Song, "The Position of Chinese Women," 19–20.

68. Song, "The Position of Chinese Women," 19–20.

69. Song, "The Position of Chinese Women," 21.

70. Song, "The Position of Chinese Women," 21

71. Song, "The Position of Chinese Women," 22–23.

72. Lim, "The Education of Our Children," 103.

73. Lew See Fah, "Straits Chinese Mothers," *Straits Chinese Magazine*, June 1901, 112–14.

74. Doran, 98.

75. Editor, "News and Noted: We Are a Peculiar People," *Straits Chinese Magazine* 24 (1902), 167; and Lim Boon Keng, "Race Deterioration in the Tropics," *Straits Chinese Annual* (1909), 5.

76. Editor, *Straits Chinese Magazine*, 1906, 176.

77. Song, "The Position of Chinese Women," 22–23.

78. Soh Poh Tong, "Concerning Our Girls," *Straits Chinese Magazine* 11 (1907), 142.

79. Lim, "The Education of Our Children," 103.

80. Lim, "The Education of Our Children," 103.

81. Lim, "The Education of Our Children," 103.

82. Lim, "The Education of Our Children," 103.

83. "Singapore Chinese Girls' School," *Singapore Free Press and Mercantile Advertiser* (April 24, 1899), 1.

84. Ooi Yu-lin, *Pieces of Jade and Gold*, 12.

85. "The Singapore Chinese Girls' School," *Singapore Free Press and Mercantile Advertiser* (August 8, 1899), 3; and Song Ong Siang, *One Hundred Years of the Chinese in Singapore* (London: John Murray, 1923), 305.

86. Ooi Yu-lin, *Pieces of Jade and Gold*, 12–16; and "Chinese Girls' School," *Straits Times* (February 5, 1921), 9.

87. The Editors, "Editorial," *Straits Chinese Magazine* (1903).

88. Editor, "Female Education for Straits Chinese," *Straits Chinese Magazine* 2 (1907), 41.

89. Ooi Yu-lin, *Pieces of Jade and Gold*, 14.

90. Ooi Yu-lin, *Pieces of Jade and Gold*, 20.

91. "Singapore Chinese Girls' School," *Singapore Free Press and Mercantile Advertiser* (November 3, 1924), 7.

92. Ooi Yu-lin, *Pieces of Jade and Gold*, 20.

93. "Chinese Girls' School," *Straits Times*.

94. Ooi Yu-lin, *Pieces of Jade and Gold*, 57.

95. Mr. M. Hellier, Inspector of Schools for Singapore and Malacca, November 10, 1910, quoted in Ooi Yu-lin, *Pieces of Jade and Gold*, 16.

96. Details on developments at SCGS under Geake in this paragraph are from Ooi Yu-lin, *Pieces of Jade and Gold*, 24, 58, 19, 23.

97. "Straits Chinese Education. Policy of Girls' School. Speech by Sir Ong Siang Song," *Straits Times* (August 18, 1936), 12.

98. Ooi Yu-lin, *Pieces of Jade and Gold*, 24.

99. Ooi Yu-lin, *Pieces of Jade and Gold*, 23.

100. Ooi Yu-lin, *Pieces of Jade and Gold*, 24.

101. Mr. Hullett, Director of Public Instruction for the Straits Settlements, SCGS Principal's Diary (November 24, 1903), quoted in Ooi Yu-lin, *Pieces of Jade and Gold*, 14.

102. Ooi Yu-lin, *Pieces of Jade and Gold*, 58.

103. Ooi Yu-lin, *Pieces of Jade and Gold*, 58.

104. Ooi Yu-lin, "The Changing Status of Chinese Women in Singapore, 1819–1961" (Academic Exercise, National University of Singapore, 1981), 20.

105. "Chinese Girls' School," *Straits Times*.

106. Ooi Yu-lin, "The Changing Status of Chinese Women," 23.

107. Lim San Neo, *My Life, My Memories, My Story* (Singapore: Epic Management Services, 1997), 14.

108. Lim San Neo, 14.

109. Florence Chan, interview with Daniel Chew, *Communities of Singapore: Peranakans*, National Archives of Singapore (Singapore: Oral History Department, 1989).

110. Florence Chan.

111. Victor Sim, *Biographies of Prominent Chinese in Singapore* (Singapore: Nan Kok Publication Company, 1950), 153.

112. Song Ong Siang, *One Hundred Years' History of the Chinese in Singapore* (Singapore: University of Malaya Press, 1967), 352–53.

113. Duncan Sutherland, "Lee Choo Neo," *Singapore Infopedia*, National Library Board Singapore, http://eresources.nlb.gov.sg/infopedia/articles/SIP_1493_2009-04-05.html (accessed October 10, 2016).

114. Seah, "Phoenix without Wings," 60–65.

115. Louis Kwan, "Careers for Educated Chinese Girls," *Straits Chinese Monthly* 2, no. 5/7 (February/April 1933): 33–34; and "The Chinese Woman in the Eyes of the Law," *Straits Chinese Monthly* 4, no. 2 (January 1933): 19–20.

116. "The Modern Eastern Woman, Ignoring the Natural Purposes of Her Life: Warnings from the Philippines," *Malaya Tribune* (August 29, 1931), 4; and "The Women of India: Their Ideals and Problems," *Malaya Tribune* (January 8, 1932), 14.

117. Seah, "Phoenix without Wings," 57.

118. Ooi Yu-lin, *Pieces of Jade and Gold*, 28–29, 30.

119. Doran, 102.

120. Frost, "Transcultural Diaspora," 26–27.

CHAPTER 4

School names are abbreviated as follows: CHGS: Chung Hwa Girls' School; JFGS: Jingfang Girls' School; KCGS: Kuen Cheng Girls' School; NHGS: Nan Hwa Girls' School; NYGHS: Nanyang Girls' High School; NYGS: Nanyang Girls' School; PCGHS: Penang Chinese Girls' High School.

1. "Huaqiao jiaoyu zhi qipa: Nanyang nügaozhongban zhuori biye" (Rare Flowers of Overseas Chinese Education: Nanyang Girls' Upper Secondary Class Graduated Yesterday), *Sin Chew Jit Poh*, December 23, 1934. Although the term *qipa* (奇葩) could be translated as "exotic," the negative connotations of "exotic" would have been known to observers at the time and would have been anathema to proponents of Chinese modernity. Even though the implication of patriarchal conservatism is appropriate for this headline, here I favor the translation "rare" to privilege the unusual status of this minority group of overseas Chinese schoolgirls, and the substantial odds they were up against at graduation.

2. Ye Weili, *Seeking Modernity in China's Name: Chinese Students in the United States, 1900–1927* (Stanford, CA: Stanford University Press, 2001), 121.

3. Lin Yuezhen, "Xiandai nüzi yingyou de renshi" (What a Modern Girl Should Know), *Kuncheng nüzhong chuzhong diqijie biye tekan* (KCGS Lower Secondary Seventh Annual Graduation Special Commemorative Magazine) (Kuala Lumpur: n.p., 1934), 8.

4. Joan Judge, "Talent, Virtue and the Nation: Chinese Nationalism and Female Subjectivities in the Early Twentieth Century," *American Historical Review* 106, no. 3 (June 2001): 765–803, 766.

5. Chai Yaling, "Xiandai nüzi yingyou de renshi" (What a Modern Girl Should Know), *Kuncheng nüzhong chuzhong diqijie biye tekan* (KCGS Lower Secondary Seventh Annual Graduation Special Commemorative Magazine) (Kuala Lumpur: n.p., 1934), 6; and He Zhenzhu, "Zenyang zuo yige hao gongmin" (How to Be a Good Citizen), *Xingzhou Jingfang Nüxuexiao bazhounian jiniankan* (Singapore JFGS Eighth Anniversary Commemorative Magazine) (Singapore: n.p., 1936), 20–21.

6. Re-migrant overseas Chinese women from Chinese girls' schools in Malaya and Singapore, personal interviews with author, Fujian and Guangdong provinces, China, 2006.

7. Paul Bailey, *Gender and Education in China: Gender Discourses and Women's Schooling in the Early Twentieth Century* (London: Routledge, 2007).

8. Fan Ruolan, *Immigration, Gender and Overseas Chinese Society: Studies on the Chinese Women in Malaya (1929–1941)* (Beijing: Zhonghua Huaqiao Publishing, 2005), 114.

9. Robert Culp, *Articulating Citizenship: Civic Education and Student Politics in Southeastern China, 1912–1940* (Cambridge, MA: Harvard University Asia Center, 2007), 12; and Joan Judge, "Citizens or Mothers of Citizens? Gender

and the Meaning of Modern Chinese Citizenship," and Christina K. Gilmartin, "Gender, Political Culture, and Women's Mobilization in the Chinese Nationalist Revolution, 1924–1927," in *Engendering China: Women, Culture, and the State*, ed. Christina K. Gilmartin et al., (Cambridge, MA: Harvard University Press, 1994), 23–43 and 207–12.

10. Fan, 116.
11. Joan Judge, *The Precious Raft of History: The Past, the West, and the Woman Question in China* (Stanford, CA: Stanford University Press, 2008); and Bailey, *Gender and Education in China*. See also Zheng Liangshu's "Xinma Huashe Zaoqide Nüzi Jiaoyu" (The Early Period of Girls' Education in Singaporean and Malayan Chinese Society), *Malaixiya Huaren Yanjiu Xuekan (Journal of Malaysian Chinese Studies)* 1 (August 1997): 47–58.
12. Judge, "Talent, Virtue and the Nation," 769.
13. Culp, 11.
14. *Kuncheng nüxiao sishiwu zhounian jiniankan* (KCGS Forty-Fifth Anniversary Commemorative Magazine) (Kuala Lumpur: n.p., 1953), 16.
15. *Kuncheng nüxiao sishiwu zhounian jiniankan* (1953), 16.
16. *Kuncheng nüxiao liushi zhounian jiniankan* (Kuen Cheng Girls' School Sixtieth Anniversary Commemorative Magazine) (Kuala Lumpur: n.p., 1968), 11.
17. John Cleverley, *The Schooling of China: Tradition and Modernity in Chinese Education*, 2nd ed. (Sydney: Allen and Unwin, 1991), 40.
18. Judge, "Talent, Virtue and the Nation," 771.
19. Fan, 126; and *Kuncheng nüxiao liushi zhounian jiniankan* (1968), 11.
20. Fan, 128–29.
21. G. William Skinner, "Creolized Chinese Societies in Southeast Asia," in *Sojourners and Settlers: Histories of Southeast Asia and the Chinese*, ed. Anthony Reid (Honolulu: University of Hawaii Press, 2001), 87–89.
22. Fan, 158–59.
23. Fan, 122–27.
24. *Xinjiapo Fujian huiguan shuxia Chongfu nüxuexiao liushi zhounian tekan, 1915–1975* (Chong Hock Girls' School, under the Auspices of the Singapore Hokkien Association, Sixtieth Anniversary Special Commemorative Magazine, 1915–1975), Singapore, 1975.
25. Cleverley, 52.
26. "List of Books Used for Various Subjects in the Normal Class Department," in "School Administration," in *Xingzhou Jingfang Nüxuexiao bazhounian jiniankan* (1936), 6. Also *Kuncheng nüxiao sishiwu zhounian jiniankan* (KCGS Forty-Fifth Anniversary Commemorative Magazine) (Kuala Lumpur: n.p., 1953), 69–70.
27. Culp, 43–45.
28. "List of Library Materials," in "Student Associations," *Xingzhou Jingfang Nüxuexiao bazhounian jiniankan* (1936), 5.
29. Zheng, "Girls' Education," 57–58; and Fan, 146–53.
30. Fan, 121, 128–29.
31. Fan, 204–5.
32. Liang Shaowen, *Nanyang lüxing manji* (A Record of Travel in the South Seas) (Shanghai: Zhonghua Publishing, 1924), 152–53.
33. Fan, 121.
34. Fan, 123.
35. Fan, 129.

36. Tan Liok Ee, *The Politics of Chinese Education in Malaya, 1945–1961* (Malaysia: Oxford University Press, 1997), 16.

37. *Binhua nüzi zhongxiaoxue bashi zhounian jinian tekan* (Penang Chinese Girls' Secondary and Primary Schools' Eightieth Anniversary Special Commemorative Issue) (Penang: Penang Chinese Girls' Secondary and Primary Schools, 2000), 24.

38. "School History," Penang Chinese Girls' High School, accessed April 21, 2017, http://www.smjk.edu.my/school/about.php?schid=17&schidx=284&page_type=pageid&pgid=A.

39. Tan Liok Ee, "Chinese Independent Schools in West Malaysia: Varying Responses to Changing Demands," in *Changing Identities of the Southeast Asian Chinese since World War II*, ed. Jennifer W. Cushman and Wang Gungwu (Hong Kong: Hong Kong University Press, 1988), 354–84.

40. Fan, 163–65.

41. Zheng and Wei, 248.

42. Zheng and Wei, 249.

43. *Nanyang nüzi zhongxue xiaokan* (NYGHS Magazine) (Singapore: n.p., 1935), 55.

44. Culp, 196.

45. *Nanyang nüzi zhongxue xiaokan* (NYGHS Magazine) (Singapore: n.p., 1948), 25.

46. *Bincheng Binhua xiaoyouhui qingzhu guangfu ershiyi zhounian, xinhuisuo luocheng jinian tekan* (PCGHS Alumni Association Special Commemorative Issue Celebrating the Twenty-First Anniversary of School Revival and Establishment of a New Centre) (Penang: PCGHS Alumni Association, March 1979); and *Nanyang nüzi zhongxue xiaokan* (1948).

47. Bailey, *Gender and Education in China*.

48. *Xingzhou Jingfang Nüxuexiao bazhounian jiniankan* (1936), 1.

49. *Xingzhou Jingfang Nüxuexiao bazhounian jiniankan* (1936), 4.

50. Denise Gimpel, "Freeing the Mind through the Body: Women's Thoughts on Physical Education in Late Qing and Early Republican China," *Nannü: Men, Women, and Gender in Early and Imperial China* 8, no. 2 (November 2006): 316–58.

51. *Xingzhou Jingfang Nüxuexiao bazhounian jiniankan* (1936), 1–3.

52. *Nanyang nüzi zhongxue xiaokan* (1935), 21.

53. *Nanyang nüzi zhongxue xiaokan* (1948), 20.

54. *Kuncheng nüxiao sishiwu zhounian jiniankan* (1953), 73.

55. Culp, 34–36.

56. Mei Yulan, "Wode huiyi" (My Reminiscences), *Binhua gaoshi tongxuehui liuzhounian jinian tekan* (The Magazine of the Penang Senior Normal Students' Union, Commemorating the Sixth Anniversary) (Penang: n.p., 1962), 32.

57. Mei, 32.

58. Hua R. Lan and Vanessa L. Fong, ed., *Women in Republican China: A Sourcebook* (Armonk, NY: M. E. Sharpe, 1999).

59. *Kuncheng nüzhong chuzhong diqijie biye tekan* (1934).

60. Lan and Fong, *passim*.

61. Chen Aihong, "Dushen yu jiehun" (Singlehood and Marriage), *Kuncheng nüzhong chuzhong diqijie biye tekan* (1934), 3.

62. Chen, "Dushen yu jiehun," 3.

63. Huang Ruigui, "Women de zeren" (Our Responsibility), *Kuncheng nüxiao sishiwu zhounian jiniankan* (1953), 118.

64. Wang Shaona, "Gaoshisheng de shenghuo" (The Life of a Normal School Student), *Kuncheng nüxiao sishiwu zhounian jiniankan* (1953), 115.
65. Liang Jingfeng, "Mian benjie gaoshi biye tongxue de hua" (Encouragement for Fellow Students in the Graduating Normal Class), *Kuncheng nüxiao sishiwu zhounian jiniankan* (1953), 112.
66. Culp, 36.
67. Yao Mengtong, "He Xiangning zai Xinjiapo" (He Xiangning in Singapore), *Yazhou Wenhua* 16 (June 1992): 163–67.
68. *Xingjiapo Nanhua nüxiao yijiusijiunian jianshi biyeban tekan* (Singapore Nan Hwa Girls' School 1949 Teacher Training Graduating Class Special Commemorative Magazine) (Singapore: n.p., 1949), 4.
69. *Xingjiapo Nanhua nüxiao yijiusijiunian jianshi biyeban tekan* (1949), 3.
70. *Xingjiapo Nanhua nüxiao yijiusijiunian jianshi biyeban tekan* (1949), 14 and 16.
71. *Nanhua nüzi zhongxuexiao gaozhong diyijie biyeban jiniankan* (NHGS Upper Secondary First Graduating Class Commemorative Magazine) (Singapore: n.p., 1960), 1.
72. Francis Hoy Kee Wong and Ee Tiang Hong, *Education in Malaysia* (Kuala Lumpur: Heinemann, 1971), 11–12.
73. Agnes Khoo, *Life as the River Flows: Women in the Malayan Anti-Colonial Struggle* (Malaysia: Strategic Information Research Development, 2004).
74. "Foreword," *Xingzhou Jingfang Nüxuexiao bazhounian jiniankan* (1936), 1.
75. Huang Siou Chin, "My View on Chinese Education in South Asia," in *Xingjiapo Nanhua nüxiao yijiusijiunian jianshi biyeban tekan* (Singapore NHGS 1949 Teacher Training Graduating Class Special Commemorative Magazine) (Singapore: n.p., 1949), 17–18.
76. Tang Meijun, personal interview with author, Guangzhou, 2006.
77. Li Yue, personal interview with author, Guangzhou, 2006.
78. He Zhenzhu, "Zenyang zuo yige hao gongmin" (How to Be a Good Citizen), in *Xingzhou Jingfang Nüxuexiao bazhounian jiniankan* (1936), "Student Writings," 20–21.
79. "Ni wei benxiao xueshenghui qing xuexiao dangju mou kuozhan xiaoshe shu" (The School Student Association's Letter Requesting School Authorities to Plan for the Expansion of School Facilities), *Xingzhou Jingfang Nüxuexiao bazhounian jiniankan* (1936), 1.
80. Biographical information in this paragraph is from Margaret Wang, "My Mother," in *Chinese Women: Their Malaysian Journey*, ed. Neil Khor (Selangor, Malaysia: MPH Group Publishing, 2010), 56–57.
81. Bailey, 118–19.
82. *Xingzhou Jingfang Nüxuexiao bazhounian jiniankan* (1936), 2.
83. *Xingzhou Jingfang Nüxuexiao bazhounian jiniankan* (1936), 8.
84. *Nanyang nüzi zhongxue xiaokan* (1935), 41.
85. *Nanyang nüzi zhongxue xiaokan* (1935), 44.
86. Culp, 171–74.
87. Culp, 174.
88. "Benxiao jianshi" (A Brief School History), *Kuncheng nüxiao liushi zhounian jiniankan* (1968), 11.
89. Lim Lee Chin, "A Study of the Early History of Chinese Women in Singapore and Malaya through *Penang Sin Pao*" (BA Honors Thesis, Singapore, National University of Singapore, 2000–01), 40.

90. "Wu Zaimin zhuo zai Nanhua nüxue yanjiang, pingji huanan nüzi e'xi, bushaofan bufengyi hunushibi zhizhixiaofei" (Wu Zaimin Yesterday Spoke at Nan Hwa Girls' School, Criticizing the Bad Habits of Southern Chinese Girls— Not Cooking, Not Sewing, Ordering Servants Around and Only Knowing How to Spend Money), in *Sin Chew Jit Poh* (Singapore Daily Newspaper), 1936.

91. *Xingjiapo Nanhua nüxiao yijiusijiunian jianshi biyeban tekan* (1949), 21–22.

92. Xiu Ming, "Lin," in *Xingzhou Jingfang Nüxuexiao bazhounian jiniankan* (1936), 1; Lin Yuezhen, "Wangshi fenji" (Reflecting on the Past), in *Kuncheng nüzhong chuzhong diqijie biye tekan* (1934), 6–7.

93. Xiu, "Lin."

94. Su Lin Lewis, "Cosmopolitanism and the Modern Girl: A Cross-Cultural Discourse in 1930s Penang," *Modern Asian Studies* 43, no. 6 (November 2009): 1385–1419. Also Weinbaum et al., eds., *The Modern Girl around the World*.

95. Louise Edwards, "Policing the Modern Woman in Republican China," *Modern China* 26, no. 2 (April 2000): 115–47; and Sarah E. Stevens, "Figuring Modernity: The New Woman and the Modern Girl in Republican China," *NWSA Journal* 15, no. 3 (Fall 2003): 82–103.

96. Lin Yuezhen, "Xiandai nüzi yingyou de renshi" (What a Modern Girl Should Know), *Kuncheng nüzhong chuzhong diqijie biye tekan* (1934), 8.

97. Hong Xiuhao, "Qiantu" (The Future), in *Xingzhou Jingfang Nüxuexiao bazhounian jiniankan* (1936), 14.

98. *Sin Chew Jit Poh* (Singapore Daily Newspaper), "Wo dui Mahua zhishi funü de yidian xiwang" (A Small Hope that I Have for Intellectual Chinese Women in Malaya) and "Xiang Jilongpo nütongxue jing yiyan" (A Word to Fellow Female Students in Kuala Lumpur), April 17, 1938.

99. Yang Ruichu, "Zeng jianshi biye tongxue" (To the Graduates of the Normal Class), in *"Xingjiapo Nanhua nüxiao yijiusijiunian jianshi biyeban tekan* (1949), 14; Li Ruoming, "Wo biye le" (I Have Graduated), in *Xinjiapo Nanhua nüxiao jianshi biyeban tongxuelu* (Singapore NHGS Teacher Training Graduating Class Student Directory) (Singapore: n.p., 1950), 39; and Xi, "Zhiye yu qiantu" (Career and Future), in *Zhonghua nüzhong gaozhong biyekan* (Singapore CHGS Upper Secondary Graduation Commemorative Magazine) (Singapore: n.p., 1957), 7.

100. Huang Peilian, "Funü yu jiaoyu wenti" (The Question of Women and Education), in *"Xingjiapo Nanhua nüxiao yijiusijiunian jianshi biyeban tekan* (1949), 69.

101. Liang, "Mian," in *Kuncheng nüxiao sishiwu zhounian jiniankan* (1953), 112.

102. Hwee Chee, "Women's Education," in *Nanyang nüzhong gaozhong dishisijie biye tekan* (NYGHS Upper Secondary Fourteenth Graduating Class Special Commemorative Magazine) (Singapore: n.p. 1960), 65.

103. Kuhn, 280–81.

104. Culp, 147.

105. Former students of Chinese girls' schools in Malaya and Singapore, personal interviews with author, Malaysia and Singapore, 2005–06.

106. Fang Bixia, "Wo lixiangzhong de zhiye" (My Ideal Career), in *Kuncheng nüxiao sishiwu zhounian jiniankan* (1953), 116.

107. Luo Bin, "Biye qianxi tan funü wenti" (Discussing Women's Issues on the Eve of Graduation), in *Nanyang nüzhong gaozhong dishisijie biye tekan* (NYGHS Upper Secondary Fourteenth Graduating Class Special Commemorative Magazine) (Singapore: n.p., 1960), 37.

108. Gilmartin, "Gender, Political Culture, and Women's Mobilization."

109. A few examples in overseas Chinese studies include Caleb Ford, "Guiqiao (Returned Overseas Chinese) Identity in the PRC," *Journal of Chinese Overseas* 10 (2014): 239–62; Hong Liu, "Old Linkages, New Networks: The Globalization of Overseas Chinese Voluntary Associations and Its Implications," *China Quarterly* 155 (September 1998): 582–609; Leo Suryadinata, ed., *Ethnic Chinese as Southeast Asians* (Singapore: Institute for Southeast Asian Studies, 1997); and Flemming Christiansen, *Overseas Chinese in Europe: An Imagined Community?* (Leeds: University of Leeds Department of East Asian Studies, 1997).

CHAPTER 5

1. Bai Xueqiao, "Bai Xueqiao de yi feng xin" (A Letter by Bai Xueqiao), May 18, 1939, in *Huaqiao yu qiaowu shiliao huibian* (A Compilation of Historical Materials on the Overseas Chinese and Overseas Chinese Affairs Commission), comp. Guangdong sheng dang'anguan (Guangdong Provincial Archives) (Guangdong, China: Guangdong renmin chubanshe, 1991), 692–93.
2. Michael R. Godley, "The Sojourners: Returned Overseas Chinese in the People's Republic of China," *Pacific Affairs* 62, no. 3 (Autumn 1989): 330–52.
3. Glen Peterson, *Overseas Chinese in the People's Republic of China* (London: Routledge, 2012). See also Maurice Freedman, "The Chinese in Southeast Asia: A Longer View," in *The Study of Chinese Society: Essays by Maurice Freedman, Selected and Introduced by G. William Skinner* (Stanford, CA: Stanford University Press, 1979), 20–21.
4. Xun Chaofang, "Bai Xueqiao: chuanqi huaqiao nüjigong" (Bai Xueqiao: A Legend of the Overseas Chinese Women's Engineer Corps), *Yangcheng Wanbao*, September 21, 2005, p. A19; and Bai Xueqiao, personal interview with author, Guangzhou, Guangdong province, 2006. The following details of Bai's story are also drawn from these two sources.
5. Bai Xueqiao, "Bai Xueqiao de yi feng xin" (A Letter by Bai Xueqiao), 1939.
6. Xun, "Bai Xueqiao."
7. Qiu Jin, "Song of the Jingwei Bird," in *Writing Women in Modern China: An Anthology of Women's Literature from the Early Twentieth Century*, ed. Amy D. Dooling and Kristina M. Torgeson (New York: Columbia University Press, 1998), 43–78.
8. Qiu, "Song of the Jingwei Bird," 78.
9. Xun, "Bai Xueqiao."
10. Philip A. Kuhn, "Revolution and 'National Salvation,'" in *Chinese among Others: Emigration in Modern Times* (Lanham, MD: Rowman and Littlefield, 2008), 239–82.
11. See Shen Huifen, *China's Left-Behind Wives: Families of Migrants from Fujian to Southeast Asia, 1930s–1950s* (Hawaii: University of Hawaii Press, 2012); Michael Szonyi, "Mothers, Sons, and Lovers: Fidelity and Frugality in the Overseas Chinese Divided Family before 1949," *Journal of Chinese Overseas* 1, no. 1 (2005): 43–64; and Peterson, *Overseas Chinese in the People's Republic of China*.
12. Stephen Fitzgerald, "China and the Overseas Chinese: Perceptions and Policies," *China Quarterly* 44 (October–December 1970), 1–37; Marilyn W. Tinsman, "China and the Returned Overseas Chinese Students" (EdD Diss., Teachers College, Columbia University, 1983); Glen D. Peterson, "Socialist China and the Huaqiao: The Transition to Socialism in the Overseas Chinese Areas of Rural Guangdong, 1949–1956," *Modern China* 14, no. 3 (July 1988), 309–35; and Godley, "The Sojourners," 1989.

13. Because my goal was to capture a subjective sense of these women's attitudes and opinions as opposed to a statistically representative set of information, and because the issue of re-migrants remains politically sensitive, I kept the scope of the interviews small and have also changed names and identifying details of some interviewees while preserving as much as possible of their individual stories.

14. Joan Judge, "Talent, Virtue, and the Nation: Chinese Nationalisms and Female Subjectivities in the Early Twentieth Century," *American Historical Review* 106, no. 3 (June 2001): 765–803.

15. Kuhn, "Revolution and 'National Salvation,'" in *Chinese among Others*.

16. Leo Suryadinata, ed., *Ethnic Relations and Nation-Building in Southeast Asia: The Case of the Ethnic Chinese* (Singapore: Institute of Southeast Asian Studies, 2004).

17. Daniel Chirot and Anthony Reid, eds., *Essential Outsiders: Chinese and Jews in the Modern Transformation of Southeast Asia and Central Europe* (Seattle: University of Washington Press, 1997).

18. Examples of such articles from *Guangdong Qiaobao* (Guangdong Overseas Chinese Newspaper) include "How I Taught My Children to Be Farm Workers," July 18, 1963, and "Pampered Overseas Chinese Maiden He Huiping Toughens Up to Become a 'Good Transfer Youth,'" April 17, 1965.

19. Gail Hershatter, "The Gender of Memory: Rural Chinese Women and the 1950s," *Signs: Journal of Women and Culture in Society* 28, no.1 (2002): 43–70, 64.

20. Kuhn, 267 and 365.

21. Tinsman, 124.

22. Tinsman, 207.

23. Godley, 332.

24. From *Fujian Qiaoxiangbao* (Fujian Overseas Chinese Newspaper), "Gedi huaqiao zinü xuesheng you henda de jinbu" (Returned Overseas Chinese Students Everywhere Are Improving Greatly), July 28, 1956; and "Yinggai zhongshi guli huaqiao banxue" (Education Efforts for Overseas Chinese Should Be Taken Seriously and Encouraged), March 7, 1957.

25. Guo Meiying, personal interview with author, Kuala Lumpur, Malaysia, 2005.

26. Chen Shilin, personal interview with author, Fuzhou, Fujian province, China, 2006.

27. Peng Anyun, personal interview with author, Guangzhou, Guangdong province, China, 2006.

28. Yen Ching-Hwang, "Ch'ing Changing Images of the Overseas Chinese (1644– 1912)," *Modern Asian Studies* 15, no. 2 (1981): 261–85.

29. "Huaqiao zinü taolun bushengxue youmeiyou qiantu—dou shengxue, jiao shui shengchan ne?" (Returned Overseas Chinese Youth Discuss Whether Not Seeking Higher Education Means They Will Have No Future—If All Seek Higher Education, Who Will Engage in Production?), *Fujian Qiaoxiangbao* (Fujian Overseas Chinese Newspaper), March 27, 1957.

30. From *Guangdong Qiaobao* (Guangdong Overseas Chinese Newspaper), "Nongcun wuxian hao" (The Village Is Limitlessly Good), January 30, 1964; and "Ta jianjue buyaoqiu teshu zhaogu" (She Resolutely Refused Special Treatment), March 5, 1964.

31. Yin Ling, personal interview with author, Xiamen, Fujian province, China, 2006.

32. "Bai Xueqiao: Zuguo weinanshi, jie wo yidi li" (Bai Xueqiao: When the ancestral nation was in difficulty, I made my modest contribution"), CCTV's Facebook

page, accessed March 3, 2017, https://www.facebook.com/CCTV.CH/videos/1178661385554752/.

33. Liu Peifen, personal interview with author, Fuzhou, Fujian province, China, 2006.

34. Bai Xueqiao, "Bai Xueqiao de yi feng xin" (A Letter by Bai Xueqiao), 1939.

35. Cai Jianyu, "Guiqiao de gushi: maya, woshi nide nü'er!" (Stories of Returned Overseas Chinese: Mother, I Am Your Daughter!), *Fujian Qiaobao*, August 27, 2004, 4.

36. Cai Jianyu, personal interview with author, Fuzhou, Fujian province, China, 2006.

37. See, for example, Sylvia Pankhurst, *The Suffragette: The History of the Women's Militant Suffrage Movement, 1905–1910* (New York: Sturgis and Walton, 1911).

38. Yin Ling, personal interview with author, Xiamen, Fujian province, China, 2006.

39. Tang Meijun, personal interview with author, Guangzhou, Guangdong province, China, 2006.

40. For more on Chinese women who joined the Malayan Communist guerilla movement, see Agnes Khoo, *Life as the River Flows: Women in the Malayan Anti-Colonial Struggle (An Oral History of Women from Thailand, Malaysia and Singapore)* (Malaysia: Strategic Information Research Development, 2004).

41. Peng Anyun, personal interview with author, 2006.

42. Yin Ling, personal interview with author, 2006.

43. Zheng Ruyue, personal interview with author, Guangzhou, Guangdong province, China, 2006.

44. Fu Mingwei, personal interview with author, Xiamen, Fujian province, China, 2006.

45. Li Yue, personal interview with author, Guangzhou, Guangdong province, China, 2006.

46. Bai, personal interview with author.

47. Meng Yue, "Female Images and National Myth," in *Gender Politics in Modern China: Writing and Feminism*, ed. Tani Barlow (Durham, NC: Duke University Press, 1993), 118–36.

48. Li Xiaojiang, "With What Discourse Do We Reflect on Chinese Women? Thoughts on Transnational Feminism in China," in *Spaces of Their Own: Women's Public Sphere in Transnational China*, ed. Mayfair Mei-hui Yang (Minneapolis: University of Minnesota Press, 1999), 261–77, 269.

49. Alys Eve Weinbaum et al., eds, *The Modern Girl around the World: Consumption, Modernity, and Globalization* (Durham, NC: Duke University Press, 2008).

50. Robert Culp, *Articulating Citizenship: Civic Education and Student Politics in Southeastern China, 1912–1940* (Cambridge, MA: Harvard University Asia Center, 2007), 13.

51. Li, "With What Discourse," 268–69.

52. Elisabeth Croll, *Feminism and Socialism in China* (London: Routledge and Kegan Paul, 1978), 3.

53. Margery Wolf and Roxane Witke, eds., *Women in Chinese Society* (Stanford, CA: Stanford University Press, 1975); Margery Wolf, *Revolution Postponed: Women in Contemporary China* (Stanford, CA: Stanford University Press, 1985); Emily Honig and Gail Hershatter, eds., *Personal Voices: Chinese Women in the 1980s* (Stanford, CA: Stanford University Press, 1988); Christina K. Gilmartin et al., eds., *Engendering China: Women, Culture, and the State*, (Cambridge, MA: Harvard University Press, 1994); Prasenjit Duara, "The

Regime of Authenticity: Timelessness, Gender, and National History in Modern China," *History and Theory: Studies in the Philosophy of History* 37, no. 3 (October 1998): 287–308; Judge, "Talent, Virtue, and the Nation," 2001; and Gail Hershatter, "The Gender of Memory: Rural Chinese Women and the 1950s," *Signs: Journal of Women and Culture in Society* 28, no. 1 (2002): 43–70.

54. Li, "With What Discourse," 272–76.
55. Bai, personal interview with author.
56. Judge, "Talent, Virtue, and the Nation," 766.
57. Lisa Rofel, *Other Modernities: Gendered Yearnings in China after Socialism* (Berkeley: University of California Press, 1999).

CONCLUSION

1. Phyllis Ghim Lian Chew, *The Singapore Council of Women and the Women's Movement* (Singapore: Singapore University Press, 1999).
2. Tey Nai Peng, "The Changing Demographic Situation of Malaysian Chinese," in *Ethnic Chinese in Singapore and Malaysia: A Dialogue between Tradition and Modernity*, ed. Leo Suryadinata (Singapore: Times Academic Press, 2002): 45–66, 46; and Francis Hoy Kee Wong and Ee Tiang Hong, *Education in Malaya* (Singapore: Heinemann Educational Books, 1971), 105.
3. Chiew Seen Kong, "Chinese Singaporeans: Three Decades of Progress and Changes," in *Ethnic Chinese in Singapore and Malaysia: A Dialogue between Tradition and Modernity*, ed. Leo Suryadinata (Singapore: Times Academic Press, 2002): 11–44; and Anthony Reid, ed., *Sojourners and Settlers: Histories of Southeast Asia and the Chinese* (Sydney: Allen and Unwin, 1996), xxiii.
4. Lee Ting Hui, *Chinese Schools in British Malaya: Policies and Politics* (Singapore: South Seas Society, 2006); Zheng Liangshu, *Malaixiya Huawen jiaoyu fazhan jianshi* (A Concise History of the Development of Chinese Education in Malaysia) (Malaysia: Nanfang xueyuan chubanshe, 2005); and Tan Liok Ee, *The Politics of Chinese Education in Malaya, 1945–1961* (Malaysia: Oxford University Press, 1997).
5. Harold E. Wilson, *Social Engineering in Singapore: Educational Policies and Social Change* (Singapore: Singapore University Press, 1978), 237.
6. Kho Ee Moi, "Construction of Femininity: Girls' Education in Singapore, 1959–2000" (PhD Diss., National University of Singapore, 2004).
7. Onn bin Jaafar, *Debates of the Dewan Rakyat*, December 5, 1959, in Lenore Manderson, "The Development and Direction of Female Education in Peninsular Malaysia," *Journal of the Malayan Branch of the Royal Asiatic Society* 51, no. 2 (December 1978): 100–22, 114.
8. Sutan Shahrir, "Education the Only Remedy—Mrs. Shahrir," *Straits Times*, October 13, 1951; and "Weaker Sex," *Singapore Free Press*, March 10, 1952, in Kho, 40.
9. Kho, 51–54.
10. Kho, 62–65.
11. "Girls Urged to Work as Hard as the Boys," *Straits Times*, July 27, 1968, in Kho, 72.
12. Singapore Ministry of Education, *Syllabus for Domestic Science* (Singapore: Ministry of Education), in Kho, 107–8.
13. Lee Sook Ching and Seow Peng Kim, *Comprehensive Domestic Science Book 1* (Singapore: Federal Publications, 1968), in Kho, 108–9.
14. *Xinjiapo Nanhua nüzi zhongxuexiao wushiwu zhounian jinian ji jiazhengshi luocheng dianli tekan* (Singapore Nan Hwa Girls' High School Fifty-Fifth Anniversary

and Official Opening of Home Economics Classroom Souvenir Magazine) (Singapore: n.p., 1971), 1.

15. Hwee Chee, "Women's Education," in *Nanyang nüzhong gaozhong dishisijie biye tekan* (NYGHS Upper Secondary Fourteenth Graduating Class Special Commemorative Magazine) (Singapore: n.p. 1960), 65.

16. Joan Judge, "Citizens or Mothers of Citizens? Gender and the Meaning of Modern Chinese Citizenship," in *Changing Meanings of Citizenship in Modern China*, ed. Merle Goldman and Elizabeth J. Perry (Cambridge, MA: Harvard University Press, 2002), 23–43.

17. Kho, 77.

18. *Singapore Teacher*, May 1968, 15; *Singapore Teacher*, March/April 1969, 42; and *Singapore Teacher*, January/February 1969, 14.

19. Christine Inglis, "The Feminisation of the Teaching Profession in Singapore," in *Women's Work and Women's Roles: Economics and Everyday Life in Indonesia, Malaysia and Singapore*, ed. Lenore Manderson (Canberra: Australian National University, 1983), 217–39, 217.

20. Inglis, 232–33.

21. Inglis, 237.

22. Loh Teik Soon, personal interview with author, Kuala Lumpur, 2005.

23. Singapore Ministry of Education, *Syllabus for Domestic Science*, 1.

24. Singapore Ministry of Education, *Syllabus for Domestic Science*, 1.

25. Kho, 77–80.

26. Mark R. Thompson, "Pacific Asia after 'Asian Values': Authoritarianism, Democracy, and 'Good Governance,'" *Third World Quarterly* 25, no. 6 (2004): 1079–95.

27. Kho, 80–82. On self-orientalization, see Huang Jianli and Lysa Hong, "Chinese Diasporic Culture and National Identity: The Taming of the Tiger Balm Gardens in Singapore," *Modern Asian Studies* 41, no. 1 (2007): 41–76.

28. Geraldine Heng and Janadas Devan, "State Fatherhood: The Politics of Nationalism, Sexuality, and Race in Singapore," in *Nationalisms and Sexualities*, ed. Andrew Parker et al. (Singapore: Routledge, 1991), 344–64.

BIBLIOGRAPHY

PRIMARY SOURCES

Annals of IJ Convent Light Street, Penang. Book 1 (1851–1905). Convent of the Holy Infant Archives.

Annual Report of the Department of Education, Singapore. 1946–56.

Annual Reports on Education in the Federated Malay States. 1931–34.

Annual Reports on Education, Federation of Malaya. 1948–57.

Annual Reports on Education in the Malayan Union. 1946–47.

Bai Xueqiao. Personal interview with author. Guangzhou, Guangdong province, China, 2006.

Bincheng Binhua xiaoyouhui qingzhu guangfu ershiyi zhounian, xinhuisuo luocheng jinian tekan (Penang Chinese Girls' High School Alumni Association Special Commemorative Issue Celebrating the Twenty-First Anniversary of School Revival and Establishment of a New Center). Penang, Malaysia: Penang Chinese Girls' High School Alumni Association, March 1979.

Binhua gaoshi tongxuehui liuzhounian jinian tekan (The Magazine of the Penang Senior Normal Students' Union, Commemorating the Sixth Anniversary). Penang, Malaysia: 1962.

Binhua nüzi zhongxiaoxue sishi zhounian jinian tekan (Penang Chinese Girls' Secondary and Primary Schools' Fortieth Anniversary Special Commemorative Issue). Penang, Malaya: Penang Chinese Girls' Secondary and Primary Schools, December 1960.

Binhua nüzi zhongxiaoxue bashi zhounian jinian tekan (Penang Chinese Girls' Secondary and Primary Schools' Eightieth Anniversary Special Commemorative Issue). Penang, Malaysia: Penang Chinese Girls' Secondary and Primary Schools, 2000.

Blackmore, Sophia. Report. *Methodist Message* (April 1899). In "Linda Lim's MGS Schooldays," by Linda Lim. Unpublished memoir, 2004.

Cai Jianyu. "Guiqiao de gushi: maya, wo shi ni de nü'er!" (Stories of Returned Overseas Chinese: Mother, I Am Your Daughter!). *Fujian Qiaobao*, August 27, 2004, 4.

Cai Jianyu. Personal interview with author. Fuzhou, Fujian province, China, 2006.

Chan, Florence. Interview with Daniel Chew. *Communities of Singapore: Peranakans.* National Archives of Singapore. Singapore: Oral History Department, 1989.

Chang, Margaret. Personal interview with author. Singapore, 2005.

The Charitable Mistresses of the Holy Infant Jesus, Known as the Dames de St Maur 1662. Published in the Mother Generalship of Reverend Mother Ste Marguerite-Marie

    Delbecq for the Missionary Exhibition Held at the Vatican December 25th, 1924.
        Dornach (Haut-Rhin): Braun & Co., 1925.

Chen Shilin. Personal interview with author. Fuzhou, Fujian province, China, 2006.

Chong Eu Ngoh. Personal interview with author. Kuala Lumpur, Malaysia, 2005.

Colonial Office Files. CO 273. Straits Settlements. Original Correspondence
    (1838–1946).

Congregation des Soeurs du Saint Enfant Jesus dites Dames de Saint-Maur 1662
    (Congregation of the Sisters of the Holy Infant Jesus called Dames de Saint
    Maur 1662). 1950. Convent of the Holy Infant Archives.

*Congregation of the Sisters of the Holy Infant Jesus called Dames de St Maur Centenary
    Souvenir: Mission of the Sisters of the Holy Infant Jesus in Malaya 1852–1952.*
    Convent of the Holy Infant Archives.

Convent Bukit Nanas: 100 Years at the Top, 1899–1999. Kuala Lumpur: Kamsiah
    Mohammad, 1998.

Convent Bukit Nanas Community Annals 1899–1942. Convent of the Holy Infant
    Archives.

Convent Bukit Nanas School Annals 1899–1956. Convent of the Holy Infant Archives.

Convent Light Street: 150 Years of Touching Hearts, 1852–2002. Penang, Malaysia:
    2002.

Convent Light Street Scrapbook 1, 1900–30. Convent of the Holy Infant Archives.

Convent Light Street Scrapbook 3, 1939–65. Convent of the Holy Infant Archives.

*Convents of the Infant Jesus (Nicolas Barre): Malaysia-Singapore, 1852–1981. Notes
    Compiled by Rev. Mother Charles DeLebarre, Provincial Superior Malaysia-
    Singapore, 1954–1970, from the Annals of the Communities of Malaysia-Singapore
    and Documents from the Archives of the Congregation, Paris.* Convent of the Holy
    Infant Archives.

*English Essays and Compositions by Junior Middle School Graduates (1935 Class) of the
    Kwan Seng [Kuen Cheng] Girls' School.* Kuala Lumpur: Union Press, 1935.

Fang Jianyi. Group interview with author, Kuen Cheng Girls' High School Alumni
    Association. Kuala Lumpur, Malaysia, 2005.

Federation of Malaya. Federal Secretariat Files 13130. 1948–54.

Fifth Educational Conference of Malaya. Official Report of the Proceedings. [1939].

"First Report of the Advisory Committee on Social Hygiene, 1925. Paper to be laid
    before the Legislative Council by Command of His Excellency the Officer
    Administering the Government. No. 48 of 1925."

Forde, Sister Brede. Personal interview with author. Kuala Lumpur, Malaysia, 2005.

Fu Mingwei. Personal interview with author. Xiamen, Fujian province, China, 2006.

Fujian sheng dang'anguan (Fujian Provincial Archives), comp. *Fujian huaqiao dang'an
    shiliao* (Historical Materials from the Fujian Overseas Chinese Archives).
    Fuzhou, China: Dang'an chubanshe, 1990.

Fujian Qiaoxiangbao (Fujian Overseas Chinese Newspaper). 1956–67.

Guangdong sheng dang'anguan (Guangdong Provincial Archives), comp. *Huaqiao yu
    qiaowu shiliao huibian* (A Compilation of Historical Materials on the Overseas
    Chinese and Overseas Chinese Affairs Commission). Guangdong: Guangzhou
    renmin chubanshe, 1991.

Guangdong Qiaobao (Guangdong Overseas Chinese Newspaper). 1963–66.

Goh Min Yee. Personal interview with author. Penang, Malaysia, 2006.

Guo Meiying. Personal interview with author. Kuala Lumpur, Malaysia, 2005.

IJ Bukit Nanas, Kuala Lumpur, Book 8. Community Annals 1548–1946. Convent of the
    Holy Infant Archives.

IJ Bukit Nanas, Kuala Lumpur School Annals—Book 1, 1899–1916. Convent of the Holy Infant Archives.

IJ Mission in Malaya, 1852–1945. Convent of the Holy Infant Archives.

Koh, Susan. Personal interview with author. Penang, Malaysia, 2006.

Kuncheng nüxiao bashi zhounian jiniankan (Kuen Cheng Girls' School Eightieth Anniversary Commemorative Magazine). Kuala Lumpur: 1993.

Kuncheng nüxiao liushi zhounian jiniankan (Kuen Cheng Girls' School Sixtieth Anniversary Commemorative Magazine). Kuala Lumpur: 1968.

Kuncheng nüxiao sishiwu zhounian jiniankan (Kuen Cheng Girls' School Forty-Fifth Anniversary Commemorative Magazine). Kuala Lumpur: 1953.

Kuncheng nüxiao wushiliu zhounian jiniankan (Kuen Cheng Girls' School Fifty-Sixth Anniversary Commemorative Magazine). Kuala Lumpur: 1964.

Kuncheng nüzhong chuzhong diqijie biye tekan (Kuen Cheng Girls' School Lower Secondary Seventh Annual Graduation Special Commemorative Magazine). Kuala Lumpur: 1934.

Kuncheng nüzhong gaozhong diqijie biye tekan (Kuen Cheng Girls' School Upper Secondary Seventh Annual Graduation Special Commemorative Magazine). Kuala Lumpur: 1963.

Lat Pau (The Straits Newspaper). 1920–40.

Li Yue. Personal interview with author. Guangzhou, Guangdong province, China, 2006.

Liang Shaowen. *Nanyang lüxing manji* (A Record of Travel in the South Seas). Shanghai: Zhonghua, 1924.

Liu Peifen. Personal interview with author. Fuzhou, Fujian province, China, 2006.

Loh Teik Soon. Personal interview with author. Kuala Lumpur, 2005.

Lu Zhao. Personal interview with author. Selangor, Malaysia, 2006.

Lu Wei. Personal interview with author. Selangor, Malaysia, 2006.

Lye Ming Pao. Personal interview with author. Selangor, Malaysia, 2005.

Malaya Tribune. 1931–35.

Nanhua nüzi zhongxuexiao gaozhong diyijie biyeban jiniankan (Nan Hwa Girls' High School Upper Secondary First Graduating Class Commemorative Magazine). Singapore: 1960.

Nanhua nüzi zhongxuexiao liushi zhounian jinian tekan (Nan Hwa Girls' High Sixtieth Anniversary Souvenir Magazine). Singapore: 1977.

Nanyang nüzhong gaozhong dishisijie biye tekan (Nanyang Girls' High School Upper Secondary Fourteenth Graduating Class Special Commemorative Magazine). Singapore: 1960.

Nanyang nüzi zhongxue xiaokan (Nanyang Girls' High School Magazine). Singapore: 1935.

Nanyang nüzi zhongxue xiaokan (Nanyang Girls' High School Magazine). Singapore: 1948.

Nanyang Siang Pau (The South Seas Trade Newspaper). 1922–51.

Ng Lay Sah. Personal interview with author. Selangor, Malaysia, 2005.

Oliveiro, Janet. Personal interview with author. Penang, Malaysia, 2006.

Ong Lay Fang. Personal interview with author. Penang, Malaysia, 2006.

Ong Li Peng. Personal interview with author. Penang, Malaysia, 2006.

Ong, Rose. Personal interview with author. Penang, Malaysia, 2006.

Oon Chiew Seng. Personal interview with author. Singapore, 2006.

Peng Anyun. Personal interview with author. Guangzhou, Guangdong province, China, 2006.

Qing xuebu (Qing Ministry of Education). *Xuebu guanbao* (Ministry of Education Official Reports). Taipei: Gugong buowuyuan, 1980.

Ryan, Sister Enda. Personal interview with author. Selangor, Malaysia, 2005.

Selangor Secretariat Files. 1875–1955.

Sin Chew Jit Poh (The Singapore Daily Newspaper). 1932–36.

The Singapore Free Press and Mercantile Advertiser. 1899–1924.

Singapore Teacher. 1968–69.

Song Ong Siang. *One Hundred Years of the Chinese in Singapore.* London: John Murray, 1923.

Straits Chinese Annual. 1909.

Straits Chinese Magazine: A Quarterly Journal of Oriental and Occidental Culture. 1897–1904.

Straits Chinese Monthly. 1933.

Straits Settlements Annual Report on Education. 1924.

Swettenham, Frank A. *The Real Malay.* London: John Lane, 1899.

Tang Meijun. Personal interview with author. Guangzhou, Guangdong province, China, 2006.

Xinjiapo Fujian huiguan shuxia Chongfu nüxuexiao liushi zhounian tekan, 1915–1975 (Chong Hock Girls' School, under the Auspices of the Singapore Hokkien Association, Sixtieth Anniversary Special Commemorative Magazine, 1915–1975). Singapore: 1975.

Xinjiapo Fujian huiguan zhuban Nanqiao nüzi zhongxue chuangxiao ershi zhounian tekan (Singapore Nan Chiao Girls' High School Tenth Anniversary Graduation Special Commemorative Magazine). Singapore: 1967.

Xinjiapo Hongxing nüzi zhiye xuexiao wu zhounian jinian tekan (Singapore Hongxing Girls' Vocational School Fifth Anniversary Special Commemorative Magazine). Singapore: 1951.

Xinjiapo Nanhua nüxiao jianshi biyeban tongxuelu (Singapore Nan Hwa Girls' School Teacher Training Graduating Class Student Directory). Singapore: 1950.

Xinjiapo Nanhua nüzi zhongxuexiao wushi zhounian jinian ji youyihui tekan (Singapore Nan Hwa Girls' High School Fiftieth Anniversary Variety Concert and Souvenir Magazine). Singapore: 1966.

Xinjiapo Nanhua nüzi zhongxuexiao wushiwu zhounian jinian ji jiazhengshi luocheng dianli tekan (Singapore Nan Hwa Girls' High School Fifty-Fifth Anniversary and Official Opening of Home Economics Classroom Souvenir Magazine). Singapore: 1971.

Xinjiapo Nanqiao nüzi zhongxuexiao dishijie biye tekan (Singapore Nan Chiao Girls' High School Tenth Anniversary Graduation Special Commemorative Magazine). Singapore: 1961.

Xinjiapo nüzi zhiye zhongxue chuangxiao ershi zhounian jinian tekan (Singapore Girls' Vocational High School Twentieth Anniversary Special Commemorative Magazine). Singapore: 1976.

Xinjiapo Zhonghua nüzhong gaoshi di'erjie biye tekan (Singapore Chung Hwa Girls' School Teacher Training Second Annual Graduation Special Commemorative Magazine). Singapore: 1950.

Xinjiapo Zhonghua nüzi zhongxue chuangxiao liushi zhounian jinian tekan (Singapore Chung Hwa Girls' School Sixtieth Anniversary Special Commemorative Magazine). Singapore: 1972.

Xingjiapo Nanhua nüxiao yijiusijiunian jianshi biyeban tekan (Singapore Nan Hwa Girls' School 1949 Teacher Training Graduating Class Special Commemorative Magazine). Singapore: 1949.

Xingzhou Jingfang Nüxuexiao bazhounian jiniankan (Singapore Jingfang Girls' School Eighth Anniversary Commemorative Magazine). Singapore: 1936.

Yin Ling. Personal interview with author. Xiamen, Fujian province, China, 2006.

Yong, Christine. Personal interview with author. Kuala Lumpur, Malaysia, 2005.

Yong, Maria. Personal interview with author. Selangor, Malaysia, 2005.

Zhang Ruiyue. Personal interview with author. Guangzhou, Guangdong province, China, 2006.

Zhonghua minguo jiaoyubu jiaoyu nianjian bian weiyuanhui (Republican China Ministry of Education Yearbook on Education Committee). *Di'erci Zhongguo jiaoyu nianjian* (Second Education in China Yearbook). Shanghai: Shangwu yinshuguan, 1948.

Zhonghua nüzhong gaozhong biyekan (Singapore Chung Hwa Girls' School Upper Secondary Graduation Commemorative Magazine). Singapore: 1957.

Zhongguo di'er lishi dang'anguan (Second Historical Archives of China). *Zhonghua minguoshi dang'an ziliao huibian* (A Compilation of Republican Historical Archive Materials). 1991.

Zhongguo minguo jiaoyubu (Republican China Ministry of Education). *Diyici Zhongguo jiaoyu nianjian* (First Education in China Yearbook). Shanghai: Kaiming shudian, 1931.

SECONDARY REFERENCES

Althusser, Louis. "Ideology and Ideological State Apparatus." In *Lenin and Philosophy and Other Essays*. London: New Left Books, 1977.

Ampalavanar, Rajeswary. *The Indian Minority and Political Change in Malaya, 1945–1957*. London: Oxford University Press, 1981.

Amrith, Sunil. *Migration and Diaspora in Modern Asia*. New York: Cambridge University Press, 2011.

Ang Siok Hui. "Pioneer Female Mission Schools in Singapore, 1842–1942." BA Honors Thesis, Department of History, National University of Singapore, 1993/94.

Appadurai, Arjun. *Modernity at Large: Cultural Dimensions of Globalization*. Minneapolis: University of Minnesota Press, 1996.

Bailey, Paul J. *Gender and Education in China: Gender Discourses and Women's Schooling in the Early Twentieth Century*. London: Routledge, 2007.

Bao Jiemin. *Marital Acts: Gender, Sexuality, and Identity among the Chinese Thai Diaspora*. Honolulu: University of Hawaii Press, 2005.

Barlow, Tani, ed. *Gender Politics in Modern China: Writing and Feminism*. Durham, NC: Duke University Press, 1993.

Barlow, Tani. *The Question of Women in Chinese Feminism*. Durham, NC: Duke University Press, 2004.

Beijer, Sharon. "Achieving Justice for the Survivors of Acid Violence in Cambodia." *Cambodia Law and Policy Journal* 1 (January 2014): 1–28.

Bellenoit, Hayden J. A. *Missionary Education and Empire in Late Colonial India, 1860–1920*. London: Pickering and Chatto, 2007.

Benei, Veronique. *Schooling Passions: Nation, History, and Language in Contemporary West India*. Stanford, CA: Stanford University Press, 2008.

Boddy, Janice. *Civilizing Women: British Crusades in Colonial Sudan*. Princeton, NJ: Princeton University Press, 2007.

Bocquet-Siek, Margaret. "The Peranakan Chinese Women at a Crossroad." In *Women's Work and Women's Roles: Economics and Everyday Life in Indonesia, Malaysia and*

Singapore, ed. Lenore Manderson. Canberra: Australian National University Press, 1983, 31–52.

Booth, Margaret Zoller. "Education for Liberation or Domestication? Female Education in Colonial Swaziland." In *Women and the Colonial Gaze*, ed. Tamara Hunt and Micheline Lessard. New York: Palgrave, 2002, 174–87.

Bourdieu, Pierre and Jean-Claude Passeron. *Reproduction in Education, Society and Culture*. Trans. Richard Nice. London: Sage, 1977.

Brownell, Susan and Jeffrey N. Wasserstrom, eds. *Chinese Femininities, Chinese Masculinities: A Reader*. Berkeley: University of California Press, 2002.

Butler, Kim D. "Defining Diaspora: Refining a Discourse." *Diaspora: A Journal of Transnational Studies* 10, no. 2 (Fall 2001): 189–219.

Carstens, Sharon A. "Pulai, Hakka, Chinese, Malaysian: A Labyrinth of Cultural Identities." In *Histories, Cultures, Identities: Studies in Malaysian Chinese Worlds*. Singapore: Singapore University Press, 2005, 57–81.

CCTV's Facebook Page. "Bai Xueqiao: Zuguo weinanshi, jie wo yidi li" (Bai Xueqiao: When the ancestral nation was in difficulty, I made my modest contribution"). Accessed March 3, 2017. https://www.facebook.com/CCTV.CH/videos/1178661385554752/.

Chaffee, John W. *The Thorny Gates of Learning in Sung China: A Social History of Examinations*. Cambridge: Cambridge University Press, 1985.

Chan, Faye Yik-Wei. "Chinese Women's Emancipation as Reflected in Two Peranakan Journals." *Archipel* 49 (1995): 45–62.

Chatterjee, Partha. "The Nationalist Resolution of the Women's Question." In *Recasting Women: Essays in Indian Colonial History*, ed. Kumkum Sangari and Sudesh Vaid. New Brunswick, NJ: Rutgers University Press, 1999.

Chelliah, D. D. *A History of the Educational Policy of the Straits Settlements, with Recommendations for a New System Based on Vernaculars*. Kuala Lumpur: Government Press, 1947.

Chew, Phyllis Ghim Lian. *The Singapore Council of Women and the Women's Movement*. Singapore: Singapore University Press, 1999.

Chirot, Daniel and Anthony Reid, eds. *Essential Outsiders: Chinese and Jews in the Modern Transformation of Southeast Asia and Central Europe*. Seattle: University of Washington Press, 1997.

Christiansen, Flemming. *Overseas Chinese in Europe: An Imagined Community?* Leeds: University of Leeds Department of East Asian Studies, 1997.

Chua Ai Lin. "The Domiciled Identity in Colonial Singapore: Understanding the Straits Chinese beyond 'Race', 'Nation' and 'Empire'." In *Peranakan Chinese in a Globalizing Southeast Asia*, ed. Leo Suryadinata. Singapore: Chinese Heritage Center, Nanyang Technological University and Baba House, National University of Singapore, 2010, 145–54.

Chua Ai Lin. "Imperial Subjects, Straits Citizens: Anglophone Asians and the Struggle for Political Rights in Inter-War Singapore." In *Paths Not Taken: Political Pluralism in Post-War Singapore*, ed. Michael D. Barr and Carl A. Trocki. Singapore: National University of Singapore Press, 2008, 16–36.

Clancy-Smith, Julia and Frances Gouda, eds. *Domesticating the Empire: Race, Gender and Family Life in French and Dutch Colonialism*. Charlottesville: University Press of Virginia, 1998.

Cleverley, John. *The Schooling of China: Tradition and Modernity in Chinese Education*. 2nd ed. Sydney: Allen and Unwin, 1991.

Cooper, Frederick and Ann Laura Stoler, eds. *Tensions of Empire: Colonial Cultures in a Bourgeois World*. Berkeley: University of California Press, 1997.

Coppel, Charles A. "Chinese Overseas: The Particular and the General." *Journal of Chinese Overseas* 8 (2012): 1–10.

Coppel, Charles. "Emancipation of the Indonesian Chinese Women." In *Studying Ethnic Chinese in Indonesia*. Asian Studies Monograph Series No. 7. Singapore: Singapore Society of Asian Studies, 2002.

Croll, Elisabeth. *Feminism and Socialism in China*. London: Routledge and Kegan Paul, 1978.

Culp, Robert. *Articulating Citizenship: Civic Education and Student Politics in Southeastern China, 1912–1940*. Cambridge, MA: Harvard University Asia Center, 2007.

Cushman, Jennifer W. and Wang Gungwu, eds. *Changing Identities of the Southeast Asian Chinese since World War II*. Hong Kong: Hong Kong University Press, 1988.

Davin, Anna. "Imperialism and Motherhood." In *Tensions of Empire: Colonial Cultures in a Bourgeois World*, ed. Frederick Cooper and Ann Laura Stoler. Berkeley: University of California Press, 1997.

DeBernardi, Jean. *Rites of Belonging: Memory, Modernity, and Identity in a Malaysian Chinese Community*. Stanford, CA: Stanford University Press, 2004.

Dennis, Barbara and David Skilton. *Reform and Intellectual Debate in Victorian England*. New York: Croom Helm, 1987.

Dirlik, Arif. "Modernity as History: Post-Revolutionary China, Globalization and the Question of Modernity." *Social History* 27, no. 1 (2002): 16–39.

Doraisamy, T. R. ed. *150 Years of Education in Singapore*. Singapore: Teachers' Training College, 1969.

Doran, Christine. "The Chinese Cultural Reform Movement in Singapore: Singapore Chinese Identities and Reconstruction of Gender." *Sojourn* 12, no. 1 (1997): 92–107.

Duara, Prasenjit. "Of Authenticity and Woman: Personal Narratives of Middle Class Women in Modern China." In *Becoming Chinese: Passages to Modernity and Beyond*, ed. Wen-Hsin Yeh. Berkeley: University of California Press, 2000, 342–64.

Duara, Prasenjit. "The Regime of Authenticity: Timelessness, Gender, and National History in Modern China." *History and Theory: Studies in the Philosophy of History* 37, no. 3 (October 1998): 287–308.

Duara, Prasenjit. *Sovereignty and Authenticity: Manchukuo and the East Asian Modern*. Lanham, MD: Rowman and Littlefield, 2003.

Dwivedi, Om Prakash, ed. *Tracing the New Indian Diaspora*. Leiden: Brill, 2014

Ebrey, Patricia Buckley. *The Inner Quarters: Marriage and the Lives of Chinese Women in the Sung Period*. Berkeley: University of California Press, 1993.

Educational Planning and Research Division, Ministry of Education, Malaysia. *Educational Statistics of Malaysia, 1938–1967*. Kuala Lumpur: Ministry of Education, 1968.

Edwards, Louise. "Policing the Modern Woman in Republican China." *Modern China* 26, no. 2 (April 2000): 115–47.

Ee, Joyce. "Chinese Migration to Singapore, 1896–1941." *Journal of Southeast Asian History* 2, no. 1 (March 1961): 33–37 , 39–51.

Fan Ruolan. *Immigration, Gender and Overseas Chinese Society: Studies on the Chinese Women in Malaya (1929–1941)*. Beijing: Zhonghua Huaqiao, 2005.

Fitzgerald, Stephen. "China and the Overseas Chinese: Perceptions and Policies." *China Quarterly* 44 (October–December 1970): 1–37.

Ford, Caleb. "Guiqiao (Returned Overseas Chinese) Identity in the PRC." *Journal of Chinese Overseas* 10 (2014): 239–62.

Freedman, Maurice. *Chinese Family and Marriage in Singapore*. London: Her Majesty's Stationery Office, 1957.

Freedman, Maurice. "The Chinese in Southeast Asia: A Longer View." In *The Study of Chinese Society: Essays by Maurice Freedman, Selected and Introduced by G. William Skinner*. Stanford, CA: Stanford University Press, 1979.

Frost, Mark Ravinder. "Emporium in Imperio: Nanyang Networks and the Straits Chinese in Singapore, 1819–1914." *Journal of Southeast Asian Studies* 36, no. 1 (February 2005): 29–66.

Frost, Mark Ravinder. "Transcultural Diaspora: The Straits Chinese in Singapore, 1819–1918." Asia Research Institute Working Paper Series, No. 10, August 2003. www.ari.nus.edu.sg/pub/wps.htm.

Gilmartin, Christina K. et al., eds. *Engendering China: Women, Culture, and the State*. Cambridge, MA: Harvard University Press, 1994.

Gilmartin, Christina K. *Engendering the Chinese Revolution: Radical Women, Communist Politics, and Mass Movements in the 1920s*. Berkeley: University of California Press, 1995.

Gimpel, Denise. "Freeing the Mind Through the Body: Women's Thoughts on Physical Education in Late Qing and Early Republican China." *Nannü: Men, Women, and Gender in Early and Imperial China* 8, no. 2 (November 2006): 316–58.

Godley, Michael R. "The Sojourners: Returned Overseas Chinese in the People's Republic of China," *Pacific Affairs* 62, no. 3 (Autumn 1989): 330–52.

Goodman, Bryna. "The New Woman Commits Suicide: The Press, Cultural Memory and the New Republic." *Journal of Asian Studies* 64, no. 1 (February 2005): 67–101.

Graves, Karen. *Girls' Schooling during the Progressive Era: From Female Scholar to Domesticated Citizen*. New York: Garland, 1998.

Gullick, J. M. *Josephine Foss and the Pudu English School: A Pursuit of Excellence*. Selangor, Malaysia: Pelanduk, 1988.

Hardwick, Patricia Ann. "'Neither Fish nor Fowl': Constructing Peranakan Identity in Colonial and Post-colonial Singapore." *Folklore Forum* 38, no. 1 (2008): 36–55.

Harper, Tim. "Globalism and the Pursuit of Authenticity: The Making of a Diasporic Public Sphere in Singapore." *Sojourn* 12, no. 2 (1997): 261–92.

Heng, Geraldine and Janadas Devan. "State Fatherhood: The Politics of Nationalism, Sexuality, and Race in Singapore." In *Nationalisms and Sexualities*, ed. Andrew Parker et al. Singapore: Routledge, 1991, 344–64.

Hershatter, Gail. "The Gender of Memory: Rural Chinese Women and the 1950s." *Signs: Journal of Women and Culture in Society* 28, no. 1 (2002): 43–70.

Higginbotham, Evelyn Brooks. "The Politics of Respectability." In *Righteous Discontent: The Women's Movement in the Black Baptist Church, 1880–1920*. Cambridge, MA.: Harvard University Press, 1993, 185–230.

Hirschman, Charles. "The Meaning and Measurement of Ethnicity in Malaysia: An Analysis of Census Classification." *Journal of Asian Studies* 46, no. 3 (1987): 555–82.

Ho Ping-ti. *The Ladder of Success in Imperial China: Aspects of Social Mobility, 1368–1911*. New York: Columbia University Press, 1962.

Holden, Philip. "A Literary History of Race: Reading Singapore Literature in English in an Historical Frame." In *Race and Multiculturalism in Malaysia and Singapore*, ed. Daniel P.S. Goh et al. London: Routledge, 2009, 19–35.

Honig, Emily and Gail Hershatter. *Personal Voices: Chinese Women in the 1980's.* Stanford, CA: Stanford University Press, 1988.

Huang Jianli and Lysa Hong. "Chinese Diasporic Culture and National Identity: The Taming of the Tiger Balm Gardens in Singapore." *Modern Asian Studies* 41, no. 1 (2007): 41–76.

Hunt, Felicity. *Gender and Policy in English Education: Schooling for Girls 1902–44.* Hertfordshire: Harvester Wheatsheaf, 1991.

Hunter, Thomas, John Smith, Archibald Swinton, and Scotland High Court of Justiciary. *Report of the trial of Thomas Hunter, Peter Hacket, Richard M'Neil, James Gibb, and William M'Lean: operative cotton-spinners in Glasgow, before the High court of justiciary, at Edinburgh, on Wednesday, January 3, 1838, and seven following days, for the crimes of illegal conspiracy and murder; with an appendix of documents and relative proceedings.* Edinburgh: Thomas Clark, 1838.

Ikeya, Chie. *Refiguring Women, Colonialism, and Modernity in Burma.* Honolulu: University of Hawaii Press, 2011.

Inglis, Christine. "Chinese Schools in Malaya during the Colonial Period." In *Kabar Seberang, Sulating Maphilindo* 7 (1980): 82–93.

Inglis, Christine. "The Feminisation of the Teaching Profession in Singapore." In *Women's Work and Women's Roles: Economics and Everyday Life in Indonesia, Malaysia and Singapore*, ed. Lenore Manderson. Canberra: Australian National University, 1983, 217–39.

Jaschok, Maria and Suzanne Miers, eds. *Women and Chinese Patriarchy: Submission, Servitude and Escape.* Hong Kong: Hong Kong University Press, 1994.

Judge, Joan. "Citizens or Mothers of Citizens? Gender and the Meaning of Modern Chinese Citizenship." In *Changing Meanings of Citizenship in Modern China*, ed. Merle Goldman and Elizabeth J. Perry. Cambridge, MA: Harvard University Press, 2002, 23–43.

Judge, Joan. *The Precious Raft of History: China's Woman Question and the Politics of Time at the Turn of the Twentieth Century.* Stanford, CA: Stanford University Press, 2008.

Judge, Joan. "Talent, Virtue and the Nation: Chinese Nationalism and Female Subjectivities in the Early Twentieth Century." *American Historical Review* 106, no. 3 (June 2001): 765–803.

Keyes, Charles F., ed. *Reshaping Local Worlds: Formal Education and Cultural Change in Rural Southeast Asia.* New Haven. CT: Yale University Southeast Asia Studies, 1991.

Kho Ee Moi. "Construction of Femininity: Girls' Education in Singapore, 1959–2000." PhD Diss., National University of Singapore, 2004.

Khoo, Agnes. *Life as the River Flows: Women in the Malayan Anti-Colonial Struggle (An Oral History of Women from Thailand, Malaysia and Singapore).* Malaysia: Strategic Information Research Development, 2004.

Khoo Boo Teik. "Ethnic Structure, Governance, and Inequality in the Public Sector: Malaysian Experiences." *Democracy, Governance and Human Rights Programme Paper 20* (December 2005). United Nations Research Institute for Social Development.

Khoo Joo Ee. *The Straits Chinese: A Cultural History.* Kuala Lumpur: Pepin Press, 1998.

Khor, Neil Jin Keong. "Economic Change and the Emergence of the Straits-Chinese in Nineteenth-century Penang." *Journal of the Malaysian Branch of the Royal Asiatic Society* 79, no. 2 (December 2006): 59–83.

Khor, Neil Jin Keong and Khoo, Keat Siew. *The Penang Po Leung Kuk: Chinese Women, Prostitution and a Welfare Organisation*. Malaysia: Malaysian Branch of the Royal Asiatic Society, 2004.

Kipp, Rita Smith. "Emancipating Each Other: Dutch Colonial Missionaries' Encounter with Karo Women in Sumatra, 1900–1942." In *Domesticating the Empire: Race, Gender, and Family Life in French and Dutch Colonialism*, ed. Julia Clancy-Smith and Frances Gouda. Charlottesville: University Press of Virginia, 1998, 211–35.

Ko, Dorothy. *Teachers of the Inner Chambers: Women and Culture in Seventeenth-Century China*. Stanford, CA: Stanford University Press, 1994.

Koh, Adeline. "Educating Malayan Gentlemen: Establishing an Anglicized Elite in Twentieth-Century Colonial Malaya." *Biblioasia* 3, no. 1 (2007): 10–15.

Koh, Adeline. "Inventing Malayanness: Race, Education and Englishness in Colonial Malaya." PhD Diss., University of Michigan at Ann Arbor, 2008.

Koh, Adeline and Yu-Mei Balasingamchow, eds. *Women and the Politics of Representation in Southeast Asia: Engendering Discourse in Singapore and Malaysia*. New York: Routledge, 2015.

Kong, Lily et al. *Convent Chronicles: History of a Pioneer Mission School for Girls in Singapore*. Singapore: Armour, 1994.

Kua Kia Soong. *A Protean Saga: The Chinese Schools of Malaysia*. Malaysia: Dong Jiao Zong Higher Learning Centre, 1999.

Kuhn, Philip A. *Chinese among Others: Emigration in Modern Times*. Lanham, MD: Rowman and Littlefield, 2008.

Lai Ah Eng. *Peasants, Proletarians and Prostitutes: A Preliminary Investigation into the Work of Chinese Women in Colonial Malaya*. Singapore: Institute of Southeast Asian Studies, 1986.

Lan, Hua R. and Vanessa L. Fong, eds. *Women in Republican China: A Sourcebook*. New York: M. E. Sharpe, 1999.

Lau Wai Har. "Bridging the Gap between the Two Worlds: The Chinese-Educated and the English-Educated." In *Our Place in Time: Exploring Heritage and Memory in Singapore*, ed. Kwok Kian Woon et al. Singapore: Singapore Heritage Society, 1999, 199–207.

Lebra, Joyce and Joy Paulson. *Chinese Women in Southeast Asia*. Singapore: Times Books International, 1980.

Lee Guan Kin. *Responding to Eastern and Western Cultures in Singapore: A Comparative Study of Khoo Seok Wan, Lim Boon Keng and Song Ong Siang*. Hong Kong: University of Hong Kong, 1998.

Lee Kam Hing and Tan Chee Beng, eds. *The Chinese in Malaysia*. Selangor, Malaysia: Oxford University Press, 2000.

Lee, Karen. "Between the 'King's Chinese' and 'Sons of Han': Fashioning Cultural Perfection in a Singaporean Chinese Status Group, 1890–1911." MA Thesis, Harvard University, 2012.

Lee Ting Hui. *Chinese Schools in British Malaya: Policies and Politics*. Singapore: South Seas Society, 2006.

Lee Yoke Ming. *Great Is Thy Faithfulness: The Story of St. Margaret's School in Singapore*. Singapore: St. Margaret's School, 2002.

Levinson, Bradley A., Douglas E. Foley, and Dorothy C. Holland, eds. *The Cultural Production of the Educated Person: Critical Ethnographies of Schooling and Local Practice*. Albany: State University of New York Press, 1996.

Leutner, Mechthild and Nicola Spakowski, eds. *Women in China: The Republican Period in Historical Perspective*. Munster: Lit, 2005.

Lewis, Su Lin. "Cosmopolitanism and the Modern Girl: A Cross-Cultural Discourse in 1930s Penang." *Modern Asian Studies* 43, no. 6 (2009): 1385–419.

Li Xiaojiang. "With What Discourse Do We Reflect on Chinese Women? Thoughts on Transnational Feminism in China." In *Spaces of Their Own: Women's Public Sphere in Transnational China*, ed. Mayfair Mei-hui Yang. Minneapolis: University of Minnesota Press, 1999, 261–77.

Lim Chor Pee. "A White Rose at Midnight." Singapore: s.n., 1964.

Lim Joo Hock. "Chinese Female Immigration into the Straits Settlements, 1860–1991." *South Seas Journal* 22 (1967): 99.

Lim Lee Chin. "A Study of the Early History of Chinese Women in Singapore and Malaya through *Penang Sin Pao*." BA Honors Thesis, Singapore, National University of Singapore, 2000–01.

Lim, Linda. "Linda Lim's MGS Schooldays." Unpublished memoir, 2004.

Lim, Linda Y. C. and L. A. Peter Gosling, eds. *The Chinese in Southeast Asia*. 2 vols. Singapore: Maruzen Asia, 1983.

Lim San Neo. *My Life, My Memories, My Story*. Singapore: Epic Management Services, 1997.

Liu, Hong. "Old Linkages, New Networks: The Globalization of Overseas Chinese Voluntary Associations and Its Implications." *China Quarterly* 155 (September 1998): 582–609.

Locher-Scholten, Elsbeth. *Women and the Colonial State: Essays on Gender and Modernity in the Netherlands Indies, 1900–1942*. Amsterdam: Amsterdam University Press, 2000.

Loh, Philip Fook Seng. *Seeds of Separatism: Educational Policy in Malaya, 1874–1940*. Kuala Lumpur: Oxford University Press, 1975.

Macilwee, Michael. *The Liverpool Underworld: Crime in the City, 1750–1900*. Liverpool: Liverpool University Press, 2011.

Makepeace, Walter, et al., eds. *One Hundred Years of Singapore*. London: CM Turnbull, 1921.

Manderson, Lenore. *Class, Ideology and Woman in Asian Societies*. Hong Kong: Asian Research Service, 1987.

Manderson, Lenore. "The Development and Direction of Female Education in Peninsular Malaysia." *Journal of the Malayan Branch of the Royal Asiatic Society* 51, no. 2 (December 1978): 100–22.

Mann, Susan. "Learned Women in the Eighteenth Century." In *Engendering China: Women, Culture, and the State*, ed. Christina K. Gilmartin et al. Cambridge, MA: Harvard University Press, 1994.

McElroy, Sarah Coles. "Forging a New Role for Women: Zhili First Women's Normal School and the Growth of Women's Education in China, 1901–21." In *Education, Culture, and Identity in Twentieth-Century China*, ed. Glen Peterson, Ruth Hayhoe, and Yongling Liu. Ann Arbor: University of Michigan Press, 2001, 348–74.

McKeown, Adam. *Chinese Migrant Networks and Cultural Change: Peru, Chicago, Hawaii, 1900–1936*. Chicago: University of Chicago Press, 2001.

Ong, Aihwa. *Flexible Citizenship: The Cultural Logics of Transnationality*. Durham, NC: Duke University Press, 1999.

Ong, Aihwa and Donald Nonini, eds. *Ungrounded Empires: The Cultural Politics of Modern Chinese Transnationalism*. New York: Routledge, 1997.

Ooi Keat Gin. "Domestic Servants par Excellence: The Black and White Amahs of Malaya and Singapore with Special Reference to Penang." *Journal of the Malaysian Branch of the Royal Asiatic Society* 65, no. 2 (1992): 69–84.

Ooi Keat Gin. *Southeast Asia: A Historical Encyclopedia, from Angkor Wat to East Timor*, Volume 1. Santa Barbara: ABC-CLIO, 2004.

Ooi Yu-lin. "The Changing Status of Chinese Women in Singapore, 1819–1961." Academic Exercise, National University of Singapore, 1981.

Ooi Yu-lin. *Pieces of Jade and Gold: Anecdotal History of the Singapore Chinese Girls' School, 1899–1999*. Singapore: Singapore Chinese Girls' School, 1999.

Owen, Norman, ed. *The Routledge Handbook of Southeast Asian History*. London: Routledge, 2014.

Paechter, Carrie F. *Educating the Other: Gender, Power and Schooling*. London: Falmer Press, 1998.

Pan, Lynn, ed. *The Encyclopedia of the Chinese Overseas*. Singapore: Archipelago Press and Landmark Books, 1998.

Pankhurst, Sylvia. *The Suffragette: The History of the Women's Militant Suffrage Movement, 1905–1910*. New York: Sturgis and Walton, 1911.

Penang Chinese Girls' High School. "School History." http://www.smjk.edu.my/school/about.php?schid=17&schidx=284&page_type=pageid&pgid=A.

Peterson, Glen. *Overseas Chinese in the People's Republic of China*. London: Routledge, 2012.

Peterson, Glen. "Socialist China and the Huaqiao: The Transition to Socialism in the Overseas Chinese Areas of Rural Guangdong, 1949–1956." *Modern China* 14, no. 3 (July 1988): 309–35.

Phua Ee Hwee. "A Study of the Early History of Chinese Women in Singapore and Malaya through *Lat Pau*." BA Honors Thesis, Singapore, National University of Singapore, 2000–01.

Por Heong Hong. "Revisiting the Kuen Cheng High School Dispute: Contestation between Gender Equality and Ethnic Nationalism Discourses." *Inter-Asia Cultural Studies* 10, no. 1 (2009): 165–77.

"Prisoners Awaiting Hearing: Throwing Vitriol. Garroting in Catharine-Street." *New York Times*, July 15, 1865.

Qian Nanxiu. "Revitalizing the Xianyuan (Worthy Ladies) Tradition: Women in the 1898 Reforms." *Modern China* 29, no. 4 (October 2003): 399–454.

Qiu Jin. "Song of the Jingwei Bird." In *Writing Women in Modern China: An Anthology of Women's Literature from the Early Twentieth Century*, ed. Amy D. Dooling and Kristina M. Torgeson. New York: Columbia University Press, 1998, 43–78.

Rankin, Mary Backus. "The Emergence of Women at the End of the Ch'ing: The Case of Ch'iu Chin." In *Women in Chinese Society*, ed. Margery Wolf and Roxane Witke. Stanford, CA: Stanford University Press, 1975, 39–66.

Reid, Anthony, ed. *Sojourners and Settlers: Histories of Southeast Asia and the Chinese*. Sydney: Allen and Unwin, 1996.

Rofel, Lisa. *Other Modernities: Gendered Yearnings in China after Socialism*. Berkeley: University of California Press, 1999.

Rudolph, Jurgen. "The 'Speak Mandarin Campaign' of the Babas." *Commentary* 11, no. 1 (1993): 93–102.

Scott, Joan W. "Gender: A Useful Category of Historical Analysis." *American Historical Review* 91, no. 5 (December 1986): 1053–75.

Seah Bee Leng. "Phoenix without Wings: The Negotiation of Modernity among Straits Chinese Women in Early Twentieth Century Singapore." MA Thesis, Department of History, National University of Singapore, 2005.

Seah Eu Chin. "The Chinese of Singapore." *Journal of the Indian Archipelago and Eastern Asia* 2 (1847): 283–90.

Shen Huifen. *China's Left-Behind Wives: Families of Migrants from Fujian to Southeast Asia, 1930s–1950s.* Honolulu: University of Hawaii Press, 2012.

Sim, Victor. *Biographies of Prominent Chinese in Singapore.* Singapore: Nan Kok, 1950.

Sinn, Elizabeth. *The Last Half Century of Chinese Overseas.* Hong Kong: Hong Kong University Press, 1998.

Skinner, G. William. "Creolized Chinese Societies in Southeast Asia." In *Sojourners and Settlers: Histories of Southeast Asia and the Chinese*, ed. Anthony Reid. Honolulu: University of Hawaii Press, 2001, 51–93.

Smith, Bonnie, ed. *Women's History in Global Perspective*, Volume 1. Champaign: University of Illinois Press, 2004.

Smith, Steven. *Modernity and Its Discontents: Making and Unmaking the Bourgeois from Machiavelli to Bellow.* New Haven, CT: Yale University Press, 2016.

St. Margaret's Secondary School. School History Exhibition. Singapore. Visited December 28, 2005.

Stevens, Sarah E. "Figuring Modernity: The New Woman and the Modern Girl in Republican China." *NWSA Journal* 15, no. 3 (Fall 2003): 82–103.

Stoler, Ann Laura. *Carnal Knowledge and Imperial Power: Race and the Intimate in Colonial Rule.* Berkeley: University of California Press, 2002.

Stoler, Ann Laura. *Race and the Education of Desire: Foucault's History of Sexuality and the Colonial Order of Things.* Durham, NC: Duke University Press, 1995.

Stoler, Ann Laura, Carole McGranahan, and Peter C. Perdue, eds. *Imperial Formations.* Santa Fe: School for Advanced Research Press, 2007.

Strassler, Karen. *Refracted Visions: Popular Photography and National Modernity in Java.* Durham, NC: Duke University Press, 2010.

Suksod-Barger, Runchana P. *Religious Influences in Thai Female Education (1889–1931).* Cambridge: James Clarke, 2014.

Suryadinata, Leo, ed. *Ethnic Chinese as Southeast Asians.* Singapore: Institute for Southeast Asian Studies, 1997.

Suryadinata, Leo, ed. *Ethnic Relations and Nation-Building in Southeast Asia: The Case of the Ethnic Chinese.* Singapore: Institute of Southeast Asian Studies, 2004.

Suryadinata, Leo. *Migration, Indigenization, and Interaction: Chinese Overseas and Globalization.* Hackensack, NJ: World Scientific, 2011.

Suryadinata, Leo. "Peranakan Chinese Identities in Malaysia and Singapore: A Re-Examination." In *Ethnic Chinese in Singapore and Malaysia: A Dialogue between Tradition and Modernity*, ed. Leo Suryadinata. Singapore: Times Academic Press, 2002, 69–84.

Suryadinata, Leo, ed. *Southeast Asian Chinese: The Socio-Cultural Dimension.* Singapore: Times Academic Press, 1995.

Sutherland, Duncan. "Lee Choo Neo." *Singapore Infopedia.* National Library Board Singapore. http://eresources.nlb.gov.sg/infopedia/articles/SIP_1493_2009-04-05.html. Accessed October 10, 2016.

Szonyi, Michael. "Mothers, Sons, and Lovers: Fidelity and Frugality in the Overseas Chinese Divided Family before 1949." *Journal of Chinese Overseas* 1, no. 1 (2005): 43–64.

Tagliacozzo, Eric and Wen-Chin Chang, eds. *Chinese Circulations: Capital, Commodities, and Networks in Southeast Asia*. Durham, NC: Duke University Press, 2011.

Tan Chee Beng. *Chinese Overseas: Comparative Cultural Issues*. Hong Kong: Hong Kong University Press, 2004.

Tan Chee Beng. "Peranakan Chinese in Northeast Kelantan with Special Reference to Chinese Religion." *Journal of the Malaysian Branch of the Royal Asiatic Society* 55, no. 1 (1982): 26–52.

Tan Liok Ee. "A Century of Change: Education in the Lives of Four Generations of Chinese Women in Malaysia." In *Asian Migrants and Education: The Tensions of Education in Immigrant Societies and among Migrant Groups*, ed. Michael W. Charney, Brenda S. A. Yeoh, and Tong Chee Kiong. Dordrecht: Kluwer Academic, 2003, 115–31.

Tan Liok Ee. "Chinese Independent Schools in West Malaysia: Varying Responses to Changing Demands." In *Changing Identities of the Southeast Asian Chinese since World War II*, ed. Jennifer W. Cushman and Wang Gungwu. Hong Kong: Hong Kong University Press, 1988, 61–74.

Tan Liok Ee. "Locating Chinese Women in Malaysian History." In *New Terrains in Southeast Asian History*, ed. Ahmad Abu Talib and Tan Liok Ee. Singapore: Singapore University Press, 2003, 354–84.

Tan Liok Ee. *The Politics of Chinese Education in Malaya, 1945–1961*. Malaysia: Oxford University Press, 1997.

Taylor, Jean Gelman. *The Social World of Batavia: European and Eurasian in Dutch Asia*. Madison: University of Wisconsin Press, 1983.

Teoh, Karen M. "The Burden of Proof: Gender, Cultural Authenticity and Overseas Chinese Women's Education in Diaspora." *Intersections: Gender and Sexuality in Asia and the Pacific* 36 (September 2014). http://intersections.anu.edu.au/issue36/teoh.htm.

Teoh, Karen M. "Domesticating Hybridity: Straits Chinese Cultural Heritage Projects in Malaysia and Singapore." *Cross-Currents: East Asian Culture and History Review* 5, no. 1 (May 2016): 115–46.

Teoh, Karen M. "Exotic Flowers, Modern Girls, Good Citizens: Female Education and Overseas Chinese Identity in British Malaya and Singapore, 1900s–1950s." *Twentieth-Century China* 35, no. 2 (April 2010): 25–51.

Tey Nai Peng. "The Changing Demographic Situation of Malaysian Chinese." In *Ethnic Chinese in Singapore and Malaysia: A Dialogue between Tradition and Modernity*, ed. Leo Suryadinata. Singapore: Times Academic Press, 2002, 45–66

Thompson, Mark R. "Pacific Asia after 'Asian Values': Authoritarianism, Democracy, and 'Good Governance.'" *Third World Quarterly* 25, no. 6 (2004): 1079–95.

"Three Years for Throwing Vitriol." *New York Times*, November 14, 1884.

Tinsman, Marilyn W. "China and the Returned Overseas Chinese Students." EdD Diss., Teachers College, Columbia University, 1983.

Venkataranam, M. "An Analysis of China's 'Overseas Chinese' Policy." *China Report* 34, no. 2 (1998): 165–78.

Wang Gungwu. *The Chinese Overseas: From Earthbound China to the Quest for Autonomy*. Cambridge, MA: Harvard University Press, 2000.

Wang Gungwu. *Community and Nation: Essays on Southeast Asia and the Chinese*. Singapore: Heinemann, 1981.

Wang Gungwu. "Patterns of Chinese Migration in Historical Perspective." In *China and the Chinese Overseas*. Singapore: Times Academic Press, 1991, 3–21.

Wang, Margaret. "My Mother." In *Chinese Women: Their Malaysian Journey*, ed. Neil Khor. Selangor, Malaysia: MPH Group, 2010, 56–57.

Warren, James F. *Ah Ku and Karayuki-San: Prostitution in Singapore 1880–1940*. Singapore: National University of Singapore Press, 2003.

Weinbaum, Alys Eve, Lynn M. Thomas, Priti Ramamurthy, Uta G. Poiger, Madeline Yue Dong, and Tani Barlow, eds. *The Modern Girl around the World: Consumption, Modernity, and Globalization*. Durham, NC: Duke University Press, 2008.

Welsh, Jane. "'It Was Like Burning in Hell:' A Comparative Exploration of Acid Attack Violence." MA Thesis, Department of Anthropology, University of North Carolina-Chapel Hill, 2009.

Wettstein, Howard, ed. *Diasporas and Exiles: Varieties of Jewish Identity*. Berkeley: University of California Press, 2002.

Whitehead, Clive. *Colonial Educators: The British Indian and Colonial Education Service, 1858–1983*. London: I. B. Tauris, 2003.

Wilson, Harold E. *Social Engineering in Singapore: Educational Policies and Social Change*. Singapore: Singapore University Press, 1978.

Williams, James H., ed. *(Re)Constructing Memory: School Textbooks and the Imagination of the Nation*. Rotterdam: Sense, 2014.

Wolf, Margery. *Revolution Postponed: Women in Contemporary China*. Stanford, CA: Stanford University Press, 1985.

Wolf, Margery and Roxane Witke, eds. *Women in Chinese Society*. Stanford, CA: Stanford University Press, 1975.

Wong, Yee Lam Elim. "Overseas-Chinese Women and Education: A Case Study of an Overseas-Chinese Women's Association in Yokohama's Chinatown." *Journal of Chinese Overseas* 12 (2016): 285–313.

Wong, Francis Hoy Kee and Ee Tiang Hong. *Education in Malaya*. Singapore: Heinemann Educational Books, 1971.

Wong Suk Siong. *A History of the Development of Education for Girls in Selangor under the Order of the Sisters of the Holy Infant Jesus, 1899–1967*. Kuala Lumpur: University of Malaya, 1967.

Xun Chaofang. "Bai Xueqiao: chuanqi huaqiao nüjigong" (Bai Xueqiao: A Legend of the Overseas Chinese Women's Engineer Corps). *Yangcheng Wanbao*, September 21, 2005, A19.

Yan, Qinghuang [Yen Ching-Hwang]. *The Chinese in Southeast Asia and Beyond: Socioeconomic and Political Dimensions Globalization*. Hackensack, NJ: World Scientific, 2008.

Yang, Mayfair Mei-hui, ed. *Spaces of Their Own: Women's Public Sphere in Transnational China*. Minneapolis: University of Minnesota Press, 1999.

Yap, Dilys. *Convent Light Street: A History of a Community, a School and a Way of Life*. Penang: Phoenix Press, 2001.

Ye Weili. *Seeking Modernity in China's Name: Chinese Students in the United States, 1900–1927*. Stanford, CA: Stanford University Press, 2001.

Yen Ching-Hwang. "Ch'ing Changing Images of the Overseas Chinese (1644–1912)." *Modern Asian Studies* 15, no. 2 (1981): 261–85

Yen Ching-Hwang. *Community and Politics: The Chinese in Colonial Singapore and Malaysia*. Singapore: Times Academic Press, 1995.

Yen Ching-Hwang. *A Social History of the Chinese in Singapore and Malaya, 1800–1911*. Singapore: Oxford University Press, 1986.

Yeoh, Brenda S. A. *Contesting Space in Colonial Singapore: Power Relations and the Urban Built Environment*. Singapore: Singapore University Press, 2003.

Yoong, S. K., and A. N. Zainab. "The Straits Chinese Contribution to Malaysian Literary Heritage: Focus on Chinese Stories Translated in Baba Malay." *Journal of Educational Media and Library Sciences* 42, no. 2 (2004): 179–98.

Yue Meng. "Female Images and National Myth." In *Gender Politics in Modern China: Writing and Feminism*, ed. Tani Barlow. Durham, NC: Duke University Press, 1993, 118–36.

Zheng Liangshu. "Female Education in Early Singaporean and Malayan Society." *Journal of Malaysian Chinese Studies* 1 (August 1997): 47–58.

Zheng Liangshu. *Malaixiya Huawen jiaoyu fazhan jianshi* (A Concise History of the Development of Chinese Education in Malaysia). Malaysia: Nanfang xueyuan chubanshe, 2005.

Zheng Liangshu and Wei Weixian, eds. *Malaixiya, Xinjiapo huawen zhongxue tekan tiyao, fu xiaoshi* (Abstracts of Special Issue Magazines of Chinese High Schools in Malaysia and Singapore, with School Histories). Malaysia: Chinese Studies Department, University of Malaya, 1975.

INDEX

China (*cont.*)
  May Fourth Movement (1919) in, 34,
      102, 106, 109, 112, 123, 159
  modernization and, 92, 96–96, 103
  National Education Plan of 1922 in, 98
  overseas Chinese re-migration to, 17,
      109, 111, 121–45, 148
  People's Liberation Army in, 137
  school structure and curricula in, 98
  Second Five-Year Plan in, 130
  Thirty-six Rules and Regulations for
      Girls' Normal Schools (1907)
      and, 95
  "woman problem" in, 92
Chinese Boys' High School
    (Singapore), 135
Chinese Communist Party
  Chinese civil war (1927–49) and, 124
  gender equity and, 126–27, 132, 142, 144
  Malayan Communist Party's conflict
      with, 137
  Overseas Chinese Affairs Office of, 128
  overseas Chinese supporters of, 10,
      109, 111, 135, 140
Chinese Ladies' Association
    (Singapore), 87
Chinese nationalism. *See under*
    nationalism
Chinese schools
  alumni associations and, 102
  anti-Communist targeting of teachers
      and students in, 38
  British colonial policies regarding, 2,
      19–20, 31–39, 101, 109, 111
  Chinese nationalism and culture in,
      6, 9, 33–35, 37, 64, 92, 94–98,
      101–2, 104, 109–10, 112, 126, 134,
      138–39, 148
  Communist influence and supporters
      in, 101, 109, 111, 129
  curricula in, 33–37, 92, 94, 102,
      104–5, 148
  dialects used in instruction in, 100
  domestic science and home economics
      in, 13, 20, 34, 37, 96, 98, 105, 153
  earliest establishment of, 22
  English-language instruction in,
      35, 105
  enrollment numbers in, 8, 34,
      97, 99–100

extracurricular activities in, 102,
    fig, 16
fees in, 97
funding problems in, 99
gender norms reinforced in, 92–95,
    103, 112–14, 116–17
Malaysian government's efforts to
    curtail, 61–62, 101, 149
modernization and, 13, 48, 92–95, 97,
    102–7, 118, 122, 138, 148
Ong's critique of, 58
physical education in, 96, 102, 105,
    fig. 19
political engagement by alumnae of,
    198–99, 122, 136, 138–39
professional opportunities for
    graduates of, 61, 91–92, 114–18
re-migration to China among alumnae
    of, 122–24, 127, 130, 132, 134–36
standardized common exams in, 101
teachers and staff in, 18, 20, 36, 93,
    96–97, 99
textbooks in, 20, 33–34, 37, 60,
    figs. 21–22
Torch Movement (Malaya) and, 38
tradition and sociocultural
    conservatism in, 92–95, 102–7,
    112–14, 117, 148
wealthier children as majority of
    students in, 11, 39
Chong Eu Ngoh, 58–59
Chong Hock Girls' School (Singapore), 98
Chung Hwa Girls' School (Penang), 95, 98
Church of England, 22, 42
colonialism. *See* imperialism
Confucianism
  Chinese schools in Southeast Asia
      and, 97
  Peranakan culture and, 67, 71,
      74–77, 83
  Singapore's promotion of, 76, 155–56
  Straits Chinese Magazine and, 76
  women and, 76–77
Contagious Disease Ordinance
    (1870), 27, 44
Convent Light Street (girls' school in
    Penang)
  domestic science and, 51, 65
  enrollment levels in, 47
  establishment of, 41

overseas Chinese and, 25–27, 29,
31–32, 34–35, 38–39
India
British colonial education system
in, 5, 23
British colonial office in, 21
girls' education and, 79
social reform movements in, 76
Indians in Southeast Asia
boys' schools and, 22
British colonial government and
policies regarding, 31–32
English schools and, 50, 54
gender imbalances among, 43
girls' schools and, 7, 20, 32, 47, 50
in Malaya and Malaysia, 6, 149–50
in Singapore, 6, 149, 156
Indonesia
Chinese girls' schools in, 84
Chinese re-migration from, 127
Peranakan in, 70, 72, 88
Singapore and, 149
Straits Chinese Magazine and, 74
inspections by government officials, 34,
66, 83, 85, *fig. 3*

Jingfang Girls' School (Singapore)
China's politics discussed in school
magazine (1936) of, 109–10
curriculum in, 104–5
founding (1928) of, 104
gender segregation as principle in, 113
Student Association's political
engagement in, 112
student reflections on importance of
girls' education in, 115
Johor (Malaya), 22

Kang Youwei, 35, 73–74
Kedah (Malaya), 22
Kelantan (Malaya), 22
Khoo Seok Wan, 83
Kuala Lumpur (Malaya)
Chinese community in, 8, 32–34,
97, 122–23
girls' schools in, 8, 32–33, 35–36, 41,
47, 50–51, 53–54, 92, 96–98,
105–7, 112, 115–16, 121–22, 140
IJ Convent in, 41, 47, 50–51, 54
May Fourth movement protests in, 34

Kuen Cheng Girls' School (Kuala
Lumpur)
Chinese nationalism and culture in, 35
curriculum in, 105
enrollment figures in, 97
founding leaders of, 96, 121
founding (1908) of, 35, 96
Li Yue as teacher with Communist
sympathies in, 111, 140
motto of, 98
professional opportunities for
alumnae of, 91
school magazine articles on gender
equity in, 106–7
student reflections on women's roles
in, 115–16
teachers and staff in, 96
Kuomintang (KMT)
China ruled (1920s–30s) by, 98, 113,
117–18, 125, 128, 136, 142
gender equity and, 144
New Life regulations and, 113, 117
Overseas Chinese Affairs Commission
of, 128
overseas Chinese supporters of, 109,
111, 117, 136, 140
publishing industry under, 98
Kwan, Louis, 88

Lee Choo Neo, 87
Lee Choon Guan, 87
Lee Kuan Yew, 156
Lee Siow Mong, 155
Lew See Fah, 77, 80–81
Liew Yuen Sien, 1–3, 9, 101
Lim, Ruth, 111–12
Lim Boon Keng
biographical background of, 71, 73
Chinese-language education
advocated by, 75
Confucianism and, 71, 74
on education's importance, 66–67
English-language education
and, 71, 75
limited Chinese language skills of, 75
modernization and, 73, 75
Peranakan community leadership
and, 71, 73
Singapore Chinese Girls' School and,
66, 82–83, 90

Straits Settlements established as
administrative government
for, 21
Melaka Free School, 23
Methodist Girls' School (MGS;
Singapore), 44–45, 47
missionaries
anti-prostitution efforts by, 44
boys' schools established by, 2, 28
British colonial policies and, 14, 20,
25, 28, 42
Catholic, 7, 16, 22–23, 40–42, 44,
46–55, 58–59, figs. 1–6
Chinese schools' competition with, 96
financial support for, 54
"Free Schools" established by,
22–23, 25, 27
girls' schools and, 4, 7, 14, 16, 20, 23,
28, 31, 33–34, 40–48, 50–51, 54,
56, 63, 82, 102, 157
government grants for schools
run by, 25
Methodist, 7, 22, 31, 42, 44–45, 47
Order of the Charitable Mistresses of
the Holy Infant Jesus (IJ) and,
23, 40–42, 44, 46–48, 50–55,
58–59, figs. 1–6
orphanages and, 21
proselytization and, 27, 45, 50
Protestant, 7, 16, 22, 31, 42, 44–45, 47
"Modern Girls," 115
modernization
Chinese schools and, 13, 48, 92–95,
97, 102–7, 118, 122, 138, 148
connotations of, 12–13
English schools and, 13, 41–42, 58, 60
gender norms and, 9, 97
girls' schools and female education
as means of advancing, 1, 3–4,
9–14, 17, 30–31, 45, 48, 66–69,
71, 78–79, 82, 86–87, 92, 96, 102,
104–7, 114, 118, 138, 147–48,
150–51, 155
Japan viewed as model for, 97
nationalism and, 30, 118
Peranakan community and, 66–71, 73,
74, 79, 82, 86–90, 104
tradition and resistance to, 10, 12, 17,
92, 95, 141, fig. 9
Westernization and, 95

women's opportunities and, 8
mui tsai. See bondmaids

Nan Ch'iao Girls' School (Singapore), 135
Nan Hwa Girls' School (Singapore)
domestic science classes in, 153
founding (1917) of, 98
gender norms reinforced in, 114
official school song in, 98
school publications in, 98, 153
student reflections on importance of
women's education in, 116
Nanyang ("Southern Seas"; Chinese term
for Southeast Asia), 6
Nanyang Girls' School (Singapore)
alumni association in, 102
Chinese culture and nationalism in, 35
Chinese-trained teachers in, 101
Communist sympathizers in, 2, 135
comportment rules in, 113
curriculum in, 105
domestic science classes in, 105, 153
extra-curricular activities in, fig. 19
founding (1917) of, 35, 98
graduation (1934) in, 91
He Xiangning's speech (1929) in, 108
Liew Yuen Sien as principal in, 1–2
re-migration to China among alumnae
of, 134–35
school publications in, figs.
14–16, 18–19
student reflections on women's roles
in, 116
textbooks in, figs. 21–22
nationalism
anti-colonialism in Southeast
Asia and, 6, 11, 21, 38, 74, 90,
94–95, 109
Chinese nationalism and, 8–9, 13, 15,
19–21, 32–35, 37–38, 42, 64, 79,
89–90, 92, 94–95, 101–4, 110–11,
117–19, 121, 125–27, 138–39,
142–44, 147–48, 153
colonial government's efforts to
encourage pro-British forms
of, 32, 60
diaspora communities and,
118–19, 157
May Fourth Movement and, 34
modernization and, 30, 118

missionary schools in, 40–41
overseas Chinese in, 8, 23, 34, 43, 97,
  fig. 17
Peranakan in, 69
Straits Settlements created as
  administrative government
  for, 21
venereal disease in, 44
Penang Chinese Girls' High School
  administrative stability in, 100–101
  Alumni Association of, 102
  athletics in, fig. 20
  Bai Xueqiao as alumna of and teacher
    in, 123–24
  domestic science classes in, 105
  enrollment figures in, 100
  founding (1919) of, 100
  Ong as headmistress of, 55
  Yong on, 59
Penang Free School, 22
Perak (Malaya), 21, 77, 83, 88, 151
Peranakan ("Straits Chinese"; people of
  mixed Chinese-Malay heritage)
  Baba (men) in, 66, 70–71, 73
  Chinese culture and
    nationalism among, 67, 69–70,
    74–75, 82, 89
  Confucianism and, 67, 71, 74–77, 83
  as diaspora community, 89
  English language and British culture
    emphasized by, 69, 72, 74
  gender ratios among, 73
  girls' schools and female education for,
    66–69, 71, 73, 80–89, 151
  hybrid identity of, 67–70, 89–90, fig. 9
  in Indonesia, 70, 72, 88
  Malay culture and, 67, 69–70,
    81–82, 90
  modernization and, 66–71, 73–74, 79,
    82, 86–90, 104
  Nyonya (women) and, 66–70, 73,
    77–82, 86–87, 89, 119
  overseas Chinese and, 71–73,
    89–90, 119
  in Singapore, 66–73, 78, 82–89
  Straits Chinese Magazine and,
    74–78, 80
  tradition and, 67–68, 88, fig. 9
Perlis (Malaya), 22
The Philippines, 70

"The Position of Chinese Women"
  (Song Ong Siang), 80
prostitution
  British colonial policies and, 25–27,
    35, 39, 44
  female education seen as means of
    preventing, 4, 28, 43, 48
  overseas Chinese settlements and, 6,
    9, 27, 35, 43–44
Protection of Women and Girls
  Ordinance (1887), 27
Pudu English Girls' School (Kuala
  Lumpur), 47

Qiu Jin, 123–24

Raffles, Stamford, 22
Raffles Girls' School (Singapore), 23–24,
  43, 48, 85
re-migrants (guiqiao) to China
  challenges in researching, 127–28
  Chinese Communist Revolution as
    impetus for, 109, 130–31
  Cultural Revolution (1965–76) and the
    targeting of, 131, 133, 135–36, 141
  early twentieth century and, 128
  educational opportunities as
    motivation for, 123
  estimated number (1949–70) of, 121, 129
  Fujian Qiaoxiangbao news story (1957)
    about, fig. 23
  girls' school alumnae among, 17, 111,
    120, 122–27, 134
  hostility in China toward, 121, 130–31,
    137–38, 145, 148
  retrospective evaluations by,
    131–33, 136–45
  women as a subgroup among,
    125–26, 141–45

St. George's School (Penang), 47
St. Margaret's School (Singapore)
  curriculum in, 44
  establishment (1842) of, 47
  extra-curricular activities in, fig. 7
  gender norms reinforced in, 30
  photo from, fig. 7
  poor and orphan students as intended
    student body in, 23, 30
  social distinctions maintained in, 52

CPSIA information can be obtained
at www.ICGtesting.com
Printed in the USA
BVHW032326180520
579769BV00005B/14